THE FUNDAMENTALS OF SOCIAL RESEARCH

This textbook provides an introduction to the scientific study of sociology and other social sciences. It offers the basic tools necessary for readers to become both critical consumers and beginning producers of scientific research on society. The authors present an integrated approach to research design and empirical analyses in which researchers can develop and test causal theories. They use examples from social science research that students will find engaging and inspiring, and that will help them to understand key concepts. The book makes technical materials accessible to students who might otherwise be intimidated by mathematical examples. This new text, with the addition of sociologist Steven A. Tuch to the author team, follows the successful format, approach, and pedagogical features in Paul M. Kellstedt and Guy D. Whitten's bestselling text, *The Fundamentals of Political Science Research*, now in its third edition. Workbooks in Stata, SPSS, and R, three of the most popular statistical analysis programs, are available as separate purchases to accompany this textbook, enabling students to connect the lessons of this book to hands-on applications of the software.

Paul M. Kellstedt is a professor of political science at Texas A&M University.

Guy D. Whitten is a professor of political science and Director of the European Union Center at Texas A&M University.

Steven A. Tuch is a professor of sociology and public policy and public administration at George Washington University.

THE FUNDAMENTALS OF
Social Research

Paul M. Kellstedt
Texas A&M University

Guy D. Whitten
Texas A&M University

Steven A. Tuch
George Washington University

CAMBRIDGE
UNIVERSITY PRESS

CAMBRIDGE
UNIVERSITY PRESS

University Printing House, Cambridge CB2 8BS, United Kingdom

One Liberty Plaza, 20th Floor, New York, NY 10006, USA

477 Williamstown Road, Port Melbourne, VIC 3207, Australia

314–321, 3rd Floor, Plot 3, Splendor Forum, Jasola District Centre, New Delhi - 110025, India

103 Penang Road, #05–06/07, Visioncrest Commercial, Singapore 238467

Cambridge University Press is part of the University of Cambridge.

It furthers the University's mission by disseminating knowledge in the pursuit of education, learning, and research at the highest international levels of excellence.

www.cambridge.org
Information on this title: www.cambridge.org/highereducation/isbn/9781107128835
DOI: 10.1017/9781316415399

First published 2023

A catalogue record for this publication is available from the British Library

ISBN 978-1-107-12883-5 Hardback
ISBN 978-1-107-56916-4 Paperback

Additional resources for this publication at www.cambridge.org/fsr

To Deb Kellstedt, Christine Lipsmeyer, and

Sandra Hanson

—PMK, GDW, and SAT

Brief Contents

Contents

Figures

Tables

Preface

Our goals in *The Fundamentals of Social Research* are twofold: first, to provide students with a rigorous introduction to the scientific study of society and, in the process, to equip them with the methodological skills necessary to be both critical consumers and beginning producers of scholarly, observational, primarily quantitative social research; and second, to highlight the connection between research design and causal inference in conceptualizing and doing social research.

The first section of the book, consisting of Chapters 1 through 3, sets the groundwork for accomplishing these goals by discussing what it means to adopt a scientific approach to the study of society. At its core, such an approach requires the development and testing of causal theories. Because there is no magical formula by which such theories are developed, we present several strategies for doing so, and develop an integrated approach to research design and empirical analysis that allows students to determine the plausibility of their causal theories. Section two of the book, Chapters 4 and 5, presents the details of research design and of one especially common type of observational design, the sample survey. The third section of the book, Chapters 6 through 11, is devoted to the statistical methods social scientists typically use in testing their causal theories. In the book's final chapter, Chapter 12, we provide fledgling researchers with a practical, step-by-step guide on how to produce an original research project that synthesizes materials from the preceding chapters.

The text's accessible presentation of mathematical concepts is a key component of our strategy, along with the integration of examples from sociology, political science, and other social sciences, to help students grasp key concepts. In every section of the book – indeed, in every chapter – we emphasize the linkage between design and causal inference in the construction and testing of causal theories.

If these goals appear to be a bit different than those of typical social science statistics textbooks, it's because they *are* a bit different. It is common practice in many social science departments, especially sociology departments, to separate undergraduate instruction in methodology and statistics into a two-course, year-long sequence, typically with research design taught in the first semester and statistics in the second. There are sound justifications for this practice, but in our experience an unintended consequence of a two-tiered approach is that many students come away from the sequence thinking that research design, on the one hand, and data analysis, on the other, are two separate, unrelated components of the research process. In this textbook we emphasize just the opposite – that the design of research and the analysis of data are two sides of a single methodological coin, and that one without the other yields fewer, and less useful, insights about the social world. Of course, this criticism of analysis that is untethered to causal theory testing is not unique to us. Rather, it is our contention that these two mutually reinforcing components of the research process, though universally agreed upon, are not often accorded the attention they deserve in either methodology or (especially) social science statistics textbooks. We aim to help fill this gap.

The book can be flexibly adapted to different courses and instructor preferences, but, as the discussion above implies, it is ideally suited to a semester-length course that covers both research design and statistics. It is useful in many other teaching contexts, though. In those courses that focus primarily on research design, it could be used as a supplement. Chapters 1–6 cover the core issues of social science methodology – the process by which scientific knowledge is produced, the ethics of doing research, criteria for establishing cause-and-effect relationships among variables, theory building, research design, measurement, and sampling. All or parts of Chapters 7–11, which introduce students to the varied quantitative toolkit that social scientists have at their disposal to examine causal relationships, could be included as time and instructor inclination permit. In courses that focus on statistics, Chapters 1–6 would provide a review of key background issues while Chapters 7–11 would constitute the primary core content. Chapter 12 is relevant to both research design and statistics courses alike.

For several reasons, the book will have strong appeal to instructors and students in advanced undergraduate and beginning graduate level social science statistics courses, though, as we just noted, it could also be used as a supplement in just about any methodology course. We give multivariate analytic techniques special attention, focusing considerable effort throughout the text on preparing students to understand these concepts. Moreover, we connect multivariate regression back to the central goal of causal inference and research design, and emphasize how regression helps us to accomplish the critical task of controlling for the effects of other possible causes of the dependent variable. Armed with nothing more than their abilities in algebra, students are capable of seeing, mathematically, how multivariate regression is connected to the central issues of research design. We know this because of our combined decades-long experience teaching this very important material, and having had students repeatedly ask us why the material isn't also in their textbooks.

In our view, today's sociology and other social science students are able to handle the statistical components of social science research methodology. Still, the book does not require students to know any mathematical material beyond high-school algebra – and we fully recognize that, in many cases, even those algebra skills will be quite rusty. In our classroom experiences, we have found a three-pronged approach of presenting technical subject matter to be very effective. This approach presents such concepts in closely integrated packages of textual explanations, graphical illustrations, and mathematical formulae. By addressing formulae head-on and explaining the meaning of each component of these formulae, we have found that students develop a much more intuitive understanding of the underlying logic of statistical hypothesis testing. These lessons are then applied in end-of-chapter exercises which are designed to bring home critical technical concepts.

The general section of the webpage for our text (www.cambridge.org/fsr) provides the data sets used throughout the book, and the instructor-only section provides PowerPoint slides for each chapter, a test-bank, and answer keys for the exercises. Finally, in parallel to this text, there are companion software books – one for SPSS, one for Stata, and one for R – that are being published.

Acknowledgments

The idea for this book emerged from discussions first proposed by Robert Dreesen, Publisher for Economics and Political Science at Cambridge University Press. The second edition of the highly regarded *The Fundamentals of Political Science Research* by Paul Kellstedt and Guy Whitten had just been published by Cambridge, and Robert was mulling over the idea of a book that mirrored the approach to methodology championed by Paul and Guy but that was accessible to a broader audience of sociology and other social science students. *The Fundamentals of Social Research* is the product of those discussions. We are indebted to Robert for initiating our collaboration, for his unwavering support and encouragement throughout the writing process, and for being a pleasure to work with. Without him this book would not have been written.

Together, we have several decades of combined methodology teaching experience at Brown University; the University of California, Los Angeles; the University of Essex; George Washington University; the University of Minnesota; and Texas A&M University. We thank our students for helping us refine our ability to convey both the excitement and the complications of studying society in a scientifically rigorous way.

We also thank Camille Sola, who provided excellent research assistance on the project while a PhD student in Public Policy and Public Administration at George Washington University.

We are indebted to the reviewers of our manuscript for sharing their expertise as well as their own experiences teaching methodology to students across a broad range of social science disciplines. Their suggestions have measurably improved the book. In particular, Steven Tuch thanks Myron Schwartz for his insights.

We owe much to the many mentors who shaped our approach to thinking about and teaching methodology. In particular, Paul Kellstedt wishes to thank Al Reynolds and Bob Terbog of Calvin College; Michael Lewis-Beck, Vicki Hesli, and Jack Wright at the University of Iowa; and Jim

Stimson and John Freeman at the University of Minnesota. Guy Whitten thanks the following, all from his days at the University of Rochester: Larry M. Bartels, Richard Niemi, G. Bingham Powell, Lynda Powell, William H. Riker, and David Weimer. Steven Tuch thanks Clifford C. Clogg, Marylee C. Taylor, Rex Warland, and James Rosenberger of Pennsylvania State University; and Martin L. Levin and S. Mitra of Emory University.

Finally, we thank our families for their endless support and for providing us with the time and space to bring this project to completion. We owe a special debt of gratitude to our spouses, to whom we dedicate the book.

Of course, we are solely responsible for any deficiencies that remain.

1 The Scientific Study of Society

OVERVIEW

As instructors, we realize that most social science students are interested in the substance of the field and not in its methodology. We begin with a discussion of the goals of this book and why a scientific approach to the study of society is more interesting and desirable than a "just the facts" approach. In this chapter we provide an overview of what it means to study society scientifically. We begin with an introduction to how we move from causal theories to scientific knowledge, and a key part of this process is thinking about the world in terms of *models* in which the concepts of interest become variables that are causally linked together by theories. We then introduce the goals and standards of social science research that will be our rules of the road to keep in mind throughout this book. The chapter concludes with a brief overview of the structure of the book.

Doubt is the beginning, not the end, of wisdom
—Chinese proverb

1.1 SOCIAL *SCIENCE*?

"You must like people." "You must enjoy helping others." These are responses that students often hear after announcing that they are taking courses in sociology. In fact, although for some sociologists such factors may have provided initial motivation for pursuing the field, this is not the focus of modern sociology. Instead, sociology is about the scientific study of social phenomena. Perhaps like you, a great many of today's sociologists were attracted to this discipline as undergraduates because of intense interest in a particular social issue. Although we are often drawn into sociology based on such passions, the most respected sociological research today is conducted in a fashion that makes it impossible to tell the personal views of the writer.

Many people taking their first sociological research course are surprised to find out how much science and, in particular, how much math are involved. We would like to encourage the students who find themselves in this position to hang in there with us – even if your answer to this encouragement is "But I'm only taking this class because they require it to graduate, and I'll never use any of this stuff again." Even if you never run a regression model after you graduate, having made your way through these materials should help you in a number of important ways. We have written this book with the following three goals in mind:

- *To help you consume academic social science research in your other courses.* One of the signs that a field of research is becoming scientific is the development of a common technical language. We aim to make the common technical language of social science accessible to you.
- *To help you become a better consumer of information.* In sociology and many other areas of scientific and popular communication, claims about causal relationships are frequently made. We want you to be better able to evaluate such claims critically.
- *To start you on the road to becoming a producer of scientific research on society.* This is obviously the most ambitious of our goals. In our teaching we often have found that once skeptical students get comfortable with the basic tools of social science, their skepticism turns into curiosity and enthusiasm.

To see the value of this approach, consider an alternative way of learning about society, one in which sociology courses would focus on "just the facts." Under this alternative, for example, a course on race and ethnicity might inform students that, in terms of residential segregation in urban areas in the U.S., African Americans are the minority group that is most highly segregated from whites, Asians are the least segregated, and Hispanics are intermediate between blacks and Asians. Moreover, data from the 2010 census indicate that, although the gradual decline in black–white segregation levels experienced in metropolitan areas between 1960 and 2000 continued into the first decade of the twenty-first century, segregation remains high. In 2010 the value of the black–white "index of dissimilarity" for all 367 metropolitan areas in the U.S. was 59 – meaning that, on average, 59 percent of either blacks or whites would have to change neighborhoods in order for the racial composition of each neighborhood to reflect the overall racial composition of the metropolitan area. The index values for Hispanic–white and Asian–white segregation were 48 and 41, respectively. Strikingly, in 2010 the average African

American urban dweller lived in a neighborhood that was 45 percent black and 35 percent white; the average white metropolitan inhabitant, on the other hand, lived in a neighborhood that was 75 percent white and only 8 percent black. Similarly, the neighborhood composition of the typical Hispanic metropolitan resident in 2010 was 46 percent Hispanic and 35 percent white, and that of the average Asian resident was 22 percent Asian and 49 percent white. In short, whites live in neighborhoods with only a minimal minority presence; blacks and Hispanics inhabit neighborhoods with high minority representation; and Asians live in neighborhoods where they are disproportionately represented, though with more whites than the neighborhoods of either African Americans or Hispanics (Logan and Stults, 2011).

As important as these facts are, however, the problem with a "just the facts" approach is that no attention is paid to the factors that cause segregation to be so high in the first place. The latter, more theoretical approach to the topic might focus on the primary explanations for persistent racial residential segregation in the U.S. discussed in the social science research literature: economic disparities among racial and ethnic groups that create differential access to quality neighborhoods; discrimination in the real estate, insurance, and mortgage-lending industries that make it difficult for minorities to rent or purchase homes in their neighborhoods of choice; and neighborhood residential preferences, not only of whites but of minority group members themselves (Massey and Denton, 1993). This approach helps us to better understand the dynamics of race and ethnicity in America today than a "just the facts" approach is capable of doing.

In this chapter we provide an overview of what it means to study society scientifically. We begin this discussion with an introduction to how we move from causal theories to scientific knowledge. A key part of this process is thinking about the world in terms of *models* in which the concepts of interest become **variables**[1] that are causally linked together by theories. We then introduce the goals and standards of social science research that will be our rules of the road to keep in mind throughout this book. We conclude this chapter with a brief overview of the structure of the book.

[1] When we introduce an important new term in this book, that term appears in boldface type. At the end of each chapter, we will provide short definitions of each bolded term that was introduced in that chapter. We discuss variables at great length later in this and other chapters. For now, a good working definition is that a variable is a definable quantity that can take on two or more values and is subject to change from one unit of analysis (e.g., a person, a neighborhood, or a city, to name a few common units of analysis) to another. An example of a variable is religion; researchers usually **measure** it in broad categories such as Protestant, Catholic, Jewish, Muslim, none, or other.

1.2 APPROACHING SOCIOLOGY SCIENTIFICALLY: THE SEARCH FOR CAUSAL EXPLANATIONS

I've said, I don't know whether it's addictive. I'm not a doctor. I'm not a scientist.

—Bob Dole, in a conversation with Katie Couric about tobacco during the 1996 U.S. presidential campaign

The question of "how do we know what we know" is, at its heart, a philosophical question. Scientists are lumped into different disciplines that develop standards for evaluating evidence. A core part of being a scientist and taking a scientific approach to studying the phenomena that interest you is always being willing to consider new evidence and, on the basis of that new evidence, change what you thought you *knew* to be true. This willingness to always consider new evidence is counterbalanced by a critical approach to the evaluation of new evidence that permeates the scientific approach. This is certainly true of the way that sociologists and other social scientists approach the study of society.

So what do social scientists do and what makes them scientists? A basic answer to this question is that, like other scientists, sociologists develop and test theories. A **theory** is a tentative conjecture about the causes of some phenomenon of interest. The development of **causal** theories about the social world requires thinking in new ways about familiar phenomena. As such, theory building is part art and part science. We discuss this in greater detail in Chapter 2, "The Art of Theory Building."

Once a theory has been developed, like all scientists, we turn to the business of testing our theory. The first step in testing a particular theory is to restate it as one or more testable hypotheses. A **hypothesis** is a theory-based statement about a relationship that we expect to observe framed in such a way that it can be empirically tested. For every hypothesis there is a corresponding **null hypothesis**. A null hypothesis is also a theory-based statement but it is about what we would observe if there were no relationship between an independent variable and the dependent variable. **Hypothesis testing** is a process in which scientists evaluate systematically collected evidence to make a judgment of whether the evidence favors their hypothesis or favors the corresponding null hypothesis. The process of setting up hypothesis tests involves both logical reasoning and creative design. In Chapter 3, "Evaluating Causal Relationships," we focus on the logical reasoning side of this process. In Chapter 4, "Research Design," we focus on the design part of this process. If a hypothesis survives rigorous testing, scientists start to gain confidence in that hypothesis rather than in the null hypothesis, and thus they also gain confidence in the theory from which they generated their hypothesis.

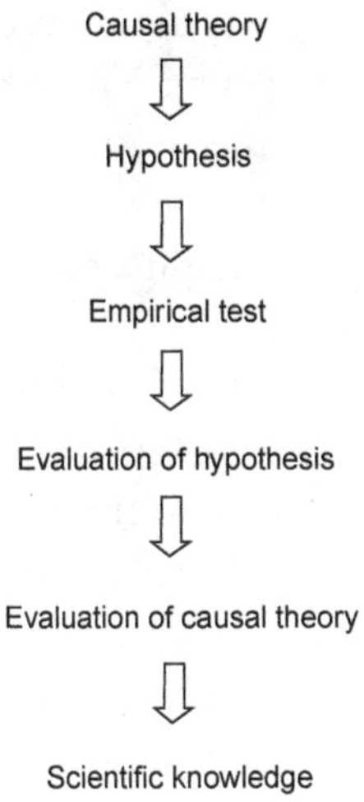

Figure 1.1 The road to scientific knowledge

Figure 1.1 presents a stylized schematic view of the path from theories to hypotheses to scientific knowledge.[2] At the top of the figure, we begin with a causal theory to explain our phenomenon of interest. We then derive one or more hypotheses about what our theory leads us to expect when we measure our concepts of interest (which we call variables – as subsequently discussed) in the real world. In the third step, we conduct **empirical** tests of our hypotheses.[3] From what we find, we evaluate our hypotheses relative to the corresponding null hypotheses. Next, from the results of our hypothesis tests, we evaluate our causal theory. In light of our evaluation of our theory, we then think about how, if at all, we should revise what we consider to be scientific knowledge concerning our phenomenon of interest.

A core part of the scientific process is skepticism. On hearing of a new theory, other scientists will challenge this theory and devise further tests. Although this process can occasionally become quite combative, it is a necessary component in the development of scientific knowledge. Indeed, a core component of scientific knowledge is that, as confident as we are in a particular theory, we remain open to the possibility that there is still a test out there that will provide evidence that makes us lose confidence in that theory.

It is important to underscore here the nature of the testing that scientists carry out. One way of explaining this is to say that scientists are *not* like lawyers in the way that they approach evidence. Lawyers work for a particular client, advocate a particular point of view (like "guilt" or "innocence"), and then accumulate evidence with a goal of proving their case to a judge or jury. This goal of *proving* a desired result determines their approach to evidence. When faced with evidence that conflicts with their case, lawyers attempt to ignore or discredit such evidence. When faced with evidence that supports their case, lawyers try to emphasize the applicability of the supportive evidence. In many ways, the scientific and legal approaches to evidence couldn't be further apart. Scientific confidence in a theory is achieved only after hypotheses derived from that theory have

[2] In practice, as we show in later chapters, the development of scientific knowledge is frequently much messier than this step-by-step diagram implies. Walter Wallace's classic, *The Logic of Science in Sociology* (1971), provides an excellent discussion of the complex interplay among these components of the scientific process.

[3] By "empirical" we simply mean "based on observations of the real world."

run a gauntlet of tough tests. At the beginning of a trial, lawyers develop a strategy to *prove* their case. In contrast, at the beginning of a research project, scientists will think long and hard about the most rigorous tests that they can conduct. A scientist's theory is never *proven* because scientists are always willing to consider new evidence that might contradict their theoretically based hypotheses.

The process of hypothesis testing reflects how hard scientists are on their own theories. As scientists evaluate systematically collected evidence to make a judgment of whether the evidence favors their hypothesis or favors the corresponding null hypothesis, they *always* favor the null hypothesis. Statistical techniques allow scientists to make probability-based statements about the empirical evidence that they have collected. You might think that, if the evidence was 50–50 between their hypothesis and the corresponding null hypothesis, the scientists would tend to give the nod to the hypothesis (from their theory) over the null hypothesis. In practice, though, this is not the case. Even when the hypothesis has an 80–20 edge over the null hypothesis, most scientists will still favor the null hypothesis. Why? Because scientists are very worried about the possibility of falsely rejecting the null hypothesis and therefore making claims that others ultimately will show to be wrong.

Once a theory has become established as a part of scientific knowledge in a field of study, researchers can build upon the foundation that this theory provides. Thomas Kuhn (1962) wrote about these processes in his famous book *The Structure of Scientific Revolutions*. According to Kuhn, scientific fields go through cycles of accumulating knowledge based on a set of shared assumptions and commonly accepted theories about the way that the world works. Together, these shared assumptions and accepted theories form what we call a **paradigm**. Once researchers in a scientific field have widely accepted a paradigm, they can pursue increasingly technical questions that make sense only because of the work that has come beforehand. This state of research under an accepted paradigm is referred to as **normal science**. When a major problem is found with the accepted theories and assumptions of a scientific field, that field will go through a revolutionary period during which new theories and assumptions replace the old paradigm to establish a new paradigm.

One of the more famous of these scientific revolutions occurred during the sixteenth century when the field of astronomy was forced to abandon its assumption that the Earth was the center of the known Universe. This was an assumption that had informed theories about planetary movement for thousands of years. In his book *De revolutionibus orbium coelestium* of 1543 (translated 2004 as *On the Revolutions of Heavenly Spheres*), Nicolaus Copernicus presented his theory that the Sun was the center of the known Universe. Although this radical theory met many challenges, an increasing body of evidence convinced astronomers that Copernicus had it right. In the aftermath of this **paradigm shift**, researchers developed new assumptions and theories that established a new paradigm, and the affected fields of study entered into new periods of normal scientific research.

It may seem hard to imagine that the field of sociology has gone through anything that can compare with the experiences of astronomers in the sixteenth century. Indeed, Kuhn and other scholars who study the evolution of scientific fields of research have a lively and ongoing debate about where the social sciences, like sociology, are in terms of their development. The more skeptical participants in this debate argue that sociology is not sufficiently mature to have a paradigm, much less a paradigm shift. If we put aside this somewhat esoteric debate about paradigms and paradigm shifts, we can see an important example of the evolution of scientific knowledge about society from the study of public opinion in the United States.

In the 1940s the study of public opinion through mass surveys was in its infancy. Prior to that time, sociologists and political scientists assumed that U.S. voters were heavily influenced by presidential campaigns – and, in particular, by campaign advertising – as they made up their minds about the candidates. To better understand how these processes worked, a team of researchers from Columbia University set up an in-depth study of public opinion in Erie County, Ohio, during the 1944 presidential election. Their study involved interviewing the same individuals at multiple time periods across the course of the campaign. Much to the researchers' surprise, they found that voters were remarkably consistent from interview to interview in terms of their vote intentions. Instead of being influenced by particular events of the campaign, most of the voters surveyed had made up their minds about how they would cast their ballots long before the campaigning had even begun. The resulting book by Paul Lazarsfeld, Bernard Berelson, and Hazel Gaudet (1948), titled *The People's Choice*, changed the way that scholars thought about public opinion and political behavior in the United States. If political campaigns were not central to vote choice, scholars were forced to ask themselves what *was* critical to determining how people voted.

At first other scholars were skeptical of the findings of the 1944 Erie County study, but as the revised theories of politics of Lazarsfeld et al. were evaluated in other studies, the field of public opinion underwent a change that looks very much like what Thomas Kuhn calls a "paradigm shift." In the aftermath of this finding, new theories were developed to attempt to explain the origins of voters' long-lasting attachments to political parties in the United States. An example of an influential study that was carried out under this shifted paradigm is Richard Niemi and Kent Jennings' seminal book from 1974, *The Political Character of Adolescence: The Influence of Families and Schools*. As the title indicates, Niemi and Jennings studied the attachments of schoolchildren to political parties. Under the pre-Erie County paradigm of public opinion, this study would not have made much sense. But once researchers had found that voters' partisan attachments were quite stable over time, studying them at the early ages at which they form became a reasonable scientific enterprise. You can see evidence of this paradigm at work in current studies of party identification and debates about its stability.

1.3 THINKING ABOUT THE WORLD IN TERMS OF VARIABLES AND CAUSAL EXPLANATIONS

So how do social scientists develop theories about society? A key element of this is that they order their thoughts about the social world in terms of concepts that scientists call *variables* and causal relationships between variables. This type of mental exercise is just a more rigorous way of expressing ideas about society that we hear on a daily basis. You should think of each variable in terms of its *label* and its *values*. The **variable label** is a description of what the variable is, and the **variable values** are the categories or metrics in which the variable occurs. So, if we're talking about the variable that reflects an individual's age, we could simply label this variable "Age" and the metric in which this variable occurs would typically be years, although months, days, or even hours might apply in some situations.

It is easier to understand the process of turning concepts into variables by using an example of an actual theory. For instance, if we're curious about the factors that shape people's attitudes toward immigrants, one possibility is that attitudes will be more positive when the U.S. economy is perceived as being relatively healthy. If we restate this in terms of a social science theory, the perceived state of the economy becomes the **independent variable** and attitudes toward immigrants becomes the **dependent variable**. One way of keeping the lingo of theories straight is to remember that the value of the "dependent" variable "depends" on the value of the "independent" variable. Recall that a theory is a tentative conjecture about the causes of some phenomenon of interest. In other words, a theory is a conjecture that the independent variable is causally related to the dependent variable; according to our theory, change in the value of the independent variable *causes* change in the value of the dependent variable.

This is a good opportunity to pause and try to come up with your own causal statement in terms of an independent and dependent variable; try filling in the following blanks with some variables that interest you:

____________________ causes ____________________

Sometimes it's easier to phrase causal propositions more specifically in terms of the values of the variables that you have in mind. For instance,

higher ________________ causes lower ________________

or

higher ________________ causes higher ________________

Once you learn to think about the world in terms of variables, you will be able to produce an almost endless slew of causal theories. In Chapter 4 we will discuss at length how we design research to evaluate the causal claims in theories, but one way to initially evaluate a particular theory is to think about the **causal explanation** behind it. The causal explanation behind a theory is the answer to the question, "*Why* do you think that this independent variable is causally related to this dependent variable?" If the answer is reasonable, then the theory has possibilities. In addition, if the answer is original and thought provoking, then you may really be on to something. Let's return now to our working example in which the perceived state of the economy is the independent variable and attitudes toward immigrants is the dependent variable. The causal explanation underlying this theory is our belief that the perceived state of the economy is *causally related* to views of immigrants *because* economic insecurity creates fear of competition for jobs and other resources among members of the host society. As a result, when the economy is thought to be performing well, attitudes toward immigrants will be more positive. When the economy is thought to be performing poorly, attitudes will be more negative. If we put this in terms of the preceding fill-in-the-blank exercise, we could write:

<u>perceptions of economic performance</u> cause

<u>attitudes toward immigrants,</u>

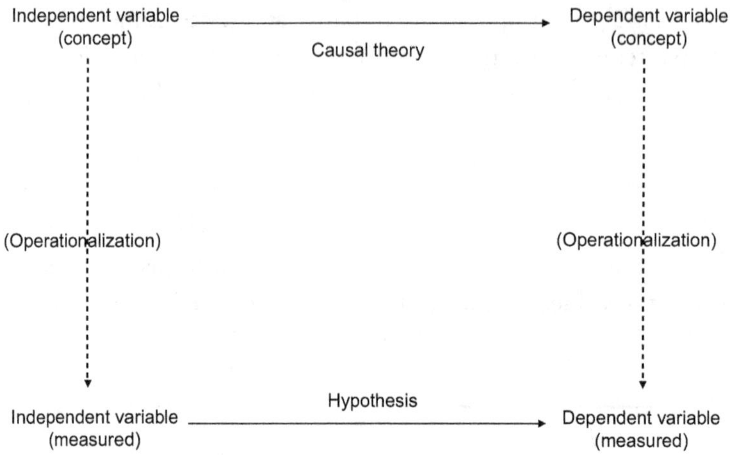

Figure 1.2 From theory to hypothesis

or, more specifically, we could write:

<u>perceptions of higher economic performance</u> cause <u>more positive views of immigrants.</u>

For now we'll refer to this theory, which has been widely advanced and tested by sociologists and political scientists alike, as "the theory of economic threat."

To test the theory of economic threat, we need to derive from it one or more testable hypotheses. Figure 1.2 provides a schematic diagram of the relationship between a theory and one of its hypotheses. At the top of this diagram are the components of the causal theory. As we move from the top part of this diagram (Causal theory) to the bottom part (Hypothesis), we are moving from a general statement about how we think the world works to a more specific statement about a relationship that we expect to find when we go out in the real world and measure (or **operationalize**) our variables.[4]

At the theory level at the top of Figure 1.2, our variables do not need to be explicitly defined. With the economic threat example, the independent variable, labeled "perceptions of economic performance," can be thought of as a concept that ranges from values of very strong to very poor. The dependent variable, labeled "attitudes toward immigrants," can be thought of as a concept that ranges from values of very positive to very negative. Our causal theory is that a stronger economic performance causes more

[4] Throughout this book we will use the terms "measure" and "operationalize" interchangeably, as is common practice in current social science literature.

positive attitudes toward immigrants by lessening fears of economic threat among members of the host society.

Because there are many ways in which we can measure each of our two variables, there are many different hypotheses that we can test to find out how well our theory holds up to real-world **data**. For instance, we can measure perceived economic performance by asking people what their expectations are regarding how the economy will be performing a year from now, among many other possibilities. Measurement (or operationalization) of concepts is an important part of the scientific process. We will discuss this in greater detail in Chapter 6, which is devoted entirely to evaluating different variable measurements and variation in variables. For now, imagine that we are operationalizing economic performance with a variable that we will label "Future Economic Performance." This measure, which is included in various surveys of the American public, asks respondents how they think the national economy will be doing in twelve months. The values for this variable range from much worse (coded 0) to much better (coded 4) on a five-point continuum. We operationalize our dependent variable, which we label "Attitudes Toward Immigrants," with what social scientists refer to as a "feeling thermometer" in which 0 indicates very negative attitudes and 100 indicates very positive attitudes.[5]

Figure 1.3 shows the axes of the graph that we could produce if we measured these two variables in a hypothetical sample of respondents. We could represent each respondent on the graph in Figure 1.3 by identifying the point that corresponds to the value of both "Future Economic Performance" (the horizontal, or X, axis) and "Attitudes Toward Immigrants" (the vertical, or Y, axis). For instance, if these values were (respectively) 2 and 50, the position for that person would be exactly in the center of the graph. Based on our theory, what would you expect to see if we collected these measures for all persons in the hypothetical sample? Remember that our theory is a stronger *expected economic performance* causes more positive *attitudes toward immigrants*. And we can restate this theory in reverse such that a weaker *expected economic performance* causes more negative *attitudes toward immigrants*.

So, what would this lead us to expect to see if we plotted real-world data onto Figure 1.3? To get this answer right, let's make sure that we know our way around this graph. If we move from left to right on the horizontal axis, which is labeled "Future Economic Performance," what

[5] If you're questioning the wisdom of these particular measures, you are thinking in the right way – any time you read about a measurement, you should think about different ways in which it might have been carried out. And, in particular, you should focus on the likely consequences of different measurement choices on the results of hypothesis tests. Evaluating measurement strategies is a major topic in Chapter 6.

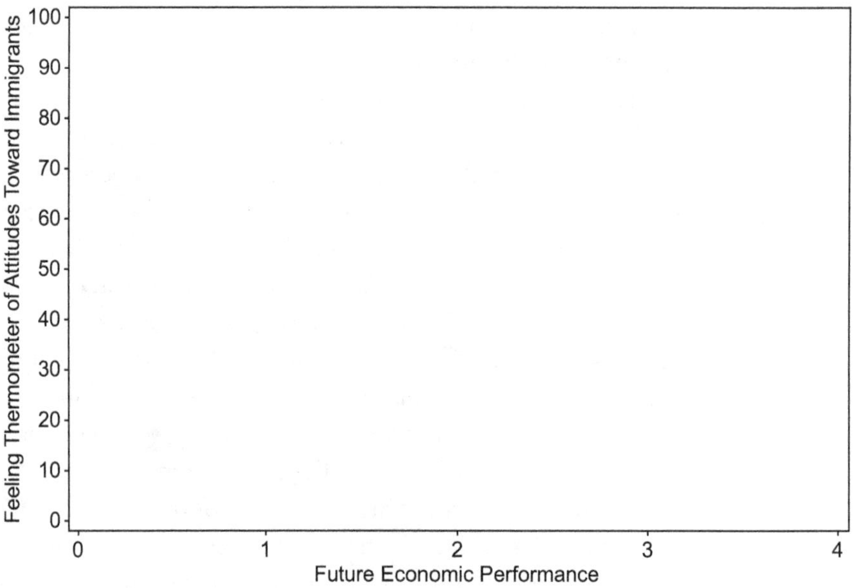

Figure 1.3 What would you expect to see based on the theory of economic threat?

is going on in real-world terms? We can see that, at the far left end of the horizontal axis, the value is 0. This would mean that respondents are very apprehensive about the one-year performance of the economy. As we move to the right on this axis, each point represents a better expected economic performance up to the point where we see a value of 4, indicating a much more sanguine view of the economy's performance over the next year. The vertical axis depicts values of "Attitudes Toward Immigrants." Moving upward on this axis represents increasingly positive, and moving downward represents increasingly negative, attitudes.

Now think about these two axes together in terms of what we would expect to see based on the economic theory of attitudes toward immigrants. In thinking through these matters, we should always start with our independent variable. This is because our theory states that the value of the independent variable exerts a causal influence on the value of the dependent variable. So, if we start with a very low value of *economic performance* – let's say 1 on the horizontal axis – what does our theory lead us to expect in terms of values for *attitudes toward immigrants*, the dependent variable? We would also expect the value of the dependent variable to be very low. This case would then be expected to be in the lower-left-hand corner of Figure 1.3. Now imagine a case in which economic performance was expected to be quite strong at 4. Under these circumstances, our theory would lead us to expect that attitudes toward immigrants would also be quite high. Such a case would be in the upper-right-hand corner of our graph.

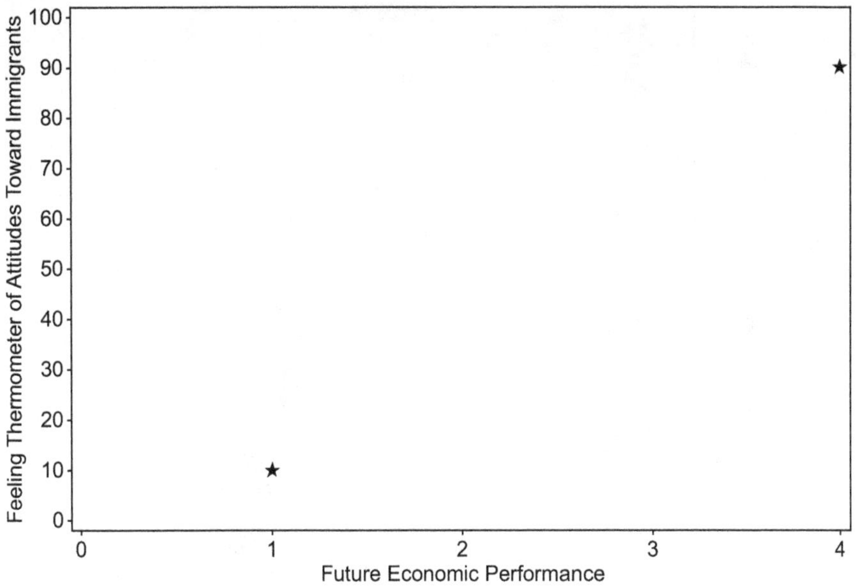

Figure 1.4 What would you expect to see based on the theory of economic threat? Two hypothetical cases

Figure 1.4 shows two such hypothetical points plotted on the same graph as Figure 1.3. If we draw a line between these two points, this line would slope upward from the lower left to the upper right. We describe such a line as having a positive slope. We can therefore hypothesize that the relationship between the variable labeled "Future Economic Performance" and the variable labeled "Attitudes Toward Immigrants" will be a **positive relationship.** A positive relationship is one for which higher values of the independent variable tend to coincide with higher values of the dependent variable.

Let's consider a different operationalization of our independent variable. Instead of "Future Economic Performance," let's use "Unemployment Percentage" as our operationalization of economic performance. We haven't changed our theory, but we need to rethink our hypothesis with this new measurement or operationalization. The best way to do so is to draw a picture like Figure 1.3 but with the changed independent variable on the horizontal axis. This is what we have in Figure 1.5. Now, as we move from left to right on the horizontal axis in Figure 1.5, the percentage of members of the workforce who are unemployed goes up. What does this mean in terms of economic performance? Rising unemployment is generally considered a poorer economic performance, whereas decreasing unemployment is considered a better performance. Based on our theory, what should we expect to see in terms of attitudes toward immigrants when the unemployment rate is low? What about when it is high?

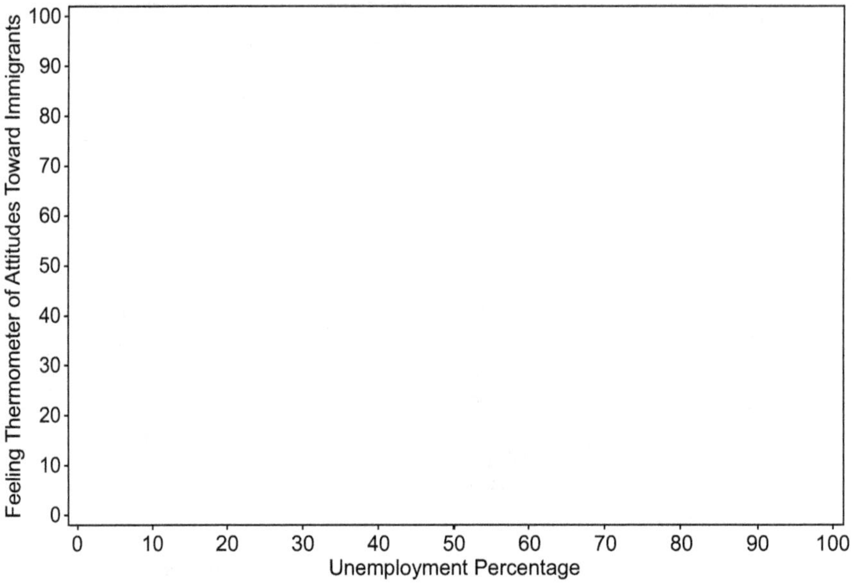

Figure 1.5 What would you expect to see based on the theory of economic threat?

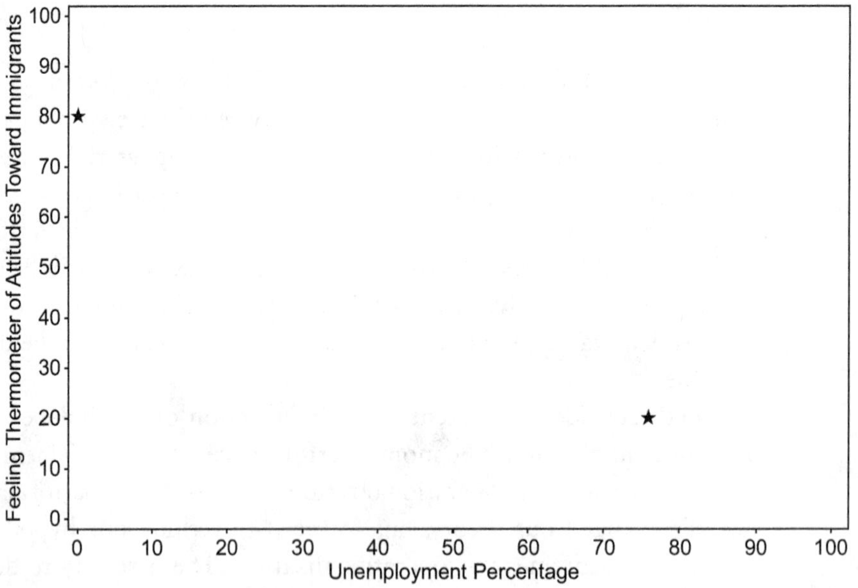

Figure 1.6 What would you expect to see based on the theory of economic threat? Two hypothetical cases

Figure 1.6 shows two such hypothetical points plotted on our graph of the "Unemployment Percentage" and "Attitudes Toward Immigrants" from Figure 1.5. The point in the upper-left-hand corner represents our expected value on the attitudes toward immigrants feeling thermometer when unemployment equals zero. Under these circumstances, our theory of economic threat leads us to expect that attitudes will be quite positive. The point in the lower-right-hand corner represents our expected value on the feeling thermometer when unemployment is very high. Under these circumstances our theory of economic threat leads us to expect that attitudes toward immigrants will be very negative. If we draw a line between these two points, this line would slope downward from the upper left to the lower right. We describe such a line as having a negative slope. We can therefore hypothesize that the relationship between the variable labeled "Unemployment Percentage" and the variable labeled "Attitudes Toward Immigrants" will be a **negative relationship**. A negative relationship is one for which higher values of the independent variable tend to coincide with lower values of the dependent variable.

In this example we have seen that the same theory can lead to a hypothesis of a positive or a negative relationship. The theory to be tested, together with the operationalization of the independent and the dependent variables, determines the direction of the hypothesized relationship. The best way to translate our theories into hypotheses is to draw a picture like Figure 1.3 or Figure 1.5. The first step is to label the horizontal axis with the variable label for the independent variable (as operationalized) and then label the low (left) and high (right) ends of the axis with appropriate value labels. The second step in this process is to label the vertical axis with the variable label for the dependent variable and then label the low and high ends of that axis with appropriate value labels. Once we have such a figure with the axes and low and high values for each properly labeled, we can determine what the expected value of our dependent variable should be if we observe both a low and a high value of the independent variable. And, once we have placed the two resulting points on our figure, we can tell whether our hypothesized relationship is positive or negative.

Once we have figured out our hypothesized relationship, we can collect data from real-world cases and see how well these data reflect our expectations of a positive or negative relationship. Once we collect all of the data on economic performance and attitudes toward immigrants, we will, however, still be a long way from confirming the theory that economic performance *causes* these attitudes. Even if a graph like Figure 1.3 produces compelling visual evidence, we will need to see more rigorous evidence than that. Chapters 6–12 focus on the use of statistics to evaluate hypotheses. The basic logic of statistical hypothesis testing is that we assess the probability that the relationship we find could be due to random chance. The stronger the evidence that such a relationship *could not* be due to random chance, the more confident we would be in our hypothesis. The stronger the evidence that such a relationship *could* be due to random chance, the more confident we would be in the corresponding null hypothesis. This in turn reflects on our theory.

We also, at this point, need to be cautious about claiming that we have "confirmed" our theory, because social scientific phenomena (such as attitudes toward immigrants) are usually complex and cannot be explained completely with a single independent variable. Take a minute or two to think about what other variables, aside from economic performance, you believe might be causally related to how people feel about immigrants. If you can come up with at least one, you are on your way to thinking like a social scientist. Because there are usually other variables that matter, we can continue to think about our theories two variables at a time, but we need to qualify our expectations to account for other variables. We will spend Chapters 3 and 4 expanding on these important issues.

1.4 MODELS OF SOCIETY

When we think about the phenomena that we want to better understand as dependent variables and develop theories about the independent variables that causally influence them, we are constructing **theoretical models**. A theoretical model is akin to a roadmap that helps us study, and (hopefully) explain, a social phenomenon that is of interest to us. The essential point about models is that they are simplifications that promote the construction and testing of theories. One of the remarkable aspects of models is that they are often more useful to us when they are inaccurate than when they are accurate. The process of thinking about the failure of a model to explain our outcome of interest can generate a new causal theory. Glaring inaccuracies often point us in the direction of fruitful theoretical progress.

1.5 RULES OF THE ROAD TO SCIENTIFIC KNOWLEDGE ABOUT SOCIETY

In the chapters that follow, we will focus on particular tools of sociological research. As we do this, try to keep in mind our larger purpose – trying to advance the state of scientific knowledge about society. As scientists, we have a number of basic rules that should never be far from our thinking:

- Make your theories causal.
- Don't let data alone drive your theories.
- Consider only empirical evidence.
- Avoid normative statements.
- Pursue both generality and parsimony.

1.5.1 Make Your Theories Causal

All of Chapter 3 deals with the issue of causality and, specifically, how we identify causal relationships. When social scientists construct theories, it is critical that they always think in terms of the causal processes that drive the phenomena in which they are interested. For us to develop a better understanding of the social world, we need to think in terms of causes and not mere **covariation.** The term covariation is used to describe a situation in which two variables vary together (or **covary**). If we imagine two variables, A and B, then we would say that A and B covary if it is the case that, when we observe higher values of variable A, we generally also observe higher values of variable B. We would also say that A and B covary if it is the case that, when we observe higher values of variable A, we generally also observe lower values of variable B.[6] It is easy to assume that when we observe covariation we are also observing causality, but it is important not to fall into this trap.

1.5.2 Don't Let Data Alone Drive Your Theories

This rule of the road is closely linked to the first. A longer way of stating it is "try to develop theories before examining the data on which you will perform your tests." The importance of this rule is best illustrated by a silly example. Suppose that we are looking at data on the murder rate (number of murders per 1000 people) in the city of Houston, Texas, by months of the year. This is our dependent variable, and we want to explain why it is higher in some months and lower in others. If we were to take as many different independent variables as possible and simply see whether they had a relationship with our dependent variable, one variable that we might find to strongly covary with the murder rate is the amount of money spent per capita on ice cream. If we perform some verbal gymnastics, we might develop a "theory" about how heightened blood sugar levels in people who eat too much ice cream lead to murderous patterns of behavior. Of course, if we think about it further, we might realize that both ice cream sales and the number of murders committed go up when temperatures rise. Do we have a causally plausible explanation for why temperatures and murder rates might be causally related? It is pretty well known that people's tempers tend to fray when the temperature is higher. People also spend a lot more time outside during hotter weather, and these two factors might

[6] A closely related term is **correlation**. For now we use these two terms interchangeably. In Chapter 9, you will see that there are precise statistical measures of covariance and correlation that are closely related to each other but produce different numbers for the same data.

combine to produce a causally plausible relationship between temperatures and murder rates.

What this rather silly example illustrates is that we don't want our theories to be crafted based entirely on observations from real-world data. We are likely to be somewhat familiar with empirical patterns relating to the dependent variables for which we are developing causal theories. This is normal; we wouldn't be able to develop theories about phenomena about which we know nothing. But we need to be careful about how much we let what we see guide our development of our theories. One of the best ways to do this is to think about the underlying causal process as we develop our theories and to let this have much more influence on our thinking than patterns that we might have observed. Chapter 2 is all about strategies for developing theories. One of these strategies is to identify interesting variation in our dependent variable. Although this strategy for theory development relies on data, it should not be done without thinking about the underlying causal processes.

1.5.3 Consider Only Empirical Evidence

As we previously outlined, we need to always remain open to the possibility that new evidence will come along that will decrease our confidence in even a well-established theory. A closely related rule of the road is that, as scientists, we want to base what we know on what we see from *empirical* evidence, which, as we have said, is simply "evidence based on observing the real world." Strong logical arguments are a good start in favor of a theory, but before we can be convinced, we need to see results from rigorous hypothesis tests.

1.5.4 Avoid Normative Statements

Normative statements are statements about how the world ought to be. Whereas politicians make and break their political careers with normative statements, social scientists need to avoid them at all costs. Most social scientists care about political issues and have opinions about how the world ought to be. On its own, this is not a problem. But when normative preferences about how the world "should" be structured creep into their scientific work, the results can become highly problematic. The best way to avoid such problems is to conduct research and report your findings in such a fashion that it is impossible for the reader to tell what are your normative preferences about the world.

This does not mean that good social science research cannot be used to change the world. To the contrary, advances in our scientific knowledge about phenomena enable policy makers to bring about changes in an effective manner. For instance, if we want to rid the world of wars (normative), we need to understand the systematic dynamics of the international system that produce wars in the first place (empirical and causal). If we want to rid America of homelessness (normative), we need to understand the pathways into and out of being homeless (empirical and causal). If we want to help our favored candidate win elections (normative), we need to understand what characteristics make people vote the way they do (empirical and causal).

1.5.5 Pursue Both Generality and Parsimony

Our final rule of the road is that we should always pursue generality and parsimony. These two goals can come into conflict. By "generality," we mean that we want our theories to be applied to as general a class of phenomena as possible. For instance, a theory that explains the causes of a phenomenon in only one country is less useful than a theory that explains the same phenomenon across multiple countries. Additionally, the more simple or **parsimonious** a theory is, the more appealing it becomes.[7]

In the real world, however, we often face trade-offs between generality and parsimony. This is the case because, to make a theory apply more generally, we need to add caveats. The more caveats that we add to a theory, the less parsimonious it becomes.

1.6 THE ETHICS OF SOCIAL RESEARCH

You may be surprised to find research ethics discussed in a textbook on *social* research, perhaps thinking instead that such concerns are the domain of medical researchers whose studies often have implications for patients' health. Although social scientists rarely face such issues, there are nevertheless several key ethical considerations that social researchers must be cognizant of as we conduct our research. We discuss those concerns in this section.

For our purposes, *ethical* refers to standards of conduct generally shared by members of a professional organization that highlight "right" and "wrong" behaviors in the context of research. In the absence of moral absolutes when it comes to defining what is right and wrong, however,

[7] The term "parsimonious" is often used in a relative sense. So, if we are comparing two theories, the theory that is simpler would be the more parsimonious. Indeed, this rule of the road might be phrased "pursue both generality and simplicity." We use the words "parsimony" and "parsimonious" because they are widely used to describe theories.

professional associations codify what are generally agreed-upon best practices. For instance, according to the American Sociological Association's *Code of Ethics*, there are four key guidelines for sociologists to follow regarding the ethical treatment of research subjects. (You will note that these guidelines are not mutually exclusive; in practice they can, and oftentimes do, overlap.)

1.6.1 Potential Harm

Not exposing subjects to potential harm is the *sine qua non* of ethical research behavior. Although this may strike you as an uncontroversial guideline, there are historical cases in which even this most basic right of research participants has been violated. Atrocities committed by Nazi scientists during World War II in the form of medical experiments performed on concentration camp prisoners are among the most egregious examples of violating the human rights of research subjects. The Tuskegee syphilis study conducted by the U.S. Public Health Service between 1932 and 1972 is another, albeit less well-known, example. The Tuskegee forty-year long study examined the effects of untreated syphilis among some 600 African American men. The mostly poor and uneducated participants were unaware of the true purpose of the study, and were even denied treatment with penicillin when it became the accepted standard of care for the disease in the early 1950s. In response to the Tuskegee scandal, the National Research Act of 1974 created Institutional Review Boards (IRBs) to guide universities and other organizations in their oversight of studies using human subjects. IRBs remain very much a part of the research landscape today.

The Nazi medical experiments and the Tuskegee syphilis study were heinous examples of human rights violations. Ethical issues arise less frequently, and typically less dramatically, in social science research, but they do arise on occasion. During the behavioral revolution in psychology in the 1960s, several famous experiments conducted at universities produced vigorous ethical debates. A commonly cited example is the so-called "prison study" conducted in 1971 by Stanford University psychologist Philip Zimbardo (Haney, Banks, and Zimbardo, 1973). Zimbardo was interested in the effect of roles on behavior. In order to examine this dynamic, he created a mock prison in a building on the campus of Stanford University and randomly assigned the male student volunteers to one of two roles, "guard" or "prisoner." Zimbardo himself assumed the role of "prison superintendent." Originally intended to last two weeks, the experiment was halted by Zimbardo after just six days because of psychological abuse inflicted by guards on prisoners amid a growing tendency by both groups to become so engrossed in their roles that they lost sight of the fact that the study was an experiment.

Another example of a social science experiment that resulted in psychological harm to participants is the famous Milgram obedience study (Milgram, 1963). Stanley Milgram, a psychologist at Yale University, conducted a study in 1961 to examine obedience to authority in the wake of atrocities committed during World War II under the rationale of following orders. Forty adult male volunteers who responded to a newspaper advertisement that solicited participants for a "learning experiment" were convened in a laboratory. The volunteers were assigned the role of "teacher" and were instructed to administer what they thought were electric shocks to "learners" when the learners failed a word pair test. (The ruse was that Milgram told the participants that he was testing how negative reinforcement – electric shocks – affected the "learning" of the "student.") The teachers were ordered to continue administering increasingly powerful shocks for each incorrect answer given by the learner even in the face of pleas from the learners to cease the experiment. It turns out, not surprisingly, that the learners were confederates of the experiment and that in reality no shocks had been administered to them. Milgram's goal was to determine how far the teachers would go in response to demands from an authority figure that the experiment continue. The disturbing answer was that fully two-thirds of the subjects administered the highest shock. What was the ethical violation in Milgram's study? Upon learning the true goal of the research during a post-experiment debriefing, many of the subjects suffered emotional distress and loss of self-esteem at the realization that they were willing to inflict what they thought was serious harm upon others. Scientific review boards consider such experiments unethical today.

1.6.2 Informed Consent

Voluntary participation is a key ingredient in social research, and participation cannot be truly voluntary without informed consent by research subjects. According to the ASA's *Code of Ethics*, "Informed consent is a basic ethical tenet of scientific research on human populations. Sociologists do not involve a human being as a subject in research without the informed consent of the subject or the subject's legally authorized representative, except as otherwise specified in this Code" (American Sociological Association, 2018:10). Of course, the Nazi medical experiments and the Tuskegee syphilis study discussed above blatantly violated this ethical guideline, in the former case by means of brutal force and in the latter by failing to provide study participants with full information about the study's risks.

1.6.3 Deception

As we just noted, informed consent is an important ethical component of research. But there are situations in which revealing to subjects the true nature of the research would so jeopardize the potential contribution of the study that it would be fruitless to conduct it at all. So the question arises, are there ever instances in which deceiving subjects about the goals of one's research is justified? Let's look again to the ASA for guidance. The *Code of Ethics* stipulates that "Sociologists do not use deceptive techniques (1) unless they have determined that their use will not be harmful to research participants; is justified by the study's prospective scientific, educational, or applied value; and that equally effective alternative procedures that do not use deception are not feasible, and (2) unless they have obtained the approval of institutional review boards or, in the absence of such boards, from another authoritative body with expertise on the ethics of research" (American Sociological Association, 2018:12).

A case in point will illustrate. In 1985 sociologist Judith Rollins published a book titled *Between Women: Domestics and Their Employers.* The study was based on in-depth interviews with domestic workers and their employers conducted by Rollins while she was a PhD student in sociology at Boston College. Rollins was interested in exploring hierarchical relationships between the mostly white, upper middle class women employers and their domestic workers, who were mostly women of color. In order to do so, Rollins became a domestic worker herself for a period of one year. She did not inform her employers that she in fact was a graduate student engaged in scholarly research. Clearly, by not being transparent about her goals, Rollins engaged in deception; and just as clearly, had she been honest about her real purposes, most if not all of her subjects would likely have declined to participate in the study. The question is whether or not her deception violated the ASA's *Code of Ethics*. In this case, since the potential harm to her subjects was likely quite low, Rollins was probably justified in using deception to gain access to her interviewees; no names, addresses, or other identifying information of employers was divulged by Rollins. Under these circumstances it is difficult to envision any tangible harm coming to participants as a consequence of being studied. Still, deceptive techniques were used, which, in the minds of some, was viewed as ethically unacceptable.

1.6.4 Anonymity and Confidentiality

It is incumbent upon researchers to protect the **anonymity** and **confidentiality** of our subjects; after all, to a greater or lesser degree, our research constitutes an invasion of others' privacy. Anonymity refers to a situation in which nobody, including the researcher, can connect a subject with his or her response; confidentiality refers to cases in which the researcher can connect responses with particular respondents but guarantees to subjects not to make that information accessible to others. Here's what the ASA has to say about this issue: "Sociologists have an obligation to ensure that confidential information is protected. They do so to ensure the integrity of research and the open communication with research participants and to protect sensitive information obtained in research, teaching, practice, and service" (American Sociological Association 2018:8). In short, subjects have a reasonable expectation of privacy that extends to any behaviors, attitudes, or beliefs revealed to the researcher in the course of a study.

As a case in point, a 1975 study by Laud Humphreys raised important questions not only about maintaining the anonymity and confidentiality of research subjects but also about informed consent and deception. Humphreys at the time was a PhD student in sociology at Washington University in St. Louis conducting research on consensual sexual encounters between men in public restrooms in St. Louis. He offered to serve as a "lookout" for the men while they engaged in sex. Using the license plates of the men's cars, Humphreys obtained the names and addresses of several of them. Months later, he contacted the men in their homes under the guise of conducting a survey on an unrelated topic. This now infamous study, *Tearoom Trade: Impersonal Sex in Public Places* (Humphreys, 1975), raised a number of troubling questions about the ethical obligation of the researcher to his or her subjects. First, a potential for harm to the subjects was clearly present if their behavior was publicly revealed. Second, the subjects were unaware that Humphreys was conducting a study and thus had no opportunity to give (or refuse) informed consent. (However, this is complicated by the fact that the behavior under study was conducted in a public place where, some observers argue, an expectation of privacy did not reasonably apply.) Third, Humphreys used deception in gaining the men's participation in the follow-up "survey." Finally, subjects' anonymity was clearly violated. Thus, the Humphreys study violated each of the ethical guidelines of the ASA's *Code of Ethics*.

With one exception, each of the social science studies mentioned here – Zimbardo's prison experiment, Milgram's obedience study, and Humphreys' *Tearoom Trade* – were conducted prior to the creation of institutional review boards in 1974. It is safe to say that none of them would have been approved by an IRB without substantial modification, and perhaps not at all. (The exception is Rollins' *Between Women*, which was published in 1985.)

1.7 A QUICK LOOK AHEAD

You now know the rules of the road. As we go through the next eleven chapters, you will acquire an increasingly complicated set of tools for developing and testing scientific theories about society, so it is crucial that, at every step along the way, you keep these rules in the back of your mind. The rest of this book can be divided into three different sections. The first section, which includes this chapter through Chapter 3, is focused on the development of theories to study causal relationships about society. In Chapter 2, "The Art of Theory Building," we discuss a range of strategies for developing theories about social phenomena. In Chapter 3, "Evaluating Causal Relationships," we provide a detailed explanation of the logic for evaluating causal claims about relationships between an independent variable, which we call "X," and a dependent variable, which we call "Y."

In the second section of this book we discuss the primary methodological approaches used by sociologists to investigate the social world. In Chapter 4, "Research Design," we examine experimental designs as well as two key "observational" designs, cross-sectional and time-series studies. Chapter 5, "Survey Research," takes a closer look at one of the most widely adopted observational methods in social science, the survey.

The third and final section of this book introduces the student to the basic quantitative tools that social scientists have at their disposal to investigate causal relationships. Chapter 6, "Measuring Concepts of Interest," is a detailed treatment of how we measure (or operationalize) our variables. Chapter 7, "Getting to Know Your Data," provides an introduction to a set of tools that can be used to summarize the characteristics of variables one at a time. Chapter 8, "Probability and Statistical Inference," introduces both the basics of probability theory as well as the logic of statistical hypothesis testing. In Chapter 9, "Bivariate Hypothesis Testing," we begin to apply the lessons from Chapter 8 to a series of empirical tests of the relationship between pairs of variables. Chapter 10, "Two-Variable Regression Models," introduces the two-variable regression model as an extension of the concepts from Chapters 8 and 9. In Chapter 11, "Multiple Regression," we introduce the multiple regression model, which allows researchers to examine the effects of independent variable X on dependent variable Y while simultaneously controlling for the effects of other independent variables. Lastly, in Chapter 12, "Putting It All Together to Produce Effective Research," we discuss how to apply the lessons learned in this book to begin to produce original research of your own.

CONCEPTS INTRODUCED IN THIS CHAPTER[8]

- anonymity – an assurance given to research participants that no one, including the researchers themselves, can connect a participant with his or her response
- causal – implying causality; a central focus of this book is on theories about "causal" relationships
- causal explanation – an attempt to explain *why* an independent variable is causally related to a dependent variable
- confidentiality – an assurance given to research participants that no identifying information about them will be provided to anyone except the researchers
- correlation – a statistical measure of covariation which summarizes the direction (positive or negative) and strength of the linear relationship between two variables
- covary (or covariation) – when two variables vary together, they are said to "covary"; the term "covariation" is used to describe circumstances in which two variables covary
- data – a collection of variable values for at least two observations
- dependent variable – a variable for which at least some of the variation is theorized to be caused by one or more independent variables
- empirical – based on real-world observation
- hypothesis – a theory-based statement about what we would expect to observe if our theory is correct; a hypothesis is a more explicit statement of a theory in terms of the expected relationship between a measure of the independent variable and a measure of the dependent variable
- hypothesis testing – the act of evaluating empirical evidence in order to determine the level of support for the hypothesis versus the null hypothesis
- independent variable – a variable that is theorized to cause variation in the dependent variable
- measure – a process by which abstract concepts are turned into real-world observations

[8] At the end of each chapter, we will provide short definitions of each bolded term that was introduced in that chapter. These short definitions are intended to help you get an initial grasp of the term when it is introduced. A full understanding of these concepts, of course, can only be gained through the context of the chapter.

- negative relationship – higher values of the independent variable tend to coincide with lower values of the dependent variable
- normal science – scientific research that is carried out under the shared set of assumptions and accepted theories of a paradigm
- normative statements – statements about how the world ought to be
- null hypothesis – a theory-based statement about what we would observe if there were no relationship between an independent variable and the dependent variable
- operationalize – another word for measurement; when a variable moves from the concept level in a theory to the real-world measure for a hypothesis test, it has been operationalized
- paradigm – a shared set of assumptions and accepted theories in a particular scientific field
- paradigm shift – when new findings challenge the conventional wisdom of a paradigm to the point where the set of shared assumptions and accepted theories in a scientific field is redefined
- parsimonious – synonym for simple or succinct
- positive relationship – higher values of the independent variable tend to coincide with higher values of the dependent variable
- theoretical model – the combination of independent variables, the dependent variable, and the causal relationships that are theorized to exist between them
- theory – a tentative conjecture about the causes of some phenomenon of interest
- variable – a definable quantity that can take on two or more values
- variable label – the label used to describe a particular variable
- variable values – the values that a particular variable can take on

EXERCISES

1. Pick another discipline in which you have taken a course and heard mention of scientific theories. How is sociology similar to and different from that discipline?
2. Think about something in the social world that you would like to better understand. Try to think about this as a variable with high and low values. This is your dependent variable at the conceptual level. Now think about what might cause the values of your dependent variable to be higher or lower. Try to phrase this in terms of an independent variable, also at the conceptual level. Write a paragraph about these two variables and your theory about why they are causally related to each other.

3. Identify something in the world that you would like to see happen (normative). What scientific knowledge (empirical and causal) would help you to pursue this goal?

4. Suppose you're a member of a Human Subjects Review Board tasked with evaluating the proposal for the Zimbardo, Milgram, Rollins, or Humphreys study. Formulate an argument, first, as to why the study should be approved by the Board (even if you do not believe that it should be), and, second, why the study should not be approved (even if you believe that it should be).

For Exercises 5 and 6, consider the following statement about the world: "If you care about economic success in a country, you should also care about the peoples' political rights in that country. In a society in which people have more political rights, the victims of corrupt business practices will work through the system to get things corrected. As a result, countries in which people have more political rights will have less corruption. In countries in which there is less corruption, there will be more economic investment and more economic success."

5. Identify at least two causal claims that have been made in the preceding statement. For each causal claim, identify which variable is the independent variable and which variable is the dependent variable. These causal claims should be stated in terms of one of the following types of phrases in which the first blank should be filled by the independent variable and the second blank should be filled by the dependent variable:

____________________ causes ____________________

higher ____________________ causes lower ____________________

higher ____________________ causes higher ____________________

6. Draw a graph like Figure 1.3 for each of the causal claims that you identified in Exercise 5. For each of your figures, do the following: Start on the left-hand side of the horizontal axis of the figure. This should represent a low value of the independent variable. What value of the dependent variable would you expect to find for such a case? Put a dot on your figure that represents this expected location. Now do the same for a case with a high value of the independent variable. Draw a line that connects these two points and write a couple of sentences that describe this picture.

7. Find an article in a social science journal that contains a model of a social dynamic that is of interest to you. Provide the citation to the article, and answer the following questions:

(a) What is the dependent variable?

(b) What is one of the independent variables?

(c) What is the causal theory that connects the independent variable to the dependent variable?

(d) Does this seem reasonable?

8. For each of the following statements, identify which, if any, rule(s) of the road to scientific knowledge about the social world has(have) been violated:

(a) This study of the relationship between economic development and the level of autocracy in a society is important because dictatorships are bad and we need to understand how to get rid of them.

(b) Did the 2019 impeachment of President Donald Trump cause him to lose the subsequent presidential election?

(c) It's just logical that poverty causes crime.

(d) This correlation supports the theory that intergroup contact reduces racial/ethnic prejudice.

2 The Art of Theory Building

OVERVIEW

In this chapter we discuss the art of theory building. Unfortunately there is no magical formula or cookbook for developing good theories about the social world. But there are strategies that will help you to develop good theories. We discuss these strategies in this chapter.

2.1 GOOD THEORIES COME FROM GOOD THEORY-BUILDING STRATEGIES

In Chapter 1 we discussed the role of theories in developing scientific knowledge. From that discussion, it is clear that a "good" theory is one that, after going through the rigors of the evaluation process, makes a contribution to scientific knowledge. In other words, a good theory is one that changes the way that we think about some aspect of the social world. We also know from our discussion of the rules of the road that we want our theories to be causal, not driven by data alone, empirical, nonnormative, general, and parsimonious. This is a tall order, and a logical question to ask at this point is "How do I come up with such a theory?"

Unfortunately, there is neither an easy answer nor a single answer. Instead, what we can offer you is a set of strategies. "Strategies?" you may ask. Imagine that you were given the following assignment: "Go out and get struck by lightning."[1] There is no cut-and-dried formula that will show you how to get struck by lightning, but certainly there are actions that you can take that will make it more likely. The first step is to look at a weather app on your smartphone and find an area where there is thunderstorm activity; if you were to go to such an area, you would increase your likelihood of

[1] Our lawyers have asked us to make clear that this is an illustrative analogy and that we are in no way encouraging you to go out and try to get struck by lightning!

getting struck. You would be even more likely to get struck by lightning if, once in the area of thunderstorms, you climbed to the top of a tall barren hill. But you would be still more likely to get struck if you carried with you a nine iron from your bag of golf clubs and, once on top of the barren hill, in the middle of a thunderstorm, you held that nine iron up to the sky. The point here is that, although there are no magical formulae that make the development of a good theory (or getting hit by lightning) a certain event, there are strategies that you can follow to increase the likelihood of it happening.

2.2 PROMISING THEORIES OFFER ANSWERS TO INTERESTING RESEARCH QUESTIONS

In the sections that follow, we discuss a series of strategies for developing theories. A reasonable question to ask before we depart on this tour of theory-building strategies is, "How will I know when I have a good theory?" Another way that we might think about this is to ask "What do good theories do?" We know from Chapter 1 that theories get turned into hypothesis tests, and then, if they are supported by empirical tests, they contribute to our scientific knowledge about what causes what. So a reasonable place to begin to answer the question of how one evaluates a new theory is to think about how that theory, if supported in empirical testing, would contribute to scientific knowledge. One of the main ways in which theories can be evaluated is in terms of the questions that they answer. If the question being answered by a theory is interesting and important, then that theory has potential. If our theory doesn't propose an answer to an interesting question, it probably needs to be redeveloped. As we consider different strategies for developing theories, we will refer back to this basic idea of answering questions.

2.3 IDENTIFYING INTERESTING VARIATION

A useful first step in theory building is to think about phenomena that vary and to focus on general patterns. Because theories are designed to explain variation in the dependent variable, identifying some variation that is of interest to you is a good jumping-off point. In Chapter 4 we present a discussion of two of the most common research designs – cross-sectional and time-series observational studies – in some detail. For now it is useful to give a brief description of each in terms of the types of variation in the dependent variable. These should help clarify the types of variation to consider as you begin to think about potential research ideas.

When we think about measuring our dependent variable, the first things that we need to identify are the time and spatial dimensions over which we would like to measure this variable. The **time dimension** identifies the point or points in time at which we would like to measure our variable. Depending on what we are measuring, typical time increments (**time units**) for social science data are annual, quarterly, monthly, or weekly measures. The **spatial dimension** identifies the unit of analysis that we want to collect information from. There is a lot of variability in terms of the **spatial units** in social science data. If we are looking at survey data, the spatial unit will be the individual people who answered the survey (known as survey respondents). If we are looking at data on the 100 largest U.S. cities, the spatial unit will be those cities. Data from comparative studies often take nations as their spatial units.

Throughout this book, we think about measuring our dependent variable such that one of these two dimensions will be static (or constant). This means that our measures of our dependent variable will be one of two types. The first is a **time-series measure**, in which the spatial dimension is the same for all cases and the dependent variable is measured at multiple points in time. The second is a **cross-sectional measure**, in which the time dimension is the same for all cases and the dependent variable is measured for multiple spatial units. Although it is possible for us to measure the same variable across both time and space, we strongly recommend thinking in terms of variation across only one of these two dimensions as you attempt to develop a theory about what causes this variation.[2] Let's consider an example of each type of dependent variable.

2.3.1 Time-Series Example

In Figure 2.1 we see the average monthly level of U.S. presidential approval displayed from 1995 to 2005. We can tell that this variable is measured as a time series because the spatial unit is the same (the United States), but the variable has been measured at multiple points in time (each month). This measure is comparable across the cases; for each month we are looking at the percentage of people who reported that they approved of the job that the President was doing. Once we have a measure like this that is comparable across cases, we can start to think about what independent variable might *cause* the level of the dependent variable to be higher or

[2] As we mentioned in Chapter 1, we will eventually theorize about multiple independent variables simultaneously causing the same dependent variable to vary. Confining variation in the dependent variable to a single dimension helps to make such multivariate considerations tractable.

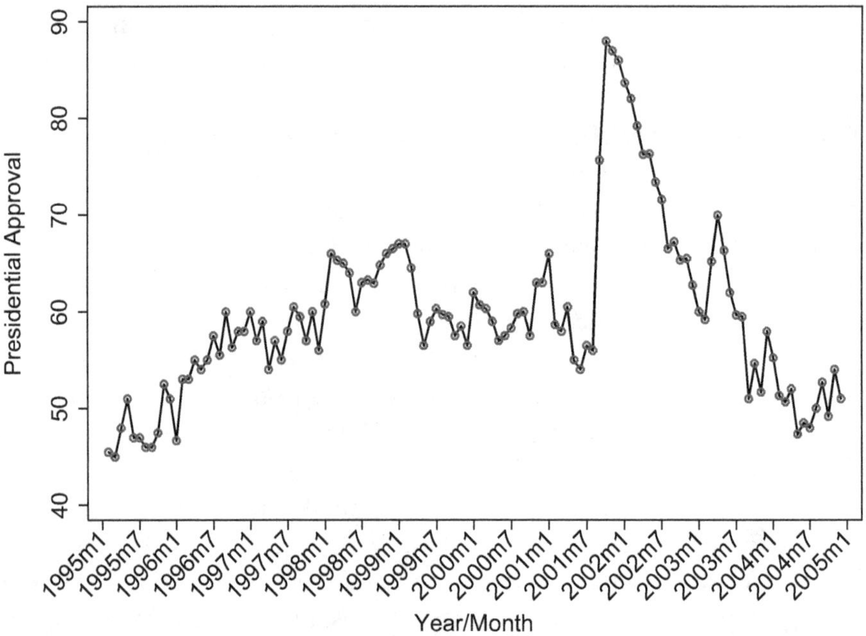

Figure 2.1 Presidential approval, 1995–2005

lower. In other words, we are looking for answers to the research question, "What causes presidential approval to go up and down?"

If you just had a mental alarm bell go off telling you that we seemed to be violating one of our rules of the road from Chapter 1, then congratulations – you are doing a good job paying attention. Our second rule of the road is "don't let data alone drive your theories." Remember that we also can phrase this rule as "try to develop theories before examining the data on which you will perform your tests." Note, however, that in this example we are only examining variation in one of our variables, in this case the dependent variable. We would start to get into real problems if we plotted pairs of variables and then developed a theory only once we observed a pair of variables that varied together. If this still seems like we are getting too close to our data before developing our theory, we could develop a theory about U.S. presidential approval using Figure 2.1, but then test that theory with a different set of data that may or may not contain the data depicted in Figure 2.1.

2.3.2 Cross-Sectional Example

In Figure 2.2 we see **Gini coefficients** in 2013 for 23 randomly selected nations. Gini coefficients measure the degree of income inequality among residents of a nation. The coefficients range from a value of 0, indicating

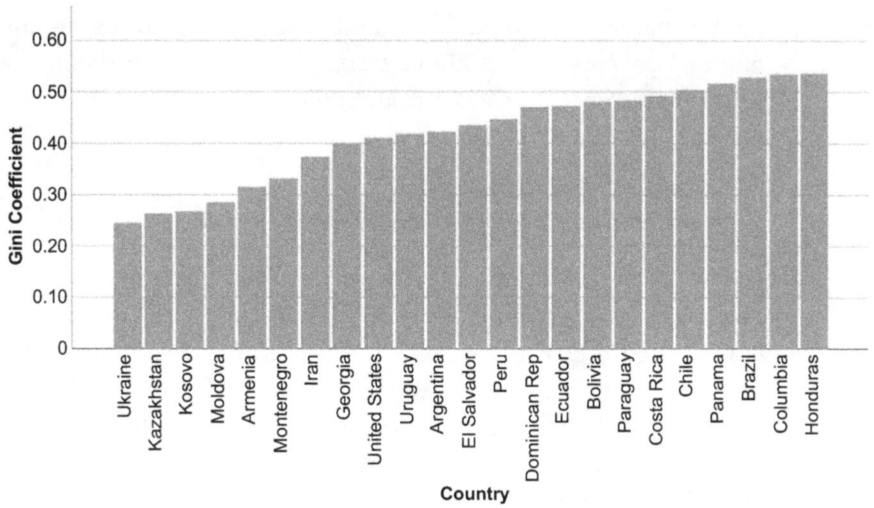

Figure 2.2 Gini coefficients in 2013

total equality in the distribution of income (each resident earns the same amount) to 1, indicating total inequality (one resident earns all the income). We can tell that this variable is measured cross-sectionally, because it varies across spatial units (nations) but does not vary across time (it is measured for the year 2013 for each case). When we measure variables across spatial units like this, we have to be careful to choose appropriate measures that are comparable across spatial units. To better understand this, imagine that we had measured our dependent variable as the amount of money that residents of each nation earn. The problem would be that country currencies – the Armenian Dram, the Moldovian Leu, and Chilean Peso – do not take on the same value. We would need to know the currency exchange rates in order to make these comparable across nations. Using currency exchange rates, we would be able to convert the absolute amounts of money that residents of each nation earn into a common measure. This would be a perfectly reasonable dependent variable. With this variation in mind, we could develop a theory to answer the question "What *causes* income inequality across nations?"

2.4 LEARNING TO USE YOUR KNOWLEDGE

One of the common problems that people have when trying to develop a theory about a phenomenon of interest is that they can't get past a particular event in time or a particular place about which they know a lot. It is helpful to know some specifics about the event, but it is also important to be able to distance yourself from the specifics of one case and to think more broadly about the underlying causal process. To use an analogy, it's fine to know something about trees, but we want to theorize about the forest. Remember, one of our rules of the road is to try to make our theories general.

2.4.1 Moving from a Specific Event to More General Theories

For an example of this, return to Figure 2.1. What is the first thing that you think most people notice when they look at Figure 2.1? Once they have figured out what the dimensions are in this figure (U.S. presidential approval over time), many people look at the fall of 2001 and notice the sharp increase in presidential approval that followed the terrorist attacks on the United States on September 11, 2001. This is a period of recent history about which many people have detailed memories. In particular, they might remember how the nation rallied around President Bush in the aftermath of these attacks. There are few people who would doubt that there was a causal linkage between these terrorist attacks and the subsequent spike in presidential approval.

At first glance, this particular incident might strike us as a unique event from which general theoretical insights cannot be drawn. After all, terrorist attacks on U.S. soil are rare events, and attacks of this magnitude are even more rare. The challenge to the scientific mind when we have strong confidence about a causal relationship in one specific incident is to push the core concepts around in what we might call thought experiments: How might a less-effective terrorist attack affect public opinion? How might other types of international incidents shape public opinion? Do we think that terrorist attacks lead to similar reactions in public opinion toward leaders in other nations? Each of these questions is posed in general terms, taking the specific events of this one incident as a jumping-off point. The answers to these more general questions should lead us to general theories about the causal impact of international incidents on public opinion.

In the 1970s John Mueller moved from the specifics of particular international incidents and their influence on presidential approval toward a general theory of what causes rallies (or short-term increases) in presidential approval.[3] Mueller developed a theory that presidential approval would increase in the short term any time that there was international conflict. Mueller thought that this would occur because, in the face of international conflict, people would tend to put aside their partisan differences and other critiques that they may have of the President's handling of his job and support him as the commander in chief of the

[3] See Mueller (1973).

nation. In Mueller's statistical analysis of time-series data on presidential approval, he found that there was substantial support for his hypothesis that international conflicts would raise presidential approval rates, and this in turn gave him confidence in his theory of public opinion rallies.

2.4.2 Know Local, Think Global: Can You Drop the Proper Nouns?

Physicists don't have theories that apply only in France, and neither should we. Yet many social scientists write articles with one particular geographic context in mind. Among these, the articles that have the greatest impact are those that advance general theories from which the proper nouns have been removed.[4] An excellent example of this is Michael Lewis-Beck's (1997) article titled "Who's the Chef?" Lewis-Beck, like many observers of French politics, had observed the particularly colorful period from 1986 to 1988 during which the president was a socialist named François Mitterand and the prime minister was Jacques Chirac, a right-wing politician from the Gaullist RPR party. The height of this political melodrama occurred when both leaders showed up to international summits of world leaders claiming to be the rightful representative of the French Republic. This led to a famous photo of the leaders of the G7 group of seven nations that contained eight people.[5] Although many people saw this as just another colorful anecdote about the ever-changing nature of the power relationship between presidents and prime ministers in Fifth Republic France, Lewis-Beck moved from the specifics of such events to develop and test a general theory about political control and public opinion.

His theory was that changing the political control of the economy would cause public opinion to shift in terms of who was held accountable for the economy. In France, during times of unified political control of the top offices, the president is dominant, and thus according to Lewis-Beck's theory the president should be held accountable for economic outcomes. However, during periods of divided control, Lewis-Beck's theory leads to the expectation that the prime minister, because of his or her control of economic management during such periods, should be held accountable for economic outcomes. Through careful analysis of time-series data on political control and economic accountability, Lewis-Beck found that his theory was indeed supported.

[4] By "proper nouns," we mean specific names of people or countries. But this logic can and should be pushed further to include specific dates, as we subsequently argue.

[5] The G7, formerly the G8 between 1997 and the 2014 suspension of Russia due to its annexation of Crimea, is composed of the heads of government from the world's most advanced industrialized nations.

Although the results of this study are important for advancing our understanding of French politics, the theoretical contribution made by Lewis-Beck was much greater because he couched it in general terms and without proper nouns. We also can use this logic to move from an understanding of a specific event to general theories that explain variation across multiple events. For example, although it might be tempting to think that every U.S. presidential election is entirely unique – with different candidates (proper names) and different historical circumstances – the better scientific theory does *not* explain only the outcome of the 2016 U.S. presidential election, but of U.S. presidential elections in general. That is, instead of asking "Why did Trump beat Clinton in the 2016 election?" we should ask either "What causes the incumbent party to win or lose in U.S. presidential elections?" or "What causes Republican candidates to fare better or worse than Democratic candidates in U.S. presidential elections?"

2.5 EXAMINE PREVIOUS RESEARCH

Once you have identified an area in which you want to conduct research, it is often useful to look at what other work has been done that is related to your areas of interest. As we discussed in Chapter 1, part of taking a scientific approach is to be skeptical of research findings, whether they are our own or those of other researchers. By taking a skeptical look at the research of others, we can develop new research ideas of our own and thus develop new theories.

We therefore suggest looking at research that seems interesting to you and, as you examine what has been done, keep the following list of questions in mind:

- What (if any) other causes of the dependent variable did the previous researchers miss?
- Can their theory be applied elsewhere?
- If we believe their findings, are there further implications?
- How might this theory work at different levels of aggregation (micro $\Longleftrightarrow$ macro)?

2.5.1 What Did the Previous Researchers Miss?

Any time that we read the work of others, the first thing that we should do is break down their theory or theories in terms of the independent and dependent variables that they claim are causally related to each other. We cannot overstate the importance of this endeavor. We understand that this can be a difficult task for a beginning student, but it gets easier with practice. A good way to start this process is to look at the figures or tables in an article and ask yourself, "What is the dependent variable here?" Once we have done this, we should think about whether the causal arguments that other researchers have advanced seem reasonable. (In Chapter 3 we present a detailed four-step process for doing this.) We should also be in the habit of coming up with other independent variables that we think might be causally related to the same dependent variable. Going through this type of mental exercise can lead to new theories that are worth pursuing.

2.5.2 Can Their Theory Be Applied Elsewhere?

When we read about the empirical research that others have conducted, we should be sure that we understand which specific cases they were studying when they tested their theory. We should then proceed with a mental exercise in which we think about what we might find if we applied the same theory to other cases. In doing so, we will probably identify some cases for which we expect to get the same results, as well as other cases for which we might have different expectations. Of course, we would have to carry out our own empirical research to know whether our speculation along these lines is correct, but replicating research can lead to interesting findings. The most useful theoretical development comes when we can identify systematic patterns in the types of cases that will fit and those that will not fit the established theory. These systematic patterns are additional variables that determine whether a theory will work across an expanded set of cases. In this way we can think about developing new theories that will subsume the original established theory.

2.5.3 If We Believe Their Findings, Are There Further Implications?

Beginning researchers often find themselves intimidated when they read convincing accounts of the research carried out by more established scholars. After all, how can we ever expect to produce such innovative theories and find such convincingly supportive results from extensive empirical tests? Instead of being intimidated by such works, we need to learn to view them as opportunities – opportunities to carry their logic further and think about what other implications might be out there. If, for example, another researcher has produced a convincing theory about how voters behave, we could ask how might this new understanding alter the behavior of strategic politicians who understand that voters behave in this fashion?

One of the best examples of this type of research extension in social science comes from our previous example of Mueller's (1973) research on rallies in presidential popularity. Because Mueller had found such convincingly supportive evidence of this "rally 'round the flag effect" in his empirical testing, other researchers were able to think through the strategic consequences of this phenomenon. This led to a new body of research on a phenomenon called "diversionary use of force" (Richards et al., 1993). The idea of this new research is that, because strategic politicians will be aware that international conflicts temporarily increase presidential popularity, they will choose to generate international conflicts at times when they need such a boost.

2.5.4 How Might This Theory Work at Different Levels of Aggregation (Micro $\Longleftrightarrow$ Macro)?

As a final way to use the research of others to generate new theories, we suggest considering how a theory might work differently at varying levels of aggregation. In sociological research, the lowest level of aggregation is usually at the level of individual people in studies of public opinion. As we saw in Section 2.5.3, when we find a trend in terms of individual-level behavior, we can develop new theoretical insights by thinking about how such trends might be utilized. Sometimes it is possible to gain these insights by simply changing the level of aggregation. As we have seen, social scientists have often studied trends in public opinion by examining data measured at the national level over time. This type of study is referred to as the study of macro trends. When we find trends in public opinion at higher (macro) levels of aggregation, it is always an interesting thought exercise to consider what types of patterns of individual-level or "micro-level" behavior are driving these aggregate-level findings.

As an example of this, return to the "rally 'round the flag" example and change the level of aggregation. We have evidence that, when there are international conflicts, public opinion toward the President becomes more positive. What types of individual-level forces might be driving this observed aggregate-level trend? It might be the case that there is a uniform shift across all types of individuals in their feelings about the President. It might also be the case that the shift is less uniform. Perhaps individuals who dislike the President's policy positions on domestic events are willing to put these differences aside in the face of international conflicts, whereas the opinions of the people who were already supporters of the President remain unchanged. Thinking about the individual-level dynamics that drive aggregate observations can be a fruitful source of new causal theories.

2.6 HOW DO I KNOW IF I HAVE A "GOOD" THEORY?

Once you have gone through some or all of the suggested courses of action for building a theory, a reasonable question to ask is, "How do I know if

I have a 'good' theory?" Unfortunately there is not a single succinct way of answering this question. Instead, we suggest that you answer a set of questions about your theory and consider your honest answers to these questions as you try to evaluate the overall quality of your theory. You will notice that some of these questions come directly from the "rules of the road" that we developed in Chapter 1:

- Does your theory offer an answer to an interesting research question?
- Is your theory causal?
- Can you test your theory on data that you have not yet observed?
- How general is your theory?
- How parsimonious is your theory?
- How new is your theory?
- How nonobvious is your theory?

2.6.1 Does Your Theory Offer an Answer to an Interesting Research Question?

As we discussed at the beginning of this chapter, promising theories offer answers to interesting research questions. Anytime that you formulate a theory, it's worth turning it around and asking what is the research question for which it offers an answer. If you can't give a straightforward answer to this question, you probably need to rethink your theory. A related question that you should also ask is whether anyone would care if you found support for your theory. If the answer to this question is "no," then you probably need to rethink your theory as well.

2.6.2 Is Your Theory Causal?

Remember that our first rule of the road to scientific knowledge about society is "Make your theories causal." If your answer to the question "Is your theory causal?" is anything other than "yes," then you need to go back to the drawing board until the answer is an emphatic "yes."

As scientists studying society, we want to know why things happen the way that they happen. As such, we will not be satisfied with mere correlations and we demand causal explanations. We know from Chapter 1 that one way initially to evaluate a particular theory is to think about the causal explanation behind it. The causal explanation behind a theory is the answer to the question "Why do you think that this independent variable is causally related to this dependent variable?" If the answer is reasonable, then you can answer this first question with a "yes."

2.6.3 Can You Test Your Theory on Data That You Have Not Yet Observed?

Our second rule of the road is "Don't let data alone drive your theories," which we restated in a slightly longer form as "Try to develop theories before examining the data on which you will perform your tests." If you have derived your theory from considering a set of empirical data, you need to be careful not to have observed all of the data on which you can test your theory. This can be a somewhat gray area, and only you know whether your theory is entirely data-driven and whether you observed all of your testing data before you developed your theory.

2.6.4 How General Is Your Theory?

We could rephrase this question for evaluating your theory as "How widely does your theory apply?" To the extent that your theory is not limited to one particular time period or to one particular spatial unit, it is more general. Answers to this question vary along a continuum – it's not the end of the world to have a fairly specific theory, but, all else being equal, a more general theory is more desirable.

2.6.5 How Parsimonious Is Your Theory?

As with the question in the preceding subsection, answers to this question also vary along a continuum. In fact, it is often the case that we face a trade-off between parsimony and generality. In other words, to make a theory more general, we often have to give up parsimony, and to make a theory more parsimonious, we often have to give up generality. The important thing with both of these desirable aspects of a theory is that we have them in mind as we evaluate our theory. If we can make our theory more general or more parsimonious and without sacrifice, we should do so.

2.6.6 How New Is Your Theory?

At first it might seem that this is a pretty straightforward question to answer. The problem is that we cannot know about all of the work that has been done before our own work in any particular area of research. It also is often the case that we may think our theory is really new, and luckily we have not been able to find any other work that has put forward the same theory on the same phenomenon. But then we discover a similar theory on a related phenomenon. There is no simple answer to this question. Rather, our scholarly peers usually answer this question of newness for us when they evaluate our work.

2.6.7 How Nonobvious Is Your Theory?

As with the question "How new is your theory?" the question "How nonobvious is your theory?" is best answered by our scholarly peers. If, when they are presented with your theory, they hit themselves in the head and say, "Wow, I never thought about it like that, but it makes a lot of sense!" then you have scored very well on this question.

Both of these last two questions illustrate an important part of the role of theory development in any science. It makes sense to think about theories as being like products and scientific fields as being very much like markets in which these products are bought and sold. Like other entrepreneurs in the marketplace, scientific entrepreneurs will succeed to the extent that their theories (products) are new and exciting (nonobvious). But, what makes a theory "new and exciting" is very much dependent on what has come before it.

2.7 CONCLUSION

We have presented a series of different strategies for developing theories of society. Each of these strategies involves some type of thought exercise in which we arrange and rearrange our knowledge about the social world in hopes that doing so will lead to new causal theories. You have, we're certain, noticed that there is no simple formula for generating a new theory and hopefully, as a result, you will appreciate our description of theory building as an "art" in the chapter's title. Theoretical developments come from many places, and being critically immersed in the ongoing literature that studies your phenomenon of choice is a good place to start.

CONCEPTS INTRODUCED IN THIS CHAPTER

- cross-sectional measure – a measure for which the time dimension is the same for all cases and the cases represent multiple spatial units
- Gini coefficient – a measure of the extent of income inequality among residents in a nation; coefficients range from a value of 0, indicating total equality in the distribution of income (i.e., each resident earns the same amount) to 1, indicating total inequality (i.e., one resident earns all the income)
- spatial dimension – the physical units on which a variable is measured
- spatial unit – the physical unit that forms the basis for observation; also referred to as a "unit of analysis"

- time dimension – the point or points in time at which a variable is measured
- time unit – the time-based unit that forms the basis for observation
- time-series measure – a measure for which the spatial dimension is the same for all cases and the cases represent multiple time units

EXERCISES

1. Table 2.1 contains the fifty most downloaded articles from American Sociological Association journals in 2018. Obtain copies of two of these articles that are of interest to you and describe what the research questions are.

Table 2.1 The fifty most downloaded articles from American Sociological Association journals in 2018
Ryan Jerome LeCount. Visualizing the Increasing Effect of Racial Resentment on Political Ideology among Whites, 1986 to 2016. *Socius* 4, September 2018
Heather McLaughlin, Christopher Uggen, and Amy Blackstone. Sexual Harassment, Workplace Authority, and the Paradox of Power. *American Sociological Review* 77(4), August 2012
Peter Conrad, and Kristin K. Barker. The Social Construction of Illness: Key Insights and Policy Implications. *Journal of Health and Social Behavior* 51(extra issue), March 2010
Stephen Vaisey, and Omar Lizardo. Cultural Fragmentation or Acquired Dispositions? A New Approach to Accounting for Patterns of Cultural Change. *Socius* 2, October 2016
Peter Hart-Brinson. The Social Imagination of Homosexuality and the Rise of Same-Sex Marriage in the United States. *Socius* 2, February 2016
Jo C. Phelan, Bruce G. Link, and Parisa Tehranifar. Social Conditions as Fundamental Causes of Health Inequalities: Theory, Evidence, and Policy Implications. *Journal of Health and Social Behavior* 51(extra issue), March 2010
Peggy A. Thoits. Stress and Health: Major Findings and Policy Implications. *Journal of Health and Social Behavior* 51(extra issue), March 2010
Katrin Auspurg, Thomas Hinz, and Carsten Sauer. Why Should Women Get Less? Evidence on the Gender Pay Gap from Multifactorial Survey Experiments. *American Sociological Review* 82(1), February 2017
Robert J. Sampson. Rethinking Crime and Immigration. *Contexts* 7(1), February 2008
Ted Thornhill. We Want Black Students, Just Not You: How White Admissions Counselors Screen Black Prospective Students. *Sociology of Race and Ethnicity* 5(4), 456–470, October 2019

Table 2.1 *(continued)*

Lauren A. Rivera. Hiring as Cultural Matching: The Case of Elite Professional Service Firms. *American Sociological Review* 77(6), December 2012
Amy Adamczyk, and Brittany E. Hayes. Religion and Sexual Behaviors: Understanding the Influence of Islamic Cultures and Religious Affiliation for Explaining Sex Outside of Marriage. *American Sociological Review* 77(5), October 2012
Debra Umberson, and Jennifer Karas Montez. Social Relationships and Health: A Flashpoint for Health Policy. *Journal of Health and Social Behavior* 51(extra issue), March 2010
Ruth Milkman. A New Political Generation: Millennials and the Post-2008 Wave of Protest. *American Sociological Review* 82(1), February 2017
Oliver Hahl, Minjae Kim, and Ezra W. Zuckerman Sivan. The Authentic Appeal of the Lying Demagogue: Proclaiming the Deeper Truth about Political Illegitimacy. *American Sociological Review* 83(1), February 2018
Sarah Brayne. Big Data Surveillance: The Case of Policing. *American Sociological Review* 82(5), October 2017
Elizabeth A. Armstrong, Paula England, and Alison C. K. Fogarty. Accounting for Women's Orgasm and Sexual Enjoyment in College Hookups and Relationships. *American Sociological Review* 77(3), June 2012
Min Zhou. Are Asian Americans Becoming "White?" *Contexts* 3(1), February 2004
Elaine Howard Ecklund, David R. Johnson, Christopher P. Scheitle, Kirstin R. W. Matthews, and Steven W. Lewis. Religion among Scientists in International Context: A New Study of Scientists in Eight Regions. *Socius* 2, September 2016
Joscha Legewie, and Thomas A. DiPrete. School Context and the Gender Gap in Educational Achievement. *American Sociological Review* 77(3), June 2012
Tanya Golash-Boza. A Critical and Comprehensive Sociological Theory of Race and Racism. *Sociology of Race and Ethnicity* 2(2), April 2016
Emily Kazyak, Kelsy Burke, and Mathew Stange. Logics of Freedom: Debating Religious Freedom Laws and Gay and Lesbian Rights. *Socius* 4, February 2018
Natasha Quadlin. The Mark of a Woman's Record: Gender and Academic Performance in Hiring. *American Sociological Review* 83(2), April 2018
Nour Dados, and Raewyn Connell. The Global South. *Contexts* 11(1), Winter 2012
Miliann Kang, and Katherine Jones. Why Do People get Tattoos? *Contexts* 6(1), Winter 2007
Matthew Desmond, Andrew V. Papachristos, and David S. Kirk. Police Violence and Citizen Crime Reporting in the Black Community. *American Sociological Review* 81(5), October 2016

(*continued*)

Table 2.1 *(continued)*

Peggy A. Thoits. Mechanisms Linking Social Ties and Support to Physical and Mental Health. *Journal of Health and Social Behavior* 52(2), June 2011
Ann Owens. Income Segregation between School Districts and Inequality in Students' Achievement. *Sociology of Education* 91(1), January 2018
Arne L. Kalleberg. Precarious Work, Insecure Workers: Employment Relations in Transition. *American Sociological Review* 74(1), February 2009
Becky Pettit, and Bruce Western. Mass Imprisonment and the Life Course: Race and Class Inequality in U.S. Incarceration. *American Sociological Review* 69(2), April 2004
Michael J. Rosenfeld, and Reuben J. Thomas. Searching for a Mate: The Rise of the Internet as a Social Intermediary. *American Sociological Review* 77(4), August 2012
Simón E. Weffer, Rodrigo Dominguez-Martinez, and Raymond Jenkins. Taking a Knee. *Contexts* 17(3), Summer 2018
Jessie Daniels. The Algorithmic Rise of the "Alt-Right". *Contexts* 17(1), Winter 2018
Kristen Schilt, and Laurel Westbrook. Bathroom Battlegrounds and Penis Panics. *Contexts* 14(3): Summer 2015
Amelia R. Branigan, Christopher Wildeman, Jeremy Freese, and Catarina I. Kiefe. Complicating Colorism: Race, Skin Color, and the Likelihood of Arrest. *Socius* 3, August 2017
Daniel L. Carlson, Amanda Jayne Miller, and Sharon Sassler. Stalled for Whom? Change in the Division of Particular Housework Tasks and Their Consequences for Middle- to Low-Income Couples. *Socius* 4, April 2018
Patrick Sharkey, Gerard Torrats-Espinosa, and Delaram Takyar. Community and the Crime Decline: The Causal Effect of Local Nonprofits on Violent Crime. *American Sociological Review* 82(6), December 2017
Dara Shifrer. Stigma of a Label: Educational Expectations for High School Students Labeled with Learning Disabilities. *Journal of Health and Social Behavior* 54(4), December 2013
Lauren A. Rivera. When Two Bodies Are (Not) a Problem: Gender and Relationship Status Discrimination in Academic Hiring. *American Sociological Review* 82(6), December 2017
Hyun Sik Kim. Consequences of Parental Divorce for Child Development. *American Sociological Review* 76(3), June 2011
Mary Romero. Trump's Immigration Attacks, in Brief. *Contexts* 17(1), Winter 2018
Annette Lareau. Cultural Knowledge and Social Inequality. *American Sociological Review* 80(1), February 2015
Landon Schnabel. Sexual Orientation and Social Attitudes. *Socius* 4, April 2018
Cedric Herring. Does Diversity Pay?: Race, Gender, and the Business Case for Diversity. *American Sociological Review* 74(2), April 2009

Table 2.1 (*continued*)
Winifred Breines. Struggling to Connect: White and Black Feminism in the Movement Years. *Contexts* 6(1), February 2007
Kamesha Spates, and Brittany C. Slatton. I've Got My Family and My Faith: Black Women and the Suicide Paradox. *Socius* 3, December 2017
Kieran Healy. Fuck Nuance. *Sociological Theory* 35(2), June 2017
Victor M. Rios. Stealing a Bag of Potato Chips and Other Crimes of Resistance. *Contexts* 11(1), Winter 2012
Daniel Schneider, Orestes P. Hastings, and Joe LaBriola. Income Inequality and Class Divides in Parental Investments. *American Sociological Review* 83(3), June 2018
Richard Florida. Cities and the Creative Class. *City & Community* 2(1): March 2003

2. From the same list read Natasha Quadlin's 2018 article "The Mark of a Woman's Record: Gender and Academic Performance in Hiring," published in the *American Sociological Review* 83(2):331–360. Answer the following questions:

   (a) What is the main dependent variable in the article?

   (b) What is the main independent variable in the article?

   (c) Briefly describe the causal theory that connects the independent and dependent variables.

   (d) Can you think of another independent variable that is not mentioned in the article that might be causally related to the dependent variable? Briefly explain why that variable might be causally related to the dependent variable.

For exercises 3 through 6, read Robert Putnam's 1995 article "Tuning In, Tuning Out: The Strange Disappearance of Social Capital in America," published in *PS: Political Science and Politics* 28(4):664–683.

3. What is the dependent variable in Putnam's study?
4. What other possible causes of the dependent variable can you think of?
5. Can Putnam's theory be applied in other countries? Why or why not?
6. If we believe Putnam's findings, are there further implications?

3 Evaluating Causal Relationships

OVERVIEW

Modern sociology fundamentally revolves around establishing whether there are *causal relationships* between important concepts. This is rarely straightforward, however, and serves as the basis for almost all scientific controversies. How do we know, for example, if intergroup contact causes racial tolerance, or if racial tolerance causes intergroup contact (in the sense that tolerant people seek out contact with racial others), or both, or neither? To speak more generally, if we wish to evaluate whether or not some X causes some Y, we need to cross four causal hurdles: (1) Is there a credible causal mechanism that connects X to Y? (2) Can we eliminate the possibility that Y causes X? (3) Is there covariation between X and Y? (4) Have we controlled for all confounding variables Z that might make the association between X and Y spurious? Many people make the mistake that crossing just the third causal hurdle – observing that X and Y covary – is tantamount to crossing all four. In short, finding a relationship is not the same as finding a *causal* relationship, and causality is what we care about as social scientists.

I would rather discover one causal law than be King of Persia
—Democritus (quoted in Pearl, 2000)

3.1 CAUSALITY AND EVERYDAY LANGUAGE

Like that of most sciences, the discipline of sociology fundamentally revolves around evaluating causal claims. Our theories – which may be right or may be wrong – typically specify that some independent variable causes some dependent variable. We then endeavor to find appropriate empirical evidence to evaluate the degree to which this theory is or is not supported. But how do we go about evaluating causal claims? In this chapter and the next, we discuss some principles for doing this. We focus in this chapter on the logic of causality and on several criteria for establishing with some confidence the degree to which a causal connection exists between two variables. Then, in Chapter 4, we discuss various ways to design research that help us to investigate causal claims. As we pursue answers to questions about causal relationships, keep our "rules of the road" from Chapter 1 in your mind, in particular the admonition to consider only empirical evidence along the way.

It is important to recognize a distinction between the nature of most scientific theories and the way the world seems to be ordered. Most of our theories are limited to descriptions of relationships between a *single* cause (the independent variable) and a *single* effect (the dependent variable). Such theories, in this sense, are very simplistic representations of reality, and necessarily so. In fact, as we noted at the end of Chapter 1, theories of this sort are laudable in one respect: They are parsimonious, the equivalent of bite-sized, digestible pieces of information. We cannot emphasize strongly enough that almost all of our theories about social and political phenomena are **bivariate** – that is, involving just two variables.

But social reality is *not* bivariate; it is **multivariate**, in the sense that any interesting dependent variable is caused by more than one factor. ("Multivariate" simply means "many variables," by which we mean involving more than two variables.) So although our theories describe the proposed relationship between some cause and some effect, we always have to keep in the forefront of our minds that the phenomenon we are trying to explain surely has many other possible causes. And when it comes time to design research to test our theoretical ideas – which is the topic of Chapter 4 – we have to try to account for, or "control for," those other causes. If we don't, then our causal inferences about whether our pet theory is right – whether X causes Y – may very well be wrong.[1] In this chapter we lay out some practical principles for evaluating whether or not, indeed, some X does cause Y. You also can apply these criteria when evaluating the causal claims made by others – be they a journalist, a candidate for office, a sociologist, a fellow classmate, a friend, or just about anyone else.

Nearly everyone, nearly every day, uses the language of causality – some of the time formally, but far more often in a very informal manner. Whenever we speak of how some event changes the course of subsequent events, we invoke causal reasoning. Even the word "because" implies that a

[1] Throughout this book, in the text as well as in the figures, we will use arrows as a shorthand for "causality." For example, the text "$X \rightarrow Y$" should be read as "X causes Y." Oftentimes, especially in figures, these arrows will have question marks over them, indicating that the existence of a causal connection between the concepts is uncertain.

causal process is in operation.[2] Yet, despite the ubiquitous use of the words "because," "affects," "impacts," "causes," and "causality," the meanings of these words are not exactly clear. Philosophers of science have long had vigorous debates over competing formulations of "causality."[3]

Although our goal here is not to wade too deeply into these debates, there is one feature of the discussions about causality that deserves brief mention. Most of the philosophy of science debates originate from the world of the physical sciences. The notions of causality that come to mind in these disciplines mostly involve **deterministic relationships** – that is, relationships such that if some cause occurs, then the effect will occur *with certainty*. In contrast, though, the world of human interactions consists of **probabilistic relationships** – such that increases in X are associated with increases (or decreases) in the probability of Y occurring, but those probabilities are not certainties. Whereas physical laws like Newton's laws of motion are deterministic – think of the law of gravity here – the social sciences (including sociology) more closely resemble probabilistic causation like that in Darwin's theory of natural selection, in which random mutations make an organism more or less fit to survive and reproduce.[4]

What does it mean to say that, in social science, our conceptions of causality must be probabilistic in nature? When we theorize, for example, that an individual's level of wealth causes her opinions on optimal tax policy, we do not at all mean that *every* wealthy person will want lower taxes, and *every* poor person will prefer higher taxes. Consider what would happen if we found a single rich person who favors high taxes or a single poor person who favors low taxes. (Perhaps you are, or know, such a person.) One case alone does not decrease our confidence in the theory. In this sense, the relationship is probabilistic, not deterministic. Instead of saying deterministically that "wealthy people will prefer lower taxes, and poorer people will prefer higher taxes," we say, probabilistically, that "wealthy people are more likely to prefer lower taxes, whereas poorer individuals are more likely to prefer higher taxes."

Take another example: Scholars of international conflict have noticed that there is a statistical relationship between the type of regime a country has and the likelihood of that country going to war. To be more precise, in

[2] This use of terms was brought to our attention by Brady (2002).

[3] You can find an excellent account of the vigor of these debates in a 2003 book by David Edmonds and John Eidinow titled *Wittgenstein's Poker: The Story of a Ten-Minute Argument Between Two Great Philosophers.*

[4] Nevertheless, in reviewing three prominent attempts within the philosophy of science to elaborate on the probabilistic nature of causality, the philosopher Wesley Salmon (1993, p. 137) notes that "In the vast philosophical literature on causality [probabilistic notions of causality] are largely ignored." We borrow the helpful comparison of probabilistic social science to Darwinian natural selection from Brady (2004).

a series of studies widely referred to as the "democratic peace" literature, many researchers have noticed that wars are much less likely to break out between two regimes that are democracies than pairs of countries where at least one is a nondemocracy. To be perfectly clear, the literature does not suggest that democracies do not engage in warfare at all, but that democracies don't fight other democracies. A variety of mechanisms have been suggested to explain this correlation, but the point here is that, if two democracies start a war with one another next year, it would be a mistake to discard the theory. A deterministic theory would say that "democracies don't go to war with one another," but a more sensible probabilistic theory would say that "democracies are highly unlikely to go to war with one another."

In sociology there will always be exceptions because human beings are not deterministic robots whose behaviors always conform to lawlike statements. In other sciences in which the subjects of study do not have free will, it may make more sense to speak of laws that describe behavior. Consider the study of planetary orbits, in which scientists can precisely predict the movement of celestial bodies hundreds of years in advance. The social world, in contrast, is extremely difficult to predict. As a result, most of the time we are happy to be able to make statements about probabilistic causal relationships.

What all of this boils down to is that the entire notion of what it means for something "to cause" something else is far from a settled matter. In the face of this, should social scientists abandon the search for causal connections? Not at all. What it means is that we should proceed cautiously and with an open mind, rather than in some exceedingly rigid fashion.

3.2 FOUR HURDLES ALONG THE ROUTE TO ESTABLISHING CAUSAL RELATIONSHIPS

If we wish to investigate whether some independent variable, which we will call X, "causes" some dependent variable, which we will call Y, what procedures must we follow before we can express our degree of confidence that a causal relationship does or does not exist? Finding some sort of covariation (or, equivalently, correlation) between X and Y is not sufficient for such a conclusion.

We encourage you to bear in mind that establishing causal relationships between variables is not at all akin to hunting for DNA evidence like some episode from a television crime drama. Social reality does not lend itself to such simple, cut-and-dried answers. In light of the preceding discussion about the nature of causality itself, consider what follows to be guidelines as to what constitutes "best practice" in sociology. With any theory about a causal relationship between X and Y, we should carefully consider the answers to the following four questions:

1. Is there a credible causal mechanism that connects X to Y?
2. Can we rule out the possibility that Y could cause X?
3. Is there covariation between X and Y?
4. Have we controlled for all **confounding variables** Z that might make the association between X and Y **spurious?**[5]

First, we must consider whether it is plausible to claim that X *could* cause Y. In effect, this hurdle represents an effort to answer the "how" and "why" questions about causal relationships. To do this, we need to go through a thought exercise in which we evaluate the mechanics of how X would cause Y. What is the process or mechanism that, logically speaking, suggests that X might be a cause of Y? In other words, what is it specifically about having more (or less) of X that will in all probability lead to more (or less) of Y? The more outlandish these mechanics would have to be, the less confident we are that our theory has cleared this first hurdle. Failure to clear this first hurdle is a very serious matter, the result being that either our theory needs to be thrown out altogether, or we need to revise it after some careful rethinking of the underlying mechanisms through which it works. It is worth proceeding to the second question only once we have a "yes" answer to this question.

Second, and perhaps with greater difficulty, we must ask whether it is possible (or even likely) that Y might cause X. As you will learn from the discussion of the various strategies for assessing causal connections in Chapter 4, this poses thorny problems for some forms of social science research, but is less problematic for others. Occasionally, this causal hurdle can be crossed logically. For example, when considering whether a person's gender (X) causes him or her to have particular attitudes about abortion policy (Y), it is a rock-solid certainty that the reverse-causal scenario can be dismissed: A person's attitudes about abortion do not "cause" them to have a particular gender identity. If our theory does not clear this particular hurdle, the race is not lost. Under these circumstances, we should proceed to the next question, while keeping in mind the possibility that our causal arrow might be reversed.

Throughout our consideration of the first two causal hurdles, we were concerned with only two variables, X and Y. The third causal hurdle can

[5] A "confounding variable" is simply a variable that is correlated with both the independent and dependent variables and which somehow alters the relationship between those two variables. "Spurious" means "not what it appears to be" or "coincidental" or "false."

involve a third variable Z, and the fourth hurdle always does. Often it is the case that there are several Z variables.

For the third causal hurdle, we must consider whether X and Y covary (or, equivalently, whether they are correlated or associated). Generally speaking, for X to cause Y, there must be some form of measurable association between X and Y, such as "more of X is associated with more of Y," or "more of X is associated with less of Y." Demonstrating a simple bivariate connection between two variables is a relatively straightforward matter, and we will cover various methods for doing so in Chapters 9 and 10. Of course, you may be familiar with the dictum "Correlation does not prove causality," and we wholeheartedly agree. It is worth noting, though, that correlation is normally an essential component of causality. But be careful. It is possible for a causal relationship to exist between X and Y even if there is no bivariate association between X and Y. Thus, even if we fail to clear this hurdle, we should not throw out our causal claim entirely. Instead, we should consider the possibility that there exists some confounding variable Z that we need to "control for" before we see a relationship between X and Y. In such a case we say that Z "suppressed" the relationship between X and Y. Thus, whether or not we find a bivariate relationship between X and Y, we should proceed to our fourth and final hurdle.

Fourth, in establishing causal connections between X and Y, we must face up to the reality that, as we noted at the outset of this chapter, we live in a world in which most of the interesting dependent variables are caused by more than one – often many more than one – independent variable. What problems does this pose for social science? It means that, when trying to establish whether a particular X causes a particular Y, we need to "control for" the effects of other causes of Y (and we call those other effects Z). If we fail to control for the effects of Z, we are quite likely to misunderstand the relationship between X and Y and make the wrong inference about whether X causes Y. This is the most serious mistake a social scientist can make. If we find that X and Y are correlated, but that, when we control for the effects of Z on both X and Y, the association between X and Y disappears, then the relationship between X and Y is said to be spurious.

3.2.1 Putting It All Together – Adding Up the Answers to Our Four Questions

As we have just seen, the process for evaluating a theoretical claim that X causes Y is complicated. Taken one at a time, each of the four questions in the introduction to this section can be difficult to answer with great clarity. But the challenge of evaluating a claim that X causes Y involves summing the answers to all four of these questions to determine our overall confidence about whether X causes Y. To understand this, think about the analogy that we have been using by calling these questions "hurdles." In track events that feature hurdles, runners must do their best to try to clear each hurdle as they make their way toward the finish line. Occasionally even the most experienced hurdler will knock over a hurdle. Although this slows them down and diminishes their chances of winning the race, all is not lost. If we think about putting a theory through the four hurdles posed by the preceding questions, there is no doubt our confidence will be greatest when we are able to answer all four questions the right way ("yes," "yes," "yes," "yes") and without reservation. As we described in the introduction to this section, failure to clear the first hurdle should make us stop and rethink our theory. This is also the case if we find our relationship to be spurious. For the second and third hurdles, however, failure to clear them completely does not mean that we should discard the causal claim in question. Figure 3.1 provides a summary of this process. In the subsections that follow, we will go through the process described in Figure 3.1 with a series of examples.

As we go through this process of answering the four questions, we will keep a **causal hurdles scorecard** as a shorthand for summarizing the answers to these four questions in square brackets. For now, we will limit our answers to "*y*" for "yes," "*n*" for "no," and "*m*" for "maybe." If a theory has cleared all four hurdles, the scorecard would read [*y y y y*] and the causal claim behind it would be strongly supported. As we described above, these hurdles are not all the same in terms of their impact on our assessments of causality. So, for instance, a causal claim for which the scorecard reads [*n y y y*] could be thrown out instantly. But, a claim for which it reads [*y n y y*] would have a reasonable level of evidence in its favor.

3.2.2 Identifying Causal Claims Is an Essential Thinking Skill

We want to emphasize that the logic just presented does not apply merely to sociological research examples. Whenever you see a story in the news, or hear a speech by a candidate for public office, or, yes, read a research article in a sociology class, it is almost always the case that some form of causal claim is embedded in the story, speech, or article. Sometimes those causal claims are explicit – indented and italicized so that you just can't miss them. Quite often, though, they are harder to spot, and most of the time not because the speaker or writer is trying to confuse you. What we want to emphasize is that spotting and identifying causal claims is a thinking skill. It does not come naturally to most people, but it can be practiced.

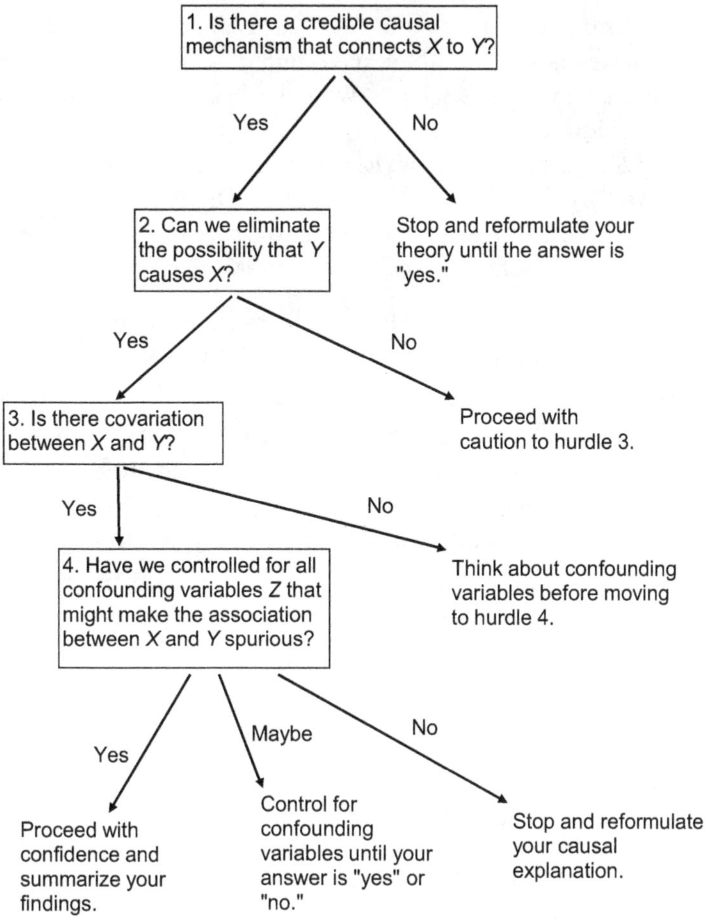

Figure 3.1 The path to evaluating a causal relationship

In our daily lives, we are often presented with causal claims by people trying to persuade us to adopt their point of view. Advocacy and attempts at persuasion, of course, are healthy features of a vibrant democracy. The health of public debate, though, will be further enhanced when citizens actively scrutinize the claims with which they are presented. Take, for example, debates in the media about the merits of private school choice programs, which have been implemented in several school districts. Among the arguments in favor of such programs is that the programs will improve student performance on standardized tests. Media reports about the successes and failures of programs like this are quite common. For example, an article in the *Washington Post* discusses a study that makes the argument that:

> African American students in the District [of Columbia] and two other cities have moved ahead of their public school classmates since they transferred to private schools with the help of vouchers, according to a new study.... The study showed that those moving to private schools scored 6 percentile points higher than those who stayed in public schools in New York City, Dayton, Ohio, and the District. The effect was biggest in the District, where students with vouchers moved 9 percentile points ahead of public school peers.[6]

Notice the causal claim here, which is: Participation (or not) in the school choice program (X) causes a child's test scores (Y) to vary. Often, the reader is presented with a bar chart of some sort in support of the argument. The reader is encouraged to think, sometimes subtly, that the differing heights of the bars, representing different average test scores for school choice children and public school children, mean that the program *caused* the school choice children to earn higher scores. When we take such information in, we might take that nugget of evidence and be tempted to jump to the conclusion that a causal relationship exists. The key lesson here is that this is a premature conclusion.

Let's be clear: School choice programs may indeed cause students to do better on standardized tests. Our objective here is not to wade into that debate, but rather to sensitize you to the thinking skills required to evaluate the causal claim made in public by advocates such as those who support or oppose school choice programs. Evidence that students in school choice programs score higher on tests than do public school students is *one piece* of the causal puzzle – namely, it satisfies crossing hurdle 3 above, that there is covariation between X and Y. At this point in our evaluation, our scorecard reads [? ? *y* ?]. And thus, before we conclude that school choice does (or does not) cause student performance, we need to subject that claim to all four of the causal hurdles, not just the third one.

So let's apply all four causal hurdles to the question at hand. First, is there a mechanism that we can use to explain how and why attending a particular type of school – public or a voucher-sponsored private school – might affect a student's test scores? Certainly. Many private schools that participate in voucher programs have smaller class sizes (among other benefits), and smaller class sizes can translate to more learning and higher test scores. *The answer to the first question is "yes"* [*y* ? *y* ?]. Second, is it possible that the causal arrow might be reversed – that is, can we rule out the possibility that test scores cause a person to participate or not participate in a school choice program? Since the test scores occur

[6] Mathews, Jay. 2000. "Scores Improve for D.C. Pupils With Vouchers." *Washington Post*, August 28. Page A1.

months or even years after the person chooses a school to attend, this is not possible. *The answer to the second question is "yes"* [*y y y* ?]. Third, is there a correlation between participation in the program and test scores? The article quoted above just noted that, in the three cities considered, there is – voucher school students scored higher on standardized tests than their public school peers. *The answer to the third question is "yes"* [*y y y* ?]. Finally, have we controlled for all confounding variables that might make the association between participation in the program and test scores spurious? Remember, a potentially confounding variable is simply a variable that is related to the independent variable and is also a cause of the dependent variable. So, can we think of something that is both related to the type of school a child attends and is also a likely cause of that child's test scores? Sure. The variable "parental involvement" is a natural candidate to be a Z variable in this instance. Some children have highly involved parents – parents who read to their children, help them with homework, and take an active role in their education – while other children have parents who are much less involved. Highly involved parents are more likely than their uninvolved counterparts to learn about the existence of school choice programs in their cities, and are more likely to apply for such programs. (So Z is almost surely related to X.) And highly involved parents are more likely to create high expectations among their children, and to instill in their children a sense that achievement in school is important, all of which probably translates into having children who score better on standardized tests. (So Z is likely to be a cause of Y.) The key question then becomes: Did the study in question manage to *control for* those effects?

We're a little ahead of the game here, because we haven't yet talked about the methods that researchers employ to control for the effects of potentially confounding variables. (That task comes in Chapter 4.) But we hope you can see why controlling for the effects of parental involvement is so key in this particular situation (and in general): If our comparison of school choice children and public school children basically amounts to a comparison between the children of highly motivated parents and the children of poorly motivated parents, then it becomes very problematic to conclude that the difference between the groups' test scores was *caused by* the program. Without a control for parental involvement (Z), in other words, the relationship between school type (X) and test scores (Y) might be spurious. So, until we see evidence that this important Z has been controlled for, our scorecard for this causal claim is [*y y y n*] and we should be highly suspicious of the study's findings. More informally, without such a control, the comparison between those sets of test scores is an unfair one, because the groups would be so different in the first place. As it happens, the article from the *Washington Post* that we mentioned did include a control for parental involvement, because the students were chosen for the program by a random lottery. We'll wait until Chapter 4 to describe exactly why this makes such a big difference, but it does.

The same process can be applied to a wide variety of causal claims and questions that we encounter in our daily lives. Does drinking red wine cause a reduction in heart disease? Does psychotherapy help people with emotional and relational problems? Do increases in government spending spur or retard economic growth? In each of these and many other examples, we might be tempted to observe a correlation between two variables and conclude that the relationship is causal. It is important for us to resist that temptation, and subject each of these claims to the more rigorous criteria that we are suggesting here. If we think about such evidence on its own in terms of our causal hurdles scorecard, what we have is [? ? *y* ?]. This is a reasonable start to the evaluation of a causal claim, but a pretty poor place to stop and draw definitive conclusions. Thinking in terms of the hurdles depicted in the scorecard, whenever someone presents us with a causal claim but fails to address each of the hurdles, we will naturally ask further questions and, when we do that, we will be much smarter consumers of information in our everyday lives.

An important part of taking a scientific approach to the study of society is that we turn the same skeptical logic loose on scholarly claims about causal relationships. Before we can evaluate a causal theory, we need to consider how well the available evidence answers each of the four questions about *X*, *Y*, and *Z*. Once we have answered each of these four questions, one at a time, we then think about the overall level of confidence that we have in the claim that *X* causes *Y*.

3.2.3 What Are the Consequences of Failing to Control for Other Possible Causes?

When it comes to any causal claim, as we have just noted, the fourth causal hurdle often trips us up, and not just for evaluating stories in the news media. This is true for scrutinizing scientific research as well. In fact, a substantial portion of disagreements between scholars boils down to this fourth causal hurdle. When one scholar is evaluating another's work, perhaps the most frequent objection is that the researcher "failed to control for" some potentially important cause of the dependent variable.

What happens when we fail to control for some plausible other cause of our dependent variable of interest? Quite simply, it means that we have failed to cross our fourth causal hurdle. *So long as a reasonable case can be made that some uncontrolled-for Z might be related to both X and Y, we cannot conclude with full confidence that X indeed causes Y*. Because the main goal of science is to establish whether causal connections between variables exist, then failing to control for other causes of *Y* is a potentially serious problem.

One of the themes of this book is that statistical analysis should not be disconnected from issues of research design – such as controlling for as many causes of the dependent variable as possible. When we discuss multiple regression (in Chapter 11), which is the most common statistical technique that sociologists use in their research, the entire point of that chapter is to learn how to control for other possible causes of the dependent variable. We will see that failures of research design, such as failing to control for all relevant causes of the dependent variable, have statistical implications, and the implications are always bad. Failures of research design produce problems for statistical analysis, but hold this thought. What is important to realize for now is that good research design will make statistical analysis more credible, whereas poor research design will make it harder for any statistical analysis to be conclusive about causal connections.

3.3 WHY IS STUDYING CAUSALITY SO IMPORTANT? THREE EXAMPLES FROM SOCIOLOGY

Our emphasis on causal connections should be clear. We turn now to several active controversies within the discipline of sociology, showing how debates about causality lie at the heart of precisely the kinds of controversies that got you (and most of us) interested in sociology in the first place.

3.3.1 Intergroup Contact and Racial Tolerance

One of the enduring controversies in the sociological study of race and ethnicity is the relationship between *intergroup contact* and *tolerance*. As attested to by six decades of social science research, perhaps no strategy for reducing racial animus has received more attention than personal contact between members of different races. What, if anything, is the causal connection between these two concepts?

According to the classic statements of the "contact hypothesis" by sociologist Gordon Allport and colleagues (1954) and social psychologist Muzafer Sherif and colleagues (1961), close interracial contact (*X*) tends, under certain circumstances at least,[7] to promote positive intergroup

[7] Experimental studies have established that favorable attitude change is likely only when contact links people of more or less equal status, involves cooperation rather than

attitudes (Y) by providing members of different races with first-hand exposure to, and accurate information about, one another's values, lifestyles, and experiences. If we think through the first of the four questions for establishing causal relationships, we can see that there is a credible causal mechanism that connects X to Y – if intergroup contact exposes people of different races to each other under favorable circumstances, racial tolerance is likely to result. *The answer to our first question is "yes"* [*y* ? ? ?]. Moving on to our second question: Can we eliminate the possibility that racial tolerance (Y) is what causes intergroup contact (X)? We cannot. It is very easy to conceive of a causal mechanism in which those who are racially tolerant seek out members of different races while those who are intolerant actively avoid such contact. *The answer to our second question is "no"* [*y n* ? ?]. We now turn to the third question. Sociologist Thomas Pettigrew (1998) has reviewed the voluminous empirical literature on the contact hypothesis and concluded that the hypothesis's predictions are generally supported, both across a wide variety of racial and ethnic groups as well as in many different societies. That is, contact and tolerance do indeed covary, with people who report greater amounts of intergroup contact also expressing more positive racial attitudes. Conversely, those who report less contact with racial others tend to harbor more negative racial outlooks. *The answer to our third question is "yes"* [*y n y* ?]. With respect to the fourth question, it is easy to imagine a myriad of other factors (Zs) that might lead to heightened (or reduced) racial animus, including region of residence, the size of one's place of primary childhood socialization, educational attainment, and many others. Whether or not studies of intergroup contact have done an adequate job of controlling for those other factors is the subject of considerable scholarly debate. *The answer to our fourth question is "maybe"* [*y n y m*]. The literature on the contact hypothesis has satisfactorily answered questions 1 and 3, but it is the answers to questions 2 and 4 that have given skeptics reason to doubt the causal claim underlying the hypothesis.

3.3.2 Race and Political Participation in the U.S.

Political participation – the extent to which individual citizens engage in voluntary political activity, such as voting, working for a campaign, or making a campaign contribution – represents one of the most frequently studied facets of mass political behavior, especially in the U.S. And with good reason: Participation in democratic societies is viewed by some as

competition in the pursuit of common goals, and is sanctioned by authority figures – conditions that often do not hold in the real world (Desforges et al., 1991).

one measure of the health of a democracy. After decades of studying the variation in Americans' rates of participation, several demographic characteristics consistently stood out as being correlated with participation, including an individual's racial classification. Anglos, surveys consistently showed, have participated in politics considerably more frequently than either Latinos or African Americans. A comprehensive survey, for example, shows that during a typical election cycle, Anglos engaged in 2.22 "participatory acts" – such as voting, working for a campaign, making a campaign contribution, attending a protest or demonstration, and similar such activities – whereas comparable rates for African Americans and Latino citizens were 1.90 and 1.41 activities (see Verba et al., 1993, figure 1).

Is the relationship between an individual's race (X) and the amount that the individual participates in politics (Y) a causal one? Before we accept the evidence above as conclusively demonstrating a *causal* relationship, we need to subject it to the four causal hurdles. Is there a reasonable mechanism that answers the "how" and "why" questions connecting race and political participation? There may be reason to think so. For long portions of American history, after all, some formal and many informal barriers existed prohibiting or discouraging the participation of non-Anglos. The notion that there might be residual effects of such barriers, even decades after they have been eradicated, is entirely reasonable. *The answer to our first question is "yes"* [*y* ? ? ?]. Can we eliminate the possibility that varying rates of participation cause an individual's racial classification? Obviously, yes. *The answer to our second question is "yes"* [*y y* ? ?]. Is there a correlation between an individual's race and their level of participation in the U.S.? The data above about the number of participatory acts among Anglos, African Americans, and Latinos clearly shows that there is a relationship; Anglos participate the most. *The answer to our third question is "yes"* [*y y y* ?].

Finally, have we controlled for all possible confounding variables Z that are related to both race (X) and participation (Y) that might make the relationship spurious? Verba and his colleagues (1993) suggest that there might be just such a confounding variable: socio-economic status. Less so today than in the past, socio-economic status (Z) is nevertheless still correlated with race (X). And unsurprisingly, socio-economic status (Z) is also a cause of political participation (Y); wealthy people donate more, volunteer more, and the like, than their less-wealthy counterparts. Once controlling for socio-economic status, the aforementioned relationship between race and political participation entirely vanishes (see Verba et al., 1993, table 8). In short, the correlation that we observe between race and political participation is spurious, or illusory; it is not a function of race, but instead a function of the disparities in wealth between Anglos and those of other races. Once we control for those socio-economic differences, the connection between race and participation goes away. *The answer to our fourth question is "no".*

In this case, the effort to answer the fourth question actually changed our answer to the third question, moving our scorecard from [*y y y* ?] to [*y y n n*]. This is one of the important ways in which our conclusions about relationships can change when we move from a bivariate analysis in which we measure the relationship between one independent variable, X, and our dependent variable, Y, to a multiple-variable analysis in which we measure the relationship between X and Y controlling for a second independent variable, Z. It is also possible for a lot of other things to happen when we move to controlling for Z. For instance, it is also possible for our scorecard to change from [*y y n n*] to [*y y y y*].

3.3.3 Evaluating Whether Head Start Is Effective

In the 1960s, as part of the War on Poverty, President Lyndon Johnson initiated the program Head Start to give economically underprivileged children a preschool experience that – the program hoped – would increase the chances that these poor children would succeed once they reached kindergarten and beyond. The program is clearly well intended, but, of course, that alone does not make it effective. Simply put: Does Head Start work? In this case, "work" would mean that Head Start could increase the chances that participants in the program would have better educational outcomes than nonparticipants.

It would be tempting, in this case, to simply compare some standardized test scores of the children who participated in Head Start with those who did not. If Head Start participants scored higher, then – voila! – case closed; the program works. If not, then not. But, as before, we need to stay focused on all four causal hurdles. First, is there some credible causal mechanism that would answer the "how" and "why" questions that connect Head Start participation (X) to educational outcomes (Y)? Yes. The theory behind the program is that exposure to a preschool environment that anticipates the actual school setting helps prepare children for what they will encounter in kindergarten and beyond. Head Start, in this sense, might help reduce discipline problems, and prepare students for reading and counting, among other skills. *The answer to our first question is "yes"* [*y* ? ? ?]. Is it possible, secondly, that the causal arrow might be reversed – in other words, can we rule out the possibility that educational outcomes (Y) could cause participation in Head Start (X)? Because testing would take place years after participation in the program, yes. *The answer to our second question is "yes"* [*y y* ? ?]. Is there an association between participation in the program and learning outcomes? Study after study has shown that Head Start participants fare better when tested, and have fewer instances of repeating a grade, than those who have no preschool experience. For example, a widely cited study shows that Head Start children do better on a vocabulary test suitable for young children than do students who have no preschool experience (Currie and Thomas, 1995). *The answer to our third question is "yes"* [*y y y* ?].

But, as was the case with the school voucher example discussed previously, a potentially confounding variable – parental involvement (*Z*) – lurks nearby. Highly involved parents (*Z*) are more likely to seek out, be aware of, and enroll their children (*X*) in programs like Head Start that might benefit their children. Parents who are less involved in their children's lives are less likely to avail themselves of the potential opportunities that Head Start creates. And, as before, highly involved parents (*Z*) are likely to have positive effects on their children's educational outcomes. The key question, then, becomes: Do parental effects (*Z*) make the relationship between Head Start and later educational outcomes spurious? The aforementioned study by Currie and Thomas (1995) uses both statistical controls as well as controls in the design of their research to account for parental factors, and they find that Head Start has lasting educational effects only for Anglo children, but not for African American children (see their table 4). Again, that phrase "statistical controls" may not be quite as transparent as it will be later on in this book. For now, suffice it to say that these researchers used all of the techniques available to them to show that Head Start does, indeed, have positive effects for some, but not all, children. *The answer to our fourth question is a highly qualified "yes"* [*y y y y*].

3.4 WRAPPING UP

Learning the thinking skills required to evaluate causal claims as conclusively as possible requires practice. They are intellectual habits that, like a good knife, will sharpen with use.

Translating these thinking skills into actively designing new research that helps to address causal questions is the subject of Chapter 4. All of the "research designs" that you will learn in that chapter are strongly linked to issues of evaluating causal claims. Keeping the lessons of this chapter in mind as we move forward is essential to making you a better consumer of information, as well as edging you forward toward being a producer of research.

CONCEPTS INTRODUCED IN THIS CHAPTER

- bivariate – involving just two variables
- causal hurdles scorecard – a shorthand for summarizing evidence about whether an independent variable causes a dependent variable
- confounding variable – a variable that is both correlated with both the independent and dependent variables and that somehow alters the relationship between those two variables
- deterministic relationship – if some cause occurs, then the effect will occur with certainty
- multivariate – involving more than two variables
- probabilistic relationship – increases in X are associated with increases (or decreases) in the probability of Y occurring, but those probabilities are not certainties
- spurious – not what it appears to be, or coincidental, or false

EXERCISES

1. Think back to your introduction to sociology class in which you learned about the "causes" of a particular societal event (for instance, the civil rights movement, racial/ethnic residential segregation, or changing racial/ethnic intergroup attitudes). How well does each causal claim perform when you try to answer the four questions for establishing causal relationships?
2. Go to your local newspaper's website (if it has one; if not, pick the website of any media outlet you visit frequently). In the site's "Search" box, type the words "research cause" (without quotes). (*Hint:* You may need to limit the search time frame, depending on the site you visit.) From the search results, find two articles that make claims about causal relationships. Print them out, and include a brief synopsis of the causal claim embedded in the article.
3. For each of the following examples, imagine that some researcher has found the reported pattern of covariation between X and Y. Can you think of a variable Z that might make the relationship between X and Y spurious?

   (a) The more firefighters (X) that go to a house fire, the greater property damage that occurs (Y).

   (b) The more money spent by an incumbent member of Congress's campaign (X), the lower their percentage of vote (Y).

   (c) Increased consumption of coffee (X) reduces the risk of depression among women (Y).

   (d) The higher the salaries of Presbyterian ministers (X), the higher the price of rum in Havana, Cuba (Y).

4. For each of the following pairs of independent and dependent variables, write both a probabilistic and a deterministic account of the likely relationship:

   (a) A person's education (X) and her/his racial/ethnic tolerance (Y).

   (b) A person's gender (X) and her/his income (Y).

   (c) A state's percentage of rural dwellers (X) and the political leanings of its citizens (Y).

5. Take a look at the codebook for the data set "GSS 2018" (which is available on the textbook's website at www.cambridge.org/fsr) and write about your answers to the following items:

   (a) Develop a causal theory about the relationship between an independent variable (X) and a dependent variable (Y) from this data set. Is it the credible causal mechanism that connects X to Y? Explain your answer.

   (b) Could Y cause X? Explain your answer.

   (c) What other variables (Z) would you like to control for in your tests of this theory?

6. Imagine causal claims for which the scorecards are listed below. Which of these claims – (a), (b), or (c) – would you evaluate as most strongly supported? Explain your answer.

   (a) [y n y y]

   (b) [y y y n]

   (c) [m y y y]

7. Researcher A and researcher B are having a scientific debate. What are they arguing about if their argument is focused on:

   (a) causal hurdle 1?

   (b) causal hurdle 2?

   (c) causal hurdle 3?

   (d) causal hurdle 4?

8. Find a social science journal article of interest to you, and of which your instructor approves, and answer the following items (be sure to provide a full citation to the chosen article with your answers):

   (a) Briefly describe the causal theory that connects the independent and dependent variables.

   (b) Create a causal hurdles scorecard for this theory and write an explanation for each of your entries in the scorecard.

9. Consider the following possible causal relationships. Following causal hurdle 4, come up with a list of some potentially confounding variables (Z) that we would need to attempt to control for in order to successfully cross hurdle 4 and be confident in our conclusion about whether or not X causes Y.

   (a) The relationship between urban (versus suburban or rural) residence (X) and racial/ethnic tolerance (Y).

   (b) The relationship between a person's educational attainment (X) and his/her attitudes toward the Black Lives Matter movement (Y).

4 Research Design

OVERVIEW

Given our focus on causality, what research strategies do sociologists use to investigate causal relationships? Generally speaking, the controlled experiment is the foundation for scientific research. And some sociologists use experiments in their work. However, owing to the nature of our subject matter, most sociologists adopt one of two types of "observational" research designs that are intended to mimic experiments. The cross-sectional observational study focuses on variation across individual units (like people or cities or countries). The time-series observational study focuses on variation in aggregate quantities (like poverty rates) over time. What is an "experiment" and why is it so useful? How do observational studies try to mimic experimental designs? Most importantly, what are the strengths and weaknesses of each of these three research designs in establishing whether or not causal relationships exist between concepts? That is, how does each one help us to get across the four causal hurdles identified in Chapter 3? Relatedly, we introduce issues concerning the selection of samples of cases to study in which we are not able to study the entire population of cases to which our theory applies. This is a subject that will feature prominently in many of the subsequent chapters.

4.1 COMPARISON AS THE KEY TO ESTABLISHING CAUSAL RELATIONSHIPS

So far, you have learned that sociologists care about causal relationships. You have learned that most phenomena we are interested in explaining have multiple causes, but our theories typically deal with only one of them while ignoring the others. In some of the research examples in the previous chapters, we have noted that the multivariate nature of the world can make our first glances at evidence misleading. In the example dealing with race and political participation, at first it appeared that race might be causally related to participation rates, with Anglos participating more than those of other races. But, we argued, in this particular case, the first glance was potentially quite misleading.

Why? Because what appeared to be straightforward comparisons between three groups – participation rates between Anglos, Latinos, and African Americans – ended up being far from simple. On some very important factors, our different groupings for our independent variable X were far from equal. That is, people of different racial groupings (X) had differing socio-economic statuses (Z), which are correlated with race (X) and also affected their levels of participation (Y). As convincing as those bivariate comparisons might have been, they would likely be misleading.

Comparisons are at the heart of science. If we are evaluating a theory about the relationship between some X and some Y, the scientist's job is to do everything possible to make sure that no other influences (Z) interfere with the comparisons that we will rely on to make our inferences about a possible causal relationship between X and Y.

The obstacles to causal inference that we described in Chapter 3 are substantial, but surmountable. We don't know whether, in reality, X causes Y. We may be armed with a theory that suggests that X does, indeed, cause Y, but theories can be (and often are) wrong or incomplete. So how do scientists generally, and sociologists in particular, go about testing whether X causes Y? There are several strategies, or **research designs**, that researchers can use toward that end. The goal of all types of research designs is to help us evaluate how well a theory fares as it makes its way over the four causal hurdles – that is, to answer as conclusively as is possible the question about whether X causes Y. In the next two sections we focus on the two strategies that sociologists use most commonly and effectively: **experiments** and (especially) **observational studies.**[1]

4.2 EXPERIMENTAL RESEARCH DESIGNS

Suppose your state legislature is considering a bill to decriminalize the recreational use of marijuana, a bill that you support. You'd like to mobilize your fellow students to join you in a grassroots effort to encourage state lawmakers to pass the bill, but you are unsure about how best to convince others of the virtue of your position. One possibility, you hypothesize, might be to produce a short documentary that compares the health effects of marijuana with those of such drugs as alcohol and cocaine. But before

[1] Throughout this book, we will use the term "experiment" in the same way that researchers in medical science use the term "randomized control trial."

embarking on your campaign, you'd like to know if your idea is worth pursuing or not. The bottom-line question is, "Will the documentary work?" That is, will marshaling scientific evidence that the long-term health effects of marijuana seem to be less serious than those of alcohol and cocaine be effective in convincing others to support the bill to legalize recreational use of marijuana?

We hope that you're becoming accustomed to spotting the causal questions embedded in this scenario: Exposure to the documentary (X) may, or may not, affect one's view of the bill (Y). And it is important to add here that the causal claim has a particular directional component to it: that is, exposure to the documentary will *increase* the chances that a person will support the bill.

How might researchers in the social sciences evaluate such a causal claim? Perhaps one idea that occurs to you is to organize a **focus group** to see how some of your classmates react to the documentary. And that's not a bad idea. Let's informally define a focus group as a group of subjects selected to be exposed to some idea (like a new kitchen knife, or a documentary comparing the health effects of marijuana, alcohol, and cocaine), and try to gather the subjects' responses to the idea. There's a problem with the focus group, though, particularly in the case at hand of the documentary: What would the subjects have said about the bill had they *not* been exposed to the documentary? There's nothing to use as a basis for comparison.

It is very important, and not at all surprising, to realize that others may either support or not support your position for a variety of reasons (Zs) that have nothing to do with exposure to the documentary – varying religious convictions, varying ideologies, and political party identifications can all cause people to favor or oppose the legalization of marijuana. So how can we establish whether, among these other influences (Z), the documentary (X) also causes others to support the bill (Y)?

Can we do better than the focus group? What would a more scientific approach look like? As the introduction to this chapter highlights, we will need a comparison of some kind, and we will want that comparison to isolate any potentially different effects that the documentary has on a person's likelihood of supporting the bill.

The standard approach to a situation like this in the physical and medical sciences is that we would need to conduct an experiment. Because the word "experiment" has such common usage, its scientific meaning is frequently misunderstood. An experiment is *not* simply any kind of analysis that is quantitative in nature; neither is it exclusively the domain of laboratories and white-coated scientists with pocket protectors. We define an experiment as follows: *An experiment is a research design in which the researcher both controls and randomly assigns values of the independent variable to the participants.*

Notice the twin components of the definition of the experiment: That the researcher both *controls* values of the independent variable – or *X*, as we have called it – as well as *randomly assigns* those values to the participants in the experiment. Together, these two features form a complete definition of an experiment, which means that there are no other essential features of an experiment beside these two.

What does it mean to say that a researcher "controls" the value of the independent variable that the participants receive? It means, most importantly, that the values of the independent variable that the participants receive are *not* determined either by the participants themselves or by nature. In our example of the documentary, this requirement means that we cannot compare people who, by their own choice, already have chosen to expose themselves to the documentary (not an issue in this case because the documentary has yet to be produced). It means that we, the researchers, have to decide which of our experimental participants will see the documentary and which ones will not.

But the definition of an experiment has one other essential component as well: We, the researchers, must not only control the values of the independent variable, but *we must also assign those values to participants randomly*. In the context of our marijuana example, this means that we must toss coins, draw numbers out of a hat, use a random-number generator, or some other such mechanism to divide our participants into a **treatment group** (who will see the documentary) and a **control group** (who will not see the documentary, but will instead watch something innocuous, in a social science parallel to a **placebo**).

What's the big deal here? Why is randomly assigning subjects to treatment groups important? What scientific benefits arise from the random assignment of people to treatment and control groups? To see why this is so crucial, recall that we have emphasized that all science is about comparisons and also that every interesting phenomenon worth exploring – every interesting dependent variable – is caused by many factors, not just one. Random assignment to treatment groups ensures that the comparison we make between the treatment group and the control group is as pure as possible, and that some other cause (*Z*) of the dependent variable will not pollute that comparison. By first taking a group of participants and then randomly splitting them into two groups on the basis of a coin flip, what we have ensured is that the participants will not be systematically different from one another. Indeed, provided that the participant pool is reasonably large, randomly assigning participants to treatment and control groups ensures that the groups, as a whole, are *identical*. If the two groups are identical, save for the coin flip, then we can be certain that any differences we observe in the groups must be because of the independent variable that we have assigned to them.

Return to our marijuana bill example. An experiment involving our documentary would involve finding a group of people – however obtained – and then randomly assigning them to view either the documentary or something that is unrelated to it (like a cartoon or a public service announcement). We fully realize that there are other causes of people's views on the legalization of marijuana and that our experiment does not negate those factors. In fact, our experiment will have nothing whatsoever to say about those other causes. What it *will* do, and do well, is to determine whether our documentary had a positive or negative effect, or no effect at all, on students' positions on the pending bill.

Contrast the comparison that results from an experiment with a comparison that arises from a non-experiment. (We'll discuss non-experimental designs in the next section.) Suppose that we don't do an experiment and just send our fellow students a link to the documentary inviting them to view it online, and then conduct a survey asking them if they've seen our documentary and whether they support (or not) the bill to legalize recreational marijuana. Let's even assume that, in conducting our survey, we obtain a random sample of students at the university. If we analyze the results of the survey and discover that, as hoped, the people who say that they have seen our documentary are more likely to support the bill than people who say they have not seen the documentary, does that mean that the documentary *caused* – see that word again? – people's opinions to shift in our favor? No. Why not? Because the people who saw our documentary and the people who did not see our documentary might be *systematically different* from one another. What does that mean? It means that those who voluntarily chose to watch the documentary might be more interested in the process of legislation than those who chose not to watch it. In this case, a person's level of interest in the legislative process could be an important Z variable. Interest in the legislative process could very well be associated with a person's likelihood to support the pending bill.

What this means is that the simple comparison in a non-experiment between those who do and those who do not see the documentary is potentially misleading because it is confounded by other factors, like interest in the legislative process. Is the higher support for the bill the result of the documentary, or is it the result of the fact that people likely to see the documentary in the first place are people with higher interest in the process of legislation? Because this particular non-experimental research design does not answer that question, it does not clear our fourth causal hurdle. It is impossible to know whether it was the documentary that caused the

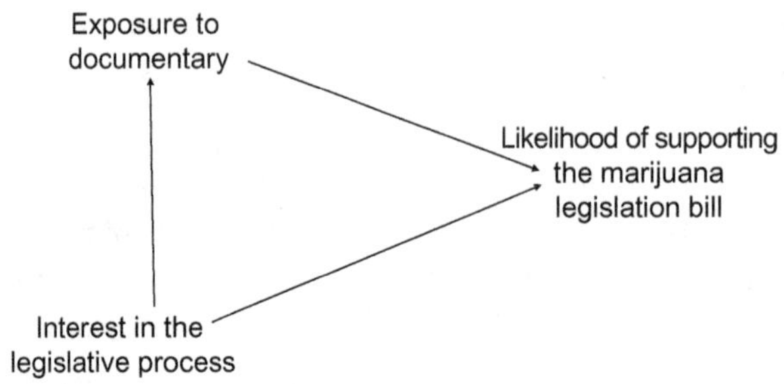

Figure 4.1 The possibly confounding effects of interest in the legislative process–bill support relationship

voters to support the bill. Because there are other factors that influence support for the bill – and, critically, because these factors are also related to whether or not people will see the documentary – it is very difficult to say conclusively that the independent variable (documentary exposure) causes the dependent variable (support, or not, of the bill). Figure 4.1 shows this graphically.

Here is where experiments differ so drastically from any other kind of research design. What experimental research designs accomplish by way of random assignment to treatment groups, then, is to decontaminate the comparison between the treatment and control groups of all other influences. Before any stimulus (like a treatment or placebo) is administered, all of the participants are in the same pool. Researchers divide them by using some random factor like a coin flip, and that difference is the only difference between the two groups.

Think of it another way. The way that the confounding variables in Figure 4.1 are correlated with the independent variable is highly improbable in an experiment. Why? Because if X is determined by randomness, like a coin flip, then (by the very definition of randomness) it is exceedingly unlikely to be correlated with anything (including confounding variables Z). When researchers control and assign values of X randomly, the comparison between the different groups will not be affected by the fact that other factors certainly do cause Y, the dependent variable. In an experiment, then, because X is only caused by randomness, it means that we can erase the connection between Z and X in Figure 4.1. And, recalling our definition of a confounding variable, if Z is not correlated with X, it cannot confound the relationship between X and Y.

Connect this back to our discussion from Chapter 3 about how researchers attempt to cross four hurdles in their efforts to establish whether some X causes Y. As we will see, experiments are not the only method that help researchers cross the four causal hurdles, but they are uniquely capable in accomplishing important parts of that task. Consider each hurdle in turn. First, we should evaluate whether there is a credible causal mechanism before we decide to run the experiment. It is worth noting that the crossing of this causal hurdle is neither easier nor harder in experiments than in non-experiments. Coming up with a credible causal scenario that links X to Y heightens our dependence on theory, not on data or research design.

Second, in an experiment, it is impossible for Y to cause X – the second causal hurdle – for two reasons. First, assigning X occurs in time before Y is measured, which makes it impossible for Y to cause X. More importantly, though, as previously noted, if X is generated by randomness alone, then nothing (including Y) can cause it. So, in Figure 4.1, we could eliminate any possible reverse-causal arrow flowing from Y to X.

Establishing, third, whether X and Y are correlated is similarly easy regardless of the chosen research design, experimental or non-experimental (as we will see in Chapter 9). What about our fourth causal hurdle? Have we controlled for all confounding variables Z that might make the association between X and Y spurious? Experiments are uniquely well equipped to help us answer this question definitively. An experiment does not, in any way, eliminate the possibility that a variety of other variables (that we call Z) might also affect Y (as well as X). What the experiment does, through the process of randomly assigning subjects to different values of X, is to equate the treatment and control groups on all possible factors. On every possible variable, whether or not it is related to X, or to Y, or to both, or to neither, the treatment and control groups should, in theory, be identical. That makes the comparison between the two values of X unpolluted by any possible Z variables because we expect the groups to be equivalent on all values of Z.

Remarkably, the experimental ability to control for the effects of outside variables (Z) applies to *all* possible confounding variables, regardless of whether we, the researchers, are aware of them. Let's make the example downright preposterous. Let's say that, twenty years from now, another team of scientists discovers that having attached (as opposed to detached) earlobes causes people to have different views on the legalization of marijuana. Does that possibility threaten the inference that we draw from our experiment about our documentary? No, not at all. Why not? Because, whether or not we are aware of it, the random assignment of participants to treatment groups means that, whether we are paying attention to it or not, we would expect our treatment and control groups to have equal numbers of people with attached earlobes, and for both groups to have equal numbers of people with detached earlobes. The key element of an experimental research design – randomly assigning subjects to different values of X, the independent variable – controls for every Z in the universe, whether or not we are aware of that Z.

In summary, if we think back to the causal hurdles scorecard from the previous chapter, all properly set-up experiments start out with a scorecard reading [? y ? y]. The ability of experimental designs to cleanly and definitively answer "yes" to the fourth hurdle question – Have we controlled for all confounding variables Z that might make the association between X and Y spurious? – is a massive advantage.[2] All that remains for establishing a causal relationship is the answers to clear the first hurdle – Is there a credible causal mechanism that connects X to Y? – and hurdle 3 – Is there covariation between X and Y? The difficulty of clearing hurdle 1 is unchanged, but hurdle 3 is much easier because we need only to make a statistical evaluation of the relationship between X and Y. As we will see in Chapter 9, such evaluations are pretty straightforward, especially when compared to statistical tests that involve controlling for other variables (Z).

Together, all of this means that experiments bring with them a particularly strong confidence in the causal inferences drawn from the analysis. In scientific parlance, this is called **internal validity.** If a research design produces high levels of confidence in the conclusions about causality, it is said to have high internal validity. Conversely, research designs that do not allow for particularly definitive conclusions about whether X causes Y are said to have low degrees of internal validity.

4.2.1 "Random Assignment" versus "Random Sampling"

It is critical that you do not confuse *the experimental process of randomly assigning subjects to treatment groups*, on the one hand, with *the process of randomly sampling subjects for participation*, on the other hand. They are entirely different, and in fact have nothing more in common than that six-letter word "random." They are, however, quite often confused for one another. **Random assignment** to treatment and control groups occurs when the participants for an experiment are assigned randomly to one of several possible values of X, the independent variable. Importantly, this definition says nothing at all about how the subjects were selected for participation. But **random sampling** is, at its very heart, about how researchers select people for participation in a study – they are selected at random, which means that every member of the underlying **population** has

[2] After all, even the best-designed and best-executed non-experimental designs must remain open to the possibility that, somewhere out there, there is a Z variable that has not yet been considered and controlled for.

an equal probability of being selected. (This is common in survey research, for example.)

Mixing up these two critical concepts will produce a good bit of confusion. In particular, confusing random sampling with random assignment to treatment groups will mean that the distinction between experiments and non-experiments has been lost, and this difference is among the more important ones in all of science. To understand how science works, keep these two very important concepts separate from one another.

4.2.2 Varieties of Experiments and Near-Experiments

Not all experiments take place in a laboratory with scientists wearing white lab coats. Some experiments in the social sciences are conducted by surveys that do use random samples (see above). Since 1990 or so, there has been a growing movement in the field of survey research – which has traditionally used random samples of the population – to use computers in the interviewing process that includes experimental randomization of variations in survey questions, in a technique called a **survey experiment.** Such designs are intended to reap the benefits of both random assignment to treatment groups, and hence have high internal validity, as well as the benefits of a random sample, and hence have high **external validity.**[3] Survey experiments may be conducted over the phone or, increasingly, over the Internet. We discuss survey experiments in more detail in Chapter 5.

Another setting for an experiment is out in the natural world. A **field experiment** is one that occurs in the natural setting where the subjects normally lead their lives. Random assignment to treatment groups has enabled researchers in the social sciences to study subjects that seemed beyond the reach of experimentation. Economists have long sought conclusive evidence about the effectiveness (or the lack thereof) of economic development policies. For example, do government fertilizer subsidies (X) affect agricultural output (Y)? Duflo, Kremer, and Robinson (2011) report the results of an experiment in a region in Western Kenya in which a subsidy of free delivery of fertilizer was offered only to randomly chosen farmers, but not to others.

Field experiments can also take place in public policy settings, sometimes with understandable controversy. Does the police officer's decision whether or not to arrest the male at a domestic violence call (X) affect the incidence of repeat violence at the same address in the subsequent months (Y)? Sherman and Berk (1984) conducted a field experiment in

[3] See Piazza, Sniderman, and Tetlock (1990) and Sniderman and Piazza (1993).

Minneapolis, randomizing whether or not the male in the household would automatically (or not) be arrested when police arrived at the house.

On occasion, situations in nature that are not properly defined as experiments – because the values of X have not been controlled and assigned by the researcher – nevertheless resemble experiments in key ways. In a **natural experiment** – which, we emphasize, does not meet our definition of an experiment – values of the independent variable arise naturally in such a way as to make it seem as if true random assignment by a researcher has occurred. For example, does the size of an ethnic group within a population (X) affect intergroup conflict or cooperation (Y)? Posner (2004) investigates why the Chewa and Tumbuka peoples are allies in Zambia but are adversaries in Malawi. Because the sizes of the groups in the different countries seem to have arisen randomly, the comparison is treated *as if* the sizes of the respective populations were assigned randomly by the researcher, when (of course) they were not.

4.2.3 Are There Drawbacks to Experimental Research Designs?

Experiments, as we have seen, have a unique ability to get social scientists across our hurdles needed to establish whether X causes Y. But that does not mean they are without disadvantages. Many of these disadvantages are related to the differences between medical and physical sciences, on the one hand, and the social sciences, on the other. We now discuss four drawbacks to experimentation.

First, especially in the social sciences, not every independent variable (X) is controllable and subject to experimental manipulation. Suppose, for example, that we wish to study the effects of gender on support for same-sex marriage. Are women more or less likely than men to favor laws that legalize same-sex marriages, or do men and women not differ on this issue? There are a variety of non-experimental ways to study this relationship, but it is impossible to experimentally manipulate a subject's gender. Recall that the definition of an experiment is that the researcher both controls and randomly assigns the values of the independent variable. In this case, the presumed cause (the independent variable) is a person's gender. Compared with drugs versus placebos, assigning a participant's gender is another matter entirely. It is, to put it mildly, impossible. People show up at an experiment either male or female, and it is not within the experimenter's power to "randomly assign" a participant to be male or female.

This is true in many, many social science examples. There are simply a myriad of substantive problems that are impossible to study in an experimental fashion. How does a person's political party (X) affect his views of race-conscious college admissions (Y)? How does a person's income level (X) affect her views of the causes of poverty (Y)? How does a country's level of democratization (X) affect its openness to international trade (Y)? How does the level of military spending in India (X) affect the level of military spending in Pakistan (Y) – and, for that matter, vice versa? How does media coverage (X) in an election campaign influence voters' priorities (Y)? In each of these examples that intrigue social scientists, the independent variable is simply not subject to experimental manipulation. Social scientists cannot, in any meaningful sense, "assign" people a party identification or an income, "assign" a country a level of democratization or a level of military spending, or "assign" a campaign a specific amount of media coverage. These variables simply exist in nature, and we cannot control exposure to them and randomly assign different values to different cases (that is, individual people or countries). And yet, social scientists feel compelled to study these phenomena, which means that, in those circumstances, we must turn to a non-experimental research design.

A second potential disadvantage of experimental research designs is that experiments often suffer from low degrees of external validity. We have noted that the key strength of experiments is that they typically have high levels of internal validity. That is, we can be quite confident that the conclusions about causality reached in the analysis are not confounded by other variables. External validity, in a sense, is the other side of the coin, as it represents the degree to which we can be confident that the results of our analysis apply not only to the participants in the study, but also to the population more broadly construed.

There are actually two types of concerns with respect to external validity. The first is the external validity of the sample itself. Recall that there is nothing whatsoever in our definition of an experiment that describes how researchers recruit or select people to participate in the experiment. To reiterate: *It is absolutely not the case that experiments require a random sample of the target population.* Indeed, it is extremely rare for experiments to draw a random sample from a population. In drug-trial experiments, for example, it is common to place advertisements in newspapers or on the radio to invite participation, usually involving some form of compensation to the participants. Clearly, people who see and respond to advertisements like this are not a random sample of the population of interest, which is typically thought of as all potential recipients of the drug. Similarly, when professors "recruit" people from their (or their colleagues') classes, the participants are not a random sample of *any* population.[4] The participant pool in this case represents what we would call a **sample of convenience**, which is to say, this is more or less the group of people we could beg, coerce, entice, or cajole to participate.

With a sample of convenience, it is simply unclear how, if at all, the results of the experiment generalize to a broader population. As we will learn in Chapter 8, this is a critical issue in the social sciences. Because most experiments make use of such samples of convenience, with any single experiment, it is difficult to know whether the results of that analysis are in any way typical of what we would find in a different sample. With experimental designs, then, scientists learn about how their results apply to a broader population through the process of **replication**, in which researchers implement the same procedures repeatedly in identical form to see if the relationships hold in a consistent fashion.

There is a second external validity concern with experiments that is more subtle, but perhaps just as important. It concerns the external validity of the stimulus. To continue our example of whether the documentary affects views on the legalization of marijuana, if we were to run an experiment to address this question, what would we do? First, we would need to obtain a sample of volunteer subjects somehow. (Remember, they need not be a random sample.) Second, we would divide them, on a random basis, into experimental and control groups. We would then sit them in a lab in front of computers, and show the documentary to the experimental group, and show something innocuous to the control group. Then we would ask the subjects from both groups their views on the legalization of marijuana, and make a comparison between our groups. Just as we might have concerns about how externally valid our sample is, because they may not be representative of the underlying population, we should also be concerned about how externally valid our stimulus is. What do we mean here? The stimulus is the X variable. In this case, it is the act of sitting the experimental and control subjects down and having them watch (different) video messages on the computer screens. How similar is that stimulus to one that a person experiences in his or her home – that is, in their more natural environment? In some respects it is quite different. In our hypothetical experiment, the individual does not choose what he or she sees. The exposure to the documentary is forced (once the subject consents to participate in the experiment). At home? People who don't

[4] Think about that for a moment. Experiments in undergraduate psychology or sociology classes are not a random sample of eighteen- to twenty-two-year-olds, or even a random sample of undergraduate students, or even a random sample of students from your college or university. Your psychology or sociology class is populated with people more interested in the social sciences than in the physical sciences or engineering or the humanities.

want to be exposed to documentaries can avoid them rather easily if they so choose, simply by not watching particular channels or programs, or by not watching TV at all, or by flipping the channel when a documentary starts up. But the comparison in our hypothetical experiment is entirely insensitive to this key difference between the experimental environment and the subject's more natural environment. To the extent that an experiment creates an entirely artificial environment, we might be concerned whether the results of that experiment will be found in a more real-world context.[5]

A third potential drawback of experimental research designs is that, when interpreting the results of an experiment, we sometimes make mistakes of emphasis. If an experiment produces a finding that some *X* does indeed cause *Y*, that does not mean that that particular *X* is the most prominent cause of *Y*. As we have emphasized repeatedly, a variety of independent variables are causally related to every interesting dependent variable in the social sciences. Experimental research designs often do not help to sort out which causes of the dependent variable have the largest effects and which ones have smaller effects.

A final possible problem with experimental research designs, as we discussed in Chapter 1, is that they can create special ethical dilemmas for the researcher.

4.3 OBSERVATIONAL STUDIES (IN TWO FLAVORS)

Taken together, the drawbacks of experiments mean that, for any given sociological research situation, implementing an experiment often proves to be unworkable, and sometimes downright impossible. As a result, experimentation is not the most common research design used by sociologists. The experiment, for many researchers and for varying reasons, remains a tool that is not applicable to many of the phenomena that we seek to study.

Does this mean that researchers have to shrug their shoulders and abandon their search for causal connections before they even begin? Not at all. But what options do scholars have when they cannot control exposure to different values of the independent variables? In such cases, the only choice is to take the world as it already exists and make the comparison between either individual units – like people, organizations, or countries – or an **aggregate** quantity that varies over time. These represent two variants of what is most commonly called an observational study. Observational

[5] For a substantive application where the issues of external validity of the stimulus are pivotal in determining the results of the experiment, see Arceneaux and Johnson (2011). See also Morton and Williams (2010, p. 264), who refer to this problem as one of "ecological validity."

studies are not experiments, but they seek to emulate them. They are known as observational studies because, unlike the controlled and somewhat artificial nature of most experiments, in these research designs researchers simply take reality as it is and "observe" it, attempting to sort out causal connections without the benefit of randomly assigning participants to treatment groups. Instead, different values of the independent variable already exist in the world, and what scientists do is observe them and then evaluate their theoretical claims by putting them through the same four causal hurdles to discover whether *X* causes *Y*.

This leads to the definition of an observational study: An observational study is a research design in which the researcher does *not* have control over values of the independent variable, which occur naturally. However, it is necessary that there be some degree of variability in the independent variable across cases, as well as variation in the dependent variable.

Because there is no random assignment to treatment groups, as in experiments, some scholars claim that it is impossible to speak of causality in observational studies, and therefore sometimes refer to them as **correlational studies**. Along with most social scientists, we do not share this view. Certainly experiments produce higher degrees of confidence about causal matters than do observational studies. However, in observational studies, if sufficient attention is paid to accounting for all of the other possible causes of the dependent variable that are suggested by current understanding, then we can make informed evaluations of our confidence that the independent variable does cause the dependent variable.

Observational studies, as this discussion implies, face exactly the same four causal hurdles as do experiments. (Recall that those hurdles are present in any research design.) So how, in observational studies, do we cross these hurdles? The first causal hurdle – Is there a credible mechanism connecting *X* and *Y*? – is identical in experimental and observational studies.

In an observational study, however, crossing the second causal hurdle – Can we eliminate the possibility that *Y* causes *X*? – can sometimes be problematic. For example, do countries with higher levels of economic development (*X*) have, as a consequence, more stable democratic regimes (*Y*)? Crossing the second causal hurdle, in this case, is a rather dicey matter. It is clearly plausible that having a stable democratic government makes economic prosperity more likely, which is the reverse-causal scenario. After all, investors are probably more comfortable taking risks with their money in democratic regimes than in autocratic ones. Those risks, in turn, likely produce greater degrees of economic prosperity. It is possible, of course, that *X* and *Y* are mutually reinforcing – that is, *X* causes *Y*, and *Y* causes *X*.

The third hurdle – Is there covariation between *X* and *Y*? – is, as we mentioned, no more difficult for an observational study than for an experiment. (The techniques for examining relationships between two variables are straightforward, and you will learn them in Chapters 9 and 10.) But, unlike in an experimental setting, if we fail to find covariation between *X* and *Y* in an observational setting, we should still proceed to the fourth hurdle because the possibility remains that we will find covariation between *X* and *Y* once we control for some variable *Z*.

The most pointed comparison between experiments and observational studies, though, occurs with respect to the fourth causal hurdle. The near-magic that happens in experiments because of random assignment to treatment groups – which enables researchers to know that no other factors interfere in the relationship between *X* and *Y* – is not present in an observational study. So, in an observational study, the comparison between groups with different values of the independent variable may very well be polluted by other factors, interfering with our ability to make conclusive statements about whether *X* causes *Y*.

Within observational studies, there are two pure types: **cross-sectional observational studies**, which focus on variation across units of analysis (such as people) at a single point in time; and **time-series observational studies**, which focus on variation within a single unit of analysis over multiple time points. There are, in addition, hybrid designs, but for the sake of simplicity we will focus on the pure types.[6] Before we get into the two types of observational studies, we need to provide a brief introduction to observational data.

4.3.1 Datum, Data, Data Set

The word "data" is one of the most grammatically misused words in the English language. Why? Because most people use this word as though it were a singular word when it is, in fact, plural. Any time you read "the data is," you have found a grammatical error. Instead, when describing data, the phrasing should be "the data are." Get used to it: You are now one of the foot soldiers in the crusade to get people to use this word appropriately. It will be a long and uphill battle.

The singular form of the word data is "**datum.**" Together, a collection of datum produces data or a "**data set.**" We define observational data sets by the variables that they contain and the units of analysis and time frames over which they are measured. Sociologists use data measured on a variety of different units of analysis. For instance, in survey research, the unit of analysis is the individual survey respondent. In comparative

[6] The classic statements of observational studies appeared in 1963 in Donald Campbell and Julian Stanley's seminal work *Experimental and Quasi-Experimental Designs for Research*.

U.S. state studies, the unit of analysis is the U.S. state. In comparative international studies, the unit of analysis is usually the nation. Commonly studied time units are months, quarters, and years. It is also common to refer to the spatial and time units that define data sets as the **data set dimensions.**

4.3.2 Cross-Sectional Observational Studies

As the name implies, a cross-sectional observational study examines a cross-section of social reality, focusing on variation between *individual units of analysis* – again, like people, states, or countries – and explaining the variation in the dependent variable across them.

For example, what, if anything, is the connection between the preferences of the voters from a district (X) and a representative's voting behavior (Y)? In a cross-sectional observational study, the strategy that a researcher would pursue in answering this question involves comparing the aggregated preferences of voters from a variety of districts (X) with the voting records of their representatives (Y). Such an analysis, of course, would have to be observational, instead of experimental, because this particular X is not subject to experimental manipulation.

Bear in mind, of course, that observational studies have to cross the same four causal hurdles as do experiments. And we have noted that, unlike experiments, with their random assignment to treatment groups, observational studies will often get stuck on our fourth hurdle. That might indeed be the case here. Assuming the other three hurdles can be cleared, consider the possibility that there are confounding variables that cause Y and are also correlated with X, which make the X–Y connection spurious. (Can you think of any such factors?) How do cross-sectional observational studies deal with this critical issue? The answer is that, in most cases, this can be accomplished through a series of rather straightforward statistical controls. In particular, beginning in Chapter 11, you will learn the most common social science research tool for "controlling for" other possible causes of Y, namely the multiple regression model. What you will learn there is that multiple regression can allow researchers to see how, if at all, controlling for another variable (like Z) affects the relationship between X and Y.

4.3.3 Time-Series Observational Studies

The other major variant of observational studies is the time-series observational study, which has, at its heart, a comparison over time within a single spatial unit. Unlike in the cross-sectional variety, which examines relationships between variables across individual units typically at a single time point, in the time-series observational study, sociologists typically examine the variation within one spatial unit over time.[7]

For example, how, if at all, do changes in media coverage about crime (X) affect public concern about crime (Y)? To be a bit more specific, when the media spend more time talking about crime, does the public show more concern about it, and when the media spend less time on the subject of crime, does public concern about crime wane? We can measure these variables in aggregate terms that vary over time. For example, how many stories about crime make it onto the nightly news in a given month? It is almost certain that that quantity will not be the same each and every month. And how much concern does the public show (through opinion polls, for example) about crime in a given month? Again, the percentage of people who identify crime as a pressing problem will almost certainly vary from month to month.

Of course, as with its cross-sectional cousin, the time-series observational study will require us to focus hard on that fourth causal hurdle. Have we controlled for all confounding variables (Z) that are related to the varying volume of news coverage about crime (X) and public concern about crime (Y)? (Exercise 5 at the end of this chapter will ask for your thoughts on this subject.) If we can identify any other possible causes of why the public is sometimes more concerned about crime, and why they are sometimes less concerned about it, then we will need to control for those factors in our analysis.

4.3.4 The Major Difficulty with Observational Studies

We noted that experimental research designs carry some drawbacks with them. So, too, do observational studies. Here, we focus only on one, but it is a big one. As the preceding examples demonstrate, when we need to control for the other possible causes of Y to cross the fourth causal hurdle, we need to control for *all of them*, not just one.[8] But how do we know whether we have controlled for all of the other possible causes of Y? In many cases, we don't know that for certain. We need to try, of course, to control statistically for all other possible causes that we can, which involves carefully considering the previous research on the subject and gathering as much data on those other causes as is possible. But in many cases, we will simply be unable to do this perfectly.

[7] The spatial units analyzed in time-series observational studies are usually aggregated.

[8] As we will see in Chapter 11, technically we need to control only for the factors that might affect Y and are also related to X. In practice, though, that is a very difficult distinction to make.

What all of this means, in our view, is that observational analysis must be a bit more tentative in its pronouncements about causality. Indeed, if we have done the very best we can to control for as many causes of Y, then the most sensible conclusion we can reach, in many cases, is that X causes Y. But in practice, our conclusions are rarely definitive, and subsequent research can modify them. That can be frustrating, we know, for students to come to grips with – and it can be frustrating for researchers, too. But the fact that conclusive answers are difficult to come by should only make us work harder to identify other causes of Y. An important part of being a scientist is that we very rarely can make definitive conclusions about causality; we must remain open to the possibility that some previously unconsidered (Z) variable will surface and render our previously found relationships to be spurious. This is especially the case in observational designs.

4.4 SUMMARY

For almost every phenomenon of interest to sociologists, there is more than one form of research design that they could implement to address questions of causal relationships. Before starting a project, researchers need to decide whether to use experimental or observational methods; and if they opt for the latter, as is common, they have to decide what type of observational study to use. And sometimes researchers choose more than one type of design.

Different research designs help shed light on different questions. Focus, for the moment, on a simple matter like the public's preferences for a more liberal or conservative government policy. Cross-sectional and time-series approaches are both useful in this respect. They simply address different types of substantive questions. Cross-sectional approaches look to see why some individuals prefer more liberal government policies, and why some other individuals prefer more conservative government policies. That is a perfectly worthwhile undertaking for a sociologist: What causes some people to be liberals and others to be conservatives? But consider the time-series approach, which focuses on why the public as an aggregated whole prefers a more liberal or a more conservative government at different points in time. That is simply a different question. Neither approach is inherently better or worse than the other, but they both shed light on different aspects of social reality. Which design researchers should choose depends on what type of question they intend to ask and answer.

CONCEPTS INTRODUCED IN THIS CHAPTER

- aggregate – a quantity that is created by combining the values of many individual cases
- control group – in an experiment, the subset of cases that is not exposed to the main causal stimulus under investigation
- correlational studies – synonymous with "observational studies"
- cross-sectional observational studies – a research design which focuses on variation across spatial units at a single time unit
- data set – a collection of variable values for at least two observations; synonym for "data"
- data set dimensions – the spatial and time units that define a data set
- datum – the singular form of the word "data"
- experiments – research designs in which the researcher both controls and randomly assigns values of the independent variable to the participants
- external validity – the degree to which we can be confident that the results of our analysis apply not only to the participants and circumstances in the study, but also to the population more broadly construed
- field experiment – an experimental study that occurs in the natural setting where the subjects normally lead their lives
- focus group – a group of people brought together to engage in discussions of a topic of interest to a researcher, such as views of political candidates or policies toward undocumented immigrants
- internal validity – the degree to which a study produces high levels of confidence about whether the independent variable causes the dependent variable
- natural experiment – situations in nature that are not properly defined as experiments but the values of the independent variable arise naturally in such a way as to make it seem as if true random assignment by a researcher has occurred
- observational studies – research designs in which the researcher does not have control over values of the independent variable, which occur naturally; it is necessary that there be some degree of variability in the independent variable across cases, as well as variation in the dependent variable
- placebo – in an experiment, an innocuous stimulus given to the control group
- population – the entire set of cases to which our theory applies
- random assignment – when the participants for an experiment are assigned randomly to one of several possible values of X, the independent variable

- random sampling – a method for selecting individual cases for a study in which every member of the underlying population has an equal probability of being selected
- replication – a scientific process in which researchers implement the same procedures repeatedly in identical form to see if the relationships hold in a consistent fashion
- research designs – the strategies that a researcher employs to make comparisons with the goal of evaluating causal claims
- sample of convenience – a sample of cases from the underlying population in which the mechanism for selecting cases is not random
- survey experiment – a survey research technique in which the interviewing process includes experimental randomization in the survey stimulus
- time-series observational studies – a research design which focuses on variation within a single spatial unit over multiple time units
- treatment group – in an experiment, the subset of cases that is exposed to the main causal stimulus under investigation

EXERCISES

1. Consider the following proposed relationships between an independent and a dependent variable. In each case, would it be realistic for a researcher to perform an experiment to test the theory? If yes, briefly describe what would be randomly assigned in the experiment; if no, briefly explain why not.

   (a) An individual's level of religiosity (X) and his or her attitudes toward interracial marriage (Y).

   (b) Exposure to negative political ads (X) and political apathy (Y).

   (c) Military service (X) and attitudes toward foreign policy (Y).

   (d) A speaker's personal characteristics (X) and persuasiveness (Y).

2. Consider the relationship between education level (X) and voting turnout (Y). How would the design of a cross-sectional observational study differ from that of a time-series observational study?
3. In the previous chapter (specifically, Section 3.3 titled "Why Is Studying Causality So Important? Three Examples from Sociology"), we gave examples of research problems. For each of these examples, identify the spatial unit(s) and time unit(s). For each, say whether the study was an experiment, a cross-sectional observational study, or a time-series observational study.
4. The beating of Rodney King by Los Angeles police officers on March 3, 1991 precipitated widespread demonstrations against police brutality. By happenstance, the 1991 General Social Survey (GSS) was being administered

at the time of the beating. Almost half (44 percent) of respondents were interviewed prior to the Rodney King incident, the remainder (56 percent) after it. Describe a research design using these data that would allow you to examine the effect of the beating on citizens' attitudes toward police. What Z variables would you include in your research?

5. In Section 4.3.3 on time-series observational studies, we introduced the idea of how varying levels of media coverage of crime (X) might cause variation in public concern about crime (Y). Can you think of any relevant Z variables that we will need to control for, statistically, in such an analysis to be reasonably confident that the relationship between X and Y is causal?

5 Survey Research

OVERVIEW

As you know by now, this book focuses on the use of statistical techniques in analyzing potentially causal relationships between variables in the social sciences. But where do the data that allow us to examine such relationships come from? In this chapter we discuss an especially important tool commonly used by sociologists and other social scientists for collecting data – survey research. From the voluminous literature on surveys, we selected several issues that are especially relevant for current purposes: modes of survey administration – face-to-face, self-administered, telephone, and web-based administrations; the use of already existing survey data sets – the General Social Survey, the American National Election Study, the International Social Survey Programme, and the World Values Survey; survey-based experiments; and types of probability sampling.

5.1 WHY SURVEYS?

Surveys are ubiquitous in social life. We typically read about (or listen to) the findings of one or more surveys every day – in newspapers; on broadcast media; in reports from local, state, or federal agencies; and, of course, in the social science research literature (Tourangeau, 2004). Political candidate preference polls, for instance, are commonplace, especially during election cycles. Surveys soliciting the public's views on a wide variety of important issues of the day – race and ethnic relations, immigration, religious beliefs, criminal justice, and LGBTQ rights, among many others – are also fielded quite often by a variety of survey research organizations. Indeed, many of the organizations that specialize in conducting social science surveys have become, if not exactly household names, at least recognizable – the Roper Center for Public Opinion Research, the Pew Research Center, the Public Religion Research Institute, and the National Opinion Research Center, among many others. The Roper Center's mission statement, as stated on its website, is typical of most such organizations: "Our mission is to collect, preserve, and disseminate public opinion data; to serve as a resource to help improve the practice of survey research; and to broaden the understanding of public opinion through the use of survey data in the United States and around the world."[1] Most (like those mentioned here) are nonpartisan. The strengths of such surveys lie in their ability to collect detailed information from large numbers of respondents on a range of topics and, assuming a probability sampling design, to allow users of the surveys to generalize findings from the sample of respondents to the population from which the sample was drawn using inferential statistics (see Section 5.3 below). As a result, surveys are especially important research tools of social scientists.

5.2 MODES OF SURVEY ADMINISTRATION

Surveys are very flexible data-gathering tools. When you think of a survey you might envision a self-administered paper-and-pencil questionnaire hand-delivered by a researcher to respondents at their workplaces, residences, or other locations (including classrooms), or sent through the (snail) mail. In practice, most modern social surveys are administered in a variety of formats, including face-to-face interviews, computer-assisted telephone interviews, and, increasingly, web-based administration, in addition to self-administered questionnaires. Each survey type has its own strengths and weaknesses, as we review next.

5.2.1 Face-to-Face In-Person Interviews

The **face-to-face interview** format has been the gold standard for social surveys going back as far as the 1940s (Yeager et al., 2011). Compared to other methods of fielding surveys, face-to-face interviews have long been considered the most adept at yielding high-quality information from probability samples of respondents. Numerous studies have shown that the data from face-to-face interviews compare favorably with the data yielded by self-administered questionnaires and telephone and web-based interviews on most – though not all – dimensions. Compared to other modes of administration, for instance, the face-to-face interview format is especially adept at administering longer questionnaires; at allowing more complex questions; at encouraging interviewees to respond to open-ended

[1] Roper Center for Public Opinion Research: https://ropercenter.cornell.edu/. The websites for the other organizations mentioned are: https://pewresearch.org; https://prri.org; and http://norc.org.

questions; and at increasing overall survey (as opposed to item) response rates. On other characteristics, however, such as the ability of the interviewer to control question order, minimize item nonresponse, and avoid contamination by nonrespondents (for example, significant others who may be at home while the respondent is being interviewed), research shows that face-to-face interviews and telephone interviews are on a par; and on still other factors, such as avoiding socially desirable responses, race-of-interviewer effects, and per-interview costs, self-administered and, especially, web-based surveys have an advantage. Overall, however, most studies have found face-to-face interviews to be the most advantageous (Berrens et al., 2003; Chang and Krosnick, 2009; Dillman, 2011; Marsden and Wright, 2010; Yeager et al., 2011).[2]

Unfortunately, the skyrocketing financial costs of face-to-face interviewing have rendered this mode of survey administration less and less feasible over time. Today, with the exception of government-sponsored surveys, face-to-face interviewing of large probability samples of respondents is more the exception than the rule (Yeager et al., 2011).[3]

5.2.2 Self-Administered Questionnaires

As we noted above, **self-administered survey questionnaires** are often mailed to a sample of respondents, who then answer the questions and (hopefully!) mail the completed questionnaire back to the researcher in the provided self-addressed, postage-paid envelope. Response rates to self-administered surveys are often quite low; as a result, systematic follow-up by the researcher in the form of contacting nonrespondents is the key to increasing the likelihood of participation (Dillman, 2011).

An alternative to mailing the questionnaire to selected respondents is to conduct what is referred to as "group interviews" in which the researcher distributes questionnaires to a group of respondents, such as a classroom of students. As a captive audience, response rates to group interviews are usually quite high. In practical terms, however, such captive audiences are rare, rendering group interviews much less common than other modes of survey administration.

5.2.3 Telephone Interviews

Telephone interviews gained prominence as a mode of survey data collection in the 1970s, for a variety of reasons. First, a large majority of U.S.

[2] In their comparison of findings yielded by full-probability face-to-face interviews with non-full-probability web-based surveys, however, Simmons and Bobo (2015) found more similarities than differences across these two modes of survey administration.

[3] See Section 5.4 below for exceptions.

households, over 90 percent, had landline telephones by 1970, a figure that increased to approximately 96 to 97 percent by the early 2000s (Blumberg and Luke, 2021). Second, the development of random digit dialing (RDD) telephone technology meant that every household with a landline telephone had a chance of being included in a sample, making lists of housing units unnecessary and improving sample representativeness. Third, advances in **computer-assisted telephone interviewing** (CATI) allowed survey questionnaires to be formatted on an interviewer's computer and the database to be compiled simultaneously with the interview, reducing the time, labor, and cost involved in administering telephone surveys. Finally, by the 1970s the logistical limitations of self-administered questionnaires, and the skyrocketing costs of face-to-face interviewing, combined to substantially increase the popularity of telephone interviewing as a cost-effective alternative mode of survey data collection.

Since the early 2000s, however, the terrain has changed dramatically, and telephone interviewing has fallen on difficult times (Couper and Bosnjak, 2010). The portion of U.S. households with landline telephones has steadily declined as cell phone use has become widespread; by 2021, 68 percent of adults lived in wireless-only households (Blumberg and Luke, 2021). The impact of this change on telephone interviewing as a mode of survey data collection has been tremendous. Diminishing rates of landline telephone use, increased rates of cellular use, and declining response rates to both has meant that RDD telephone samples of U.S. households are now infrequently used as the sole method of survey data collection (Lavrakas et al., 2017). Instead, the trend is now toward mixed-mode surveys that combine two or more modes of data collection (Olson et al., 2021).

5.2.4 Web-Based Surveys

Web-based surveys are the most recent innovation in survey data collection. This mode of administration has experienced a substantial surge in popularity among social scientists over the past two decades. There are now several professional survey research firms and organizations that specialize in conducting web-based surveys for their clients, who may include academic, government, media, and/or private sector practitioners. The best of these firms combine probability sampling methods with the reach and capabilities of the Internet to yield samples of respondents more quickly and affordably than other modes of survey administration, especially face-to-face interviews (Dillman, Smyth, and Christian, 2014).

One example among many of the kind of social science research that can be conducted using a web-based survey is a study by Weitzer and Tuch (2006) in which they contracted with the survey research firm Knowledge

Networks, Inc. (hereafter, KN) to survey a national sample of African American, Latino, and white respondents in an analysis of racial and ethnic differences in experiences with policing.[4] KN used a two-stage process of sample selection: first, they selected an RDD sample of households from a sampling frame consisting of the entire U.S. telephone population;[5] and second, they contacted the sampled households to solicit their participation in KN's "KnowledgePanel" of households. Any household with a landline telephone had a chance of being selected for the KN panel, including computer users and nonusers alike.[6] At the time of the study KN had a web-enabled panel of more than 25,000 households from which adults were randomly selected to respond to a maximum of four surveys a month for a period of two to three years, after which they were rotated off the panel. In essence, national probability samples of respondents were readily available to participate in online interviewing, which drastically reduced the time and cost required to collect data from large, representative samples of respondents. The data yielded by KN closely mirrored the U.S. population at the time on key demographic, geographic, economic, and social characteristics.[7]

Given their popularity and advantages, are web-based surveys likely to replace other modes of survey data collection anytime soon? We agree with the conclusion of Couper and Bosnjak (2010) that, for the foreseeable future at least, web-based surveys are likely to remain one, but not the only, data collection tool available to survey researchers.[8]

5.2.5 Survey-Based Experiments

In Chapter 4 (Section 4.2.2) we briefly mentioned **survey-based experiments.** In this section we delve a bit deeper into this increasingly common

[4] Knowledge Networks, Inc. was founded in 1998. Between 1998 and 2011, when it became part of the global market research firm GfK (which stands for "Growth for Knowledge"), KN was one of the preeminent web-based survey research firms in the U.S. Other organizations that specialize in probability panels include NORC's AmeriSpeak, Gallup, and Pew.

[5] The survey was fielded in 2002, before the widespread popularity of cell phones.

[6] Households without computers were provided hardware and connectivity by KN.

[7] It is important to note that, when using panels for survey research, sample bias can occur at different stages. First, respondents consent to become panel members; this is referred to as the panel acceptance rate. At the time of the study, KN's panel acceptance rate was 40 percent, calculated by standards established by the American Association for Public Opinion Research (Olson et al., 2021). Second, the within-survey completion rate – or percentage of panel members who completed the questionnaire among those who received it – was 67 percent. The margin of sampling error for parameter estimates was ±2 percent for the total sample and ±4 percent for each racial/ethnic group. See Weitzer and Tuch (2006) for a full discussion of the sample design.

[8] See Couper (2017) for an excellent review of recent changes in, and challenges facing, survey research.

method of combining the best of survey and experimental designs – the high *external* validity of surveys and the high *internal* validity of experiments – in order to increase confidence in our causal inferences.

As we saw in Chapter 4, surveys that are based on probability sampling have the major advantage of being able to generalize findings from the sample to the population from which the sample was drawn. Experiments, on the other hand, typically do not use probability sampling methods to generate pools of subjects and so suffer from low external validity. Conversely, experiments are much stronger than surveys on internal validity, i.e., the ability to clearly identify cause and effect, due to the randomization of respondents to experimental conditions. Survey-based experiments are designed to maximize *both* internal *and* external validity. Such population-based survey experiments – as they are often referred to because the samples analyzed are drawn from a population – are viewed by many social scientists as one of the most consequential changes in survey research methodology in decades (Sniderman and Druckman, 2011, page 102).

How might a survey-based experiment actually be designed and implemented? Let's consider an example. Hanson (2006) examined the effects of race and gender on young African American and white women's perceptions of discrimination in high-school STEM (Science, Technology, Engineering, and Math) classrooms. Using a web-based, nationally representative survey, she embedded a series of four randomly assigned vignettes in the questionnaire that allowed her to isolate the effects of race and gender on perceived barriers in science education. Three of the vignettes were narrated by a young African American woman and the fourth was narrated by a young white woman. Respondents clicked on the narrator's picture to hear her vignette story. Both the race of the narrator and the content of her vignette, focusing either on race- or gender-based barriers in the science classroom, were varied. Thus, in one vignette the narrator identified race as the key obstacle to her pursuit of science education; in one she identified gender; and in one both race and gender were identified as problems. There was also a race- and gender-neutral vignette that served as the comparison group. The vignettes were then randomly assigned to young African American and white women survey respondents, with each respondent assigned a single vignette. This design allowed the researcher to isolate the effects of race and gender on young African American and white women's evaluations of science experiences.

The results of Hanson's study showed that young African American women were more likely than young white women to report both race and gender as inhibiting factors in their high-school science class experiences. They were also more likely to view race as opposed to gender as the more important problem. Moreover, African American women were more likely to mention race as a problem for young women in the science classroom when they were asked about the narrator in the vignette than when they were asked about their own experiences. A traditional survey format could not have as effectively teased out the complex interplay of race and gender in shaping the science education experiences of young African American women.

5.3 ALREADY EXISTING SURVEY DATA SETS

In practice, the decision as to which mode of administration a survey researcher employs reflects, in substantial part, the availability of resources. Due to the prohibitive costs involved, individual researchers are rarely in a position to field large, representative surveys – whether face-to-face, telephone, or web-based – without substantial external funding. Fortunately, a number of very high-quality existing survey data sets are available that allow social scientists to pursue their research interests. Such data sets are often referred to as **secondary data** because they are not collected by an individual researcher her- or himself, in which case the methodology would be referred to as **primary data collection.**[9] Below, we review several of the most widely analyzed of these.

5.3.1 General Social Survey (GSS)

The GSS is based on a full-probability sampling design and is representative of the noninstitutionalized adult (eighteen years of age and older) population of the United States. The GSS has been fielded yearly between 1972 and 1993 and biennially since 1994 by the National Opinion Research Center (NORC) at the University of Chicago.[10] Sample sizes are large, averaging approximately 1500 respondents per year in the 1972 through 1993 surveys and 2500 respondents per year in the 1994 through 2018 surveys. The GSS is one of the most highly respected and widely analyzed omnibus surveys in the social sciences.[11] It includes questions on a broad range of topics – attitudes, values, beliefs, and demographics, among many others – of interest to sociologists, political scientists, social psychologists, and other social scientists.

[9] Data collection in which the researcher constructs the questionnaire and contracts with a professional survey research firm (such as GfK) to administer the survey qualifies as primary data collection.

[10] There was no GSS in 1979, 1981, or 1992.

[11] For a complete discussion of sampling methodology in the GSS, see Smith et al. (2019).

5.3.2 American National Election Study (ANES)

The ANES is a survey fielded biennially by the University of Michigan to a nationally representative sample of the noninstitutionalized adult population of the United States. The ANES has been conducted in every presidential and midterm election year since 1948, mostly by face-to-face interviews; since 2012 the ANES has employed both face-to-face and web-based modes of administration.[12] In presidential election years, both a pre-election and a post-election interview are administered; in midterm election years, only a post-election interview is fielded. Panel studies are also periodically administered by the ANES. The ANES is a highly respected source of survey data on elections and voter behavior as well as public opinion on important issues of the day, including topics that are not directly related to elections (for instance, immigration, race, and ethnicity). Information on the data and sampling methodology can be found in ANES (2021) at www.electionstudies.org.

5.3.3 International Social Survey Programme (ISSP)

The ISSP has fielded annual surveys since 1985 in a growing number of countries worldwide (currently, 43). The surveys are administered to national probability samples of adult respondents by professional survey research organizations in each participating nation either by self-administered supplements to regular annual surveys or by stand-alone mail surveys, depending on the country and the year.[13] The ISSP is a source of high-quality secondary data especially useful for social science researchers interested in comparative/international studies. Unlike the GSS, which (as noted above) includes a few questions about a vast array of issues, the ISSP is a topical or "modular" data set. Each ISSP survey focuses on a single substantive issue such as the environment, inequality, gender roles, health and healthcare, and the role of government, among many others. By focusing on one rather than a multitude of areas, ISSP data provide more in-depth coverage on that topic than a traditional survey is able to do. Moreover, the ISSP topical modules are replicated periodically so that researchers can analyze change over time. Of the eleven different topical modules that have been fielded since the inaugural ISSP survey in 1985, all but two have been replicated at least once, with several having been

[12] Originally known as the Michigan Election Studies, the "ANES" moniker came into being in 1977 when the National Science Foundation began funding the data collection. For a detailed comparison of face-to-face and web-based modes of survey administration, including an analysis of mode differences in findings, see Guggenheim et al. (2019).

[13] For full details on the survey methodology of the ISSP, see ISSP (2016).

replicated multiple times. The advantages of replicated administrations are that they allow for a richer, more nuanced study of the topic at hand because of the sheer number of questions asked and the fact that they allow for analysis of over-time trends. The disadvantage is that if we have no scholarly interest in the topic of a particular module, that year – as well as all of the years in which the module was replicated – is lost to us as a source of data.

5.3.4 World Values Survey (WVS)

The WVS (Inglehart et al., 2014) is the product of an international network of social scientists. First fielded in 1981, the surveys explore changing cultural values; attitudes about family, gender roles, and religion; tolerance; and a range of other issues among respondents in nearly 100 countries using representative samples of adults in each participating nation. Data are collected in waves: wave 1 data were collected in 1981–84, wave 2 in 1989–93, wave 3 in 1994–98, wave 4 in 1999–2004, wave 5 in 2005–09, wave 6 in 2010–15, and wave 7 in 2017–19.[14] Samples are representative of all people aged eighteen years and older who are residing in private households in each country, regardless of their nationality, citizenship, or language.

5.4 PROBABILITY SAMPLING

We conclude our treatment of survey research with an overview of the various kinds of probability sampling plans that are part of the methodological toolkits of social scientists.

The primary distinction in sampling methodology is between *probability* and *nonprobability* sampling. Consistent with our focus on inferential statistical methods in this book, we discuss probability sampling only. This is not to say that nonprobability samples have no place in social science research, nor that quantitative research is the only "good" kind of research. It is to say, however, that probability sampling is a necessary prerequisite for yielding representative samples.

The distinguishing feature of probability sampling is that every element – often, though not necessarily, people – in the population to which we want to generalize our findings has a known, nonzero probability of being included in the sample.[15] Because it is rarely if ever possible for an

[14] At the time of this writing, wave 7 data collection was still ongoing.

[15] Contrast this with nonprobability sampling plans. If we stand on a street corner asking passersby to participate in a survey, only those people who happen to be walking by at

individual researcher to collect data from all subjects in a large population, sampling is an essential part of survey design. Indeed, much of empirical social science depends upon meticulously planned and executed sampling plans in order to assure that the data we collect, and which we use to test our causal explanations, are unbiased. Otherwise, the generalizability of our findings will be unacceptably low.

5.4.1 Simple Random Samples

Simple random samples (SRS) are the most basic kinds of **EPSEM samples** (*e*qual *p*robability of *se*lection *m*ethod). In an SRS not only does every member of the population have a known, nonzero probability of being included in the sample, the probabilities of selection are all equal. For instance, say you wish to learn how the 2000 freshmen at your university are adjusting to college life. Lacking the time and financial resources necessary to interview all 2000 members of the population, you decide instead to take an SRS of 250 students to whom a self-administered questionnaire will subsequently be sent. You first obtain a comprehensive list of all freshman (the sampling frame), number the list from 1 to 2000, and then consult a table of random numbers, selecting for inclusion in the sample the first 250 students whose numbers appear in the table. This procedure yields a simple random sample of freshmen in which each student in the population has the same probability of being included in the sample, 250/2000, or 0.125.

5.4.2 Systematic Random Samples

When the population from which a sample is to be drawn is large, constructing a simple random sample can be quite tedious and time-consuming. A commonly used alternative to an SRS that requires less effort in sample selection is referred to as **systematic random sampling**. In this method the researcher selects for inclusion in the sample every *n*th case after a random start. Returning to our example above, in order to draw a systematic random sample of 250 freshmen from our population of 2000, we would randomly choose a number between 1 and 8 (2000/250, which is the sampling fraction) to identify the first student selected for the sample and then choose every eighth student thereafter. So, for example, if we began with student #3, the second student selected would be #11, followed by #19, etc., until we reach the sample size of 250.

the time we are soliciting participants for our study have any chance of being included in our sample.

Strictly speaking, systematic random samples do not meet the EPSEM equal probability of selection requirement because after the first student is randomly chosen for inclusion in the sample, the remaining students do not all have the same probability of being selected; rather, only students who are separated by eight cases have a nonzero probability of inclusion. Nevertheless, if there is no periodicity in the list of population elements, systematic random sampling and simple random sampling are essentially the same.

5.4.3 Stratified Random Sampling

It is oftentimes the case that researchers possess information about the population from which they plan to sample. If, for instance, we wish to study differences among urban, suburban, and rural dwellers on attitudes toward capital punishment, information about the share of the population each of these three groups represent could be used to improve the accuracy of our sample. Let's say we know that 45 percent of the population resides in urban areas, 40 percent in suburban areas, and 15 percent in rural areas. Armed with this information we would stratify, i.e., divide, the population into three groups according to residence type and then randomly sample individuals from each group, being sure to include in the sample 45 percent urban dwellers, 40 percent suburban dwellers, and 15 percent rural dwellers. This kind of sampling plan, known as *proportionate* **stratified random sampling**, eliminates sampling error on the place of residence variable because each group's representation in the sample is exactly proportional to its population share. Most large surveys incorporate stratified random sampling.

5.4.4 Multistage Cluster Sampling

Each of the sampling plans discussed above requires a sampling frame – a listing of population elements from which the sample is to be drawn. In the case of large-scale social surveys, however, such listings do not typically exist. In such instances a cluster sample is the appropriate alternative. Clusters are usually geographic units such as counties or metropolitan areas or city blocks, all of which *can* be enumerated. The first stage of a **multistage cluster sample** consists of a random sample of clusters, which are referred to as the primary sampling units, or PSUs. In many large surveys the PSUs are metropolitan areas; block groups within the PSUs are often the second stage; individual blocks are sampled at the third stage; households at the fourth stage; and, ultimately, randomly chosen individuals from within the selected households.

Multistage cluster sampling is a common method of generating representative samples from large populations. Its primary disadvantage is that sampling error exists at each stage of the process – the selected clusters are representative of all clusters within a margin of sampling error, as are, analogously, the selected block groups, households, and individuals. On balance, though, multistage cluster sampling is an accepted method of sampling from large, geographically dispersed populations.

CONCEPTS INTRODUCED IN THIS CHAPTER

- computer-assisted telephone interviewing (CATI) – a method of administering telephone surveys in which interviewers ask questions of respondents and enter their answers into a preprogramed questionnaire, substantially reducing the labor and cost of data collection compared to face-to-face interviewing
- EPSEM samples – samples of respondents collected by equal probability of selection methods that assure every element in the population has a known, nonzero probability of being included in the sample
- face-to-face interview – a mode of survey data collection in which the interviewer and respondent are in the same physical space while conducting the interview, often though not necessarily the respondent's home
- multistage cluster samples – a sampling design used in surveys of large populations when a listing of population elements to be sampled from is not feasible
- primary data collection – data that are collected by the individual researcher him- or herself
- secondary data – data that are collected by entities other than the individual researcher, such as government or nonprofit organizations, that are subsequently made available to researchers so they can conduct their studies
- self-administered survey questionnaires – paper-and-pencil questionnaires that are mailed or hand-delivered to respondents to fill out and return to the researcher
- simple random samples – samples in which each element in the population has the same probability of being included in the sample
- stratified random samples – samples that use demographic information about the population in order to stratify, or divide, the population into homogeneous subgroups from which to sample in an effort to reduce the sampling error of the sample and thereby improve representativeness
- survey-based experiments – surveys that embed random assignment to conditions in the context of a probability sample survey in order to maximize both the internal and external validity of a study

- survey research – a commonly used method of collecting information from large numbers of respondents who are usually selected by probability sampling plans
- systematic random samples – a method of random sampling that reduces the effort involved in selecting elements from the population to be included in the sample by selecting every *n*th case after a random start
- web-based surveys – a mode of survey administration that combines probability sampling with the reach and availability of the Internet in order to yield large representative samples of respondents at less cost than most other methods of survey data collection

EXERCISES

1. Surveys are very flexible data gathering tools. What features of surveys justify this statement?
2. Surveys are often used to measure public opinion. Discuss the ways in which surveys are likely to be more optimal than experiments in this context.
3. Surveys tend to be high on external validity but low on internal validity. Conversely, experiments tend to be low on external validity but high on internal validity. Discuss what these terms mean, and their implications for research design in the social sciences.
4. Discuss how survey-based experiments address the issues raised in Exercise 3. How do survey-based experiments increase the likelihood of identifying cause and effect between independent and dependent variables?
5. Describe a research question that you might be interested in examining using either the GSS or ANES data sets. Then describe how that research question could be expanded by using either the ISSP or WVS data sets.
6. Select an area of research interest to you. How would you create a survey-based experiment that might provide some special insights into your research question?
7. Survey research is normally done using probability samples. Under what circumstances would you be justified in analyzing data from a non-probability sample?

6 Measuring Concepts of Interest

OVERVIEW

Although what social scientists care about is discovering whether causal relationships exist between concepts, what we *actually* examine is statistical associations between variables. Therefore it is critical that we have a clear understanding of the concepts that we care about so we can measure them in a valid and reliable way. In this chapter we focus on one of the critical tasks in the process of evaluating causal theories: measurement. As we discuss the importance of measurement, we use several examples from the sociological literature, such as the concept of racial tolerance. We know that racial tolerance and intolerance is a "real" thing – that it exists to varying degrees in the hearts and minds of people. But how do we go about measuring it?

I know it when I see it

—Associate Justice of the United States Supreme Court Potter Stewart, in an attempt to define "obscenity" in a concurring opinion in *Jacobellis v. Ohio* (1964)

6.1 GETTING TO KNOW YOUR DATA: EVALUATING MEASUREMENT

We have emphasized the role of theory in social science. That is, we care about causal relationships between concepts that interest us as sociologists. At this point, you are hopefully starting to develop theories of your own about society. If these original theories are in line with the rules of the road that we laid out in Chapter 1, they will be causal, general, and parsimonious. They may even be elegant and clever.

But at this point, it is worth pausing and thinking about what a theory really *is* and *is not*. To help us in this process, take a look back at Figure 1.2. A theory, as we have said, is merely a conjecture about the possible causal relationship between two or more concepts. As scientists, we must always resist the temptation to view our theories as somehow supported until we have evaluated evidence from the real world, and until we have done everything we can with empirical evidence to evaluate how well our theory does through the four causal hurdles we identified in Chapter 3. In other words, we cannot evaluate a theory until we have gone through the rest of the process depicted in Figure 1.2. The first part of this chapter deals with operationalization, or the movement of variables from the rather abstract conceptual level to the very real measured level. We can conduct hypothesis tests and make reasonable evaluations of our theories only after we have gone carefully through this important process with all of our variables.

If our theories are statements about relationships *between concepts*, when we look for evidence to test our theories, we are immediately confronted with the reality that we do not actually *observe* those concepts. Many of the concepts that we care about in sociology, as we will see shortly, are inherently elusive and downright impossible to observe empirically in a direct way, and sometimes incredibly difficult to measure quantitatively. For this reason, we need to think very carefully about the data that we choose to evaluate our theories.

Until now, we have seen many examples of data, but we have not discussed the process of obtaining data and putting them to work. If we think back to Figure 1.2, we are now at the stage where we want to move from the theoretical-conceptual level to the empirical-measured level. For every theoretical concept, there are multiple operationalization or measurement strategies. As we discussed in the Chapter 4, one of the first major decisions that one needs to make is whether to conduct an experiment or some form of observational test. In this chapter, we assume that you have a theory and that you are going to conduct an observational test of your theory.

A useful exercise, once you have developed an original theory, is to draw your version of Figure 1.2 and to think about what would be the ideal setup for testing your theory. What would be the best setup, a cross-sectional design or a time-series design? Once you have answered this question and have your ideal time and spatial dimensions in hand, what would be the ideal measure of your independent and dependent variables?

Having gone through the exercise of thinking about the ideal data, the first instinct of most students is to collect their own data, perhaps even to do so through a survey.[1] In our experience, beginning researchers almost

[1] A survey is a particularly cumbersome choice because, at least at most universities, you would need to have approval for conducting your survey from the Human Subjects Research Committee.

always underestimate the difficulties and the costs (in terms of both time and money) of collecting one's own data. We *strongly* recommend that you look to see what data are already available for you to use.

For a social science researcher, one of the great things about the era in which we live is that there is a nearly endless supply of data that are available from websites and other easily accessible resources.[2] But a few words of caution: Just because data are easily available on the Web does not mean that these data will be perfectly suitable to the particular needs of your hypothesis test. What follows in the rest of this chapter is a set of considerations that you should have in mind to help you determine whether or not a particular set of data that you have found is appropriate for your purposes, and to help you to get to know your data once you have loaded them into a statistical program. We begin with the all-important topic of variable measurement. We describe the problems of measurement and the importance of measuring the concepts in which we are interested as precisely as possible. During this process, you will learn some thinking skills for evaluating the measurement strategies of scholarship that you read, as well as learn about evaluating the usefulness of measures that you are considering using to test your hypotheses.

We begin the section on measurement in the social sciences generally. We focus on examples from economics and psychology, two social sciences that are at rather different levels of agreement about the measurement of their major variables. In sociology, we have a complete range of variables in terms of the levels of agreement about how they should be measured. We discuss the core concepts of measurement and give some examples from sociological research. Throughout our discussion of these core concepts, we focus on the measurements of variables that take on a numeric range of values we feel comfortable treating the way that we normally treat numeric values. Toward the end of the chapter, when we discuss the basics of getting to know your data with a software program, we will discuss this further and focus on some variable types that can take different types of nonnumeric values.

6.2 SOCIAL SCIENCE MEASUREMENT: THE VARYING CHALLENGES OF QUANTIFYING HUMANITY

Measurement is a "problem" in all sciences – from the physical sciences of physics and chemistry to the social sciences of sociology, economics,

[2] One resource that is often overlooked is your school's library. While libraries may seem old-fashioned, your school's library may have purchased access to data sources and librarians are often experts in the location of data from the Web.

political science, psychology, and the rest. But in the physical sciences, the problem of measurement is often reduced to a problem of instrumentation, in which scientists develop well-specified protocols for measuring, say, the amount of gas released in a chemical reaction or the amount of light given off by a star. The social sciences, by contrast, are younger sciences, and scientific consensus on how to measure our important concepts is rare. Perhaps more crucial, though, is the fact that the social sciences deal with an inherently difficult-to-predict subject matter: human beings.

The problem of measurement exists in all of the social sciences. It would be wrong, though, to say that it is equally problematic in all of the social science disciplines. Some disciplines pay comparatively little heed to issues of measurement, whereas others are mired nearly constantly in measurement controversies and difficulties.

Consider the subject matter in much research in economics: dollars (or euros, or yen, or what have you). If the concept of interest is "economic output" (or "Gross Domestic Product," GDP), which is commonly defined as the total sum of goods and services produced by labor and property in a given time period, then it is a relatively straightforward matter to obtain an empirical observation that is consistent with the concept of interest.[3] Such measures will not be controversial among the vast majority of scholars. To the contrary, once economists agree on a measure of economic output, they can move on to the next (and more interesting) step in the scientific process – to argue about what forces *cause* greater or less growth in economic output. (That's where the agreement among economists ends.)

Not every concept in economics is measured with such ease, however. Many economists are concerned with poverty: Why are some individuals poor whereas others are not? What forces cause poverty to rise or fall over time? Despite the fact that we all know that poverty is a very real thing, measuring who is poor and who is not poor turns out to be a bit tricky. The federal government defines the concept of poverty as "a set of income cutoffs adjusted for household size, the age of the head of the household, and the number of children under age 18."[4] The intent of the cutoffs is to describe "minimally decent levels of consumption."[5] There are difficulties in obtaining empirical observations of poverty, though. Among them, consider the reality that most Western democracies (including the United

[3] For details about how the federal government measures GDP, see www.bea.gov.

[4] See www.census.gov/hhes/www/poverty/poverty.html.

[5] Note a problem right off the bat: What is "minimally decent"? Do you suspect that what qualified as "minimally decent" in 1950 or 1985 would be considered "minimally decent" today? This immediately raises issues of how sensible it is to compare the poverty rates from the past with those of today. If the floor of what is considered minimally decent continues to rise, then the comparison is problematic at best, and meaningless at worst.

States) have welfare states that provide transfer payments – in the form of cash payments, food stamps, or services like subsidized healthcare – to their citizens below some income threshold. Such programs, of course, are designed to minimize or eliminate the problems that afflict the poor. When economists seek to measure a person's income level to determine whether or not he is poor, should they use a "pretransfer" definition of income – a person's or family's income level *before* receiving any transfer payments from the government – or a "posttransfer" definition? Either choice carries some negative consequences. Choosing a pretransfer definition of income gives a sense of how much the private sector of the economy is failing. On the other hand, a posttransfer definition gives a sense of how much welfare-state programs are falling short and how people are actually living. As the "Baby Boom" generation in the United States continues to age, though, more and more people are retiring from work. Using a pretransfer measure of poverty means that researchers will not consider Social Security payments – the U.S.'s largest source of transfer payments by far – and therefore the (pretransfer) poverty rate should grow rather steadily over the next few decades, regardless of the health of the overall economy. This might not accurately represent what we mean by "poverty" (Danziger and Gottschalk, 1983).

If, owing to their subject matter, economists rarely (but occasionally) have measurement obstacles, the opposite end of the spectrum would be the discipline of psychology. The subject matter of psychology – human behavior, cognition, and emotion – is rife with concepts that are extremely difficult to measure. Consider a few examples. We all know that the concept of "depression" is a real thing; some individuals are depressed, and others are not. Some individuals who are depressed today will not be depressed as time passes, and some who are not depressed today will become depressed. Yet how is it possible to assess scientifically whether a person is or is not depressed?[6] Why does it matter if we measure depression accurately? Recall the scientific stakes described at the beginning of this chapter: If we don't measure depression well, how can we know whether remedies like clinical therapy or chemical antidepressants are effective?[7] Psychology deals with a variety of other concepts that are notoriously slippery, such as the clinical

[6] Since 1952, the American Psychological Association has published the *Diagnostic and Statistical Manual of Mental Disorders*, now in its fifth edition (called DSM 5), which diagnoses depression by focusing on four sets of symptoms that indicate depression: mood, behavioral symptoms such as withdrawal, cognitive symptoms such as concentration, and somatic symptoms such as insomnia.

[7] In fact, the effectiveness of clinical "talk" therapy is a matter of some contention among psychologists. See "Married with Problems? Therapy May Not Help," *The New York Times*, April 19, 2005.

focus on "anxiety," or the social-psychological focus on concepts such as "stereotyping" or "prejudice" (which, of course, are also of concern to sociologists).

Sociology, in our view, lies somewhere between the extremes of economics and psychology in terms of how frequently we encounter serious measurement problems. In Section 6.4 we describe the measurement controversies surrounding a concept that is especially important to sociology – racial/ethnic tolerance. But first, in the next section, we describe some key issues that social scientists need to grapple with when measuring their concepts of interest.

6.3 PROBLEMS IN MEASURING CONCEPTS OF INTEREST

We can summarize the problems of measuring concepts of interest in preparation for hypothesis testing as follows: First, you need to make sure that you have conceptual clarity. Next, settle on a reasonable level of measurement. Finally, ensure that your measure is both valid and reliable. After you repeat this process for each variable in your theory, you are ready to test your hypothesis.

Unfortunately, there is no clear map to follow as we go through these steps with our variables. Some variables are very easy to measure, whereas others, because of the nature of what we are trying to measure, will always be elusive. As we will see, debates over issues of measurement are at the core of many interesting fields of study in sociology.

6.3.1 Conceptual Clarity

The first step in measuring any phenomenon of interest to sociologists is to have a clear sense of what the concept is that we are trying to measure. In some cases, like the ones we subsequently discuss, this is an exceedingly revealing and difficult task. It requires considerably disciplined thought to ferret out precisely what we mean by the concepts about which we are theorizing. But even in some seemingly easy examples, this is more difficult than might appear at first glance.

Consider a survey in which we needed to measure a person's *income*. That would seem easy enough. Once we draw our sample of adults, why not just ask each respondent, "What is your income?" and offer a range of values, perhaps in increments of $10,000 or so, on which respondents could place themselves. What could be the problem with such a measure? Imagine a nineteen-year-old college student whose parents are very wealthy, but who has never worked herself, answering such a question.

How much income has that person earned in the last year? Zero. In such a circumstance, this is the true answer to such a question. But it is not a particularly valid measure of her income. We likely want a measure of income that reflects the fact that her parents earn a good deal of money, which affords her the luxury of not having to work her way through school as many other students do. That measure should place the daughter of wealthy parents ahead of a relatively poor student who works forty hours a week and carries a full load just to pay her tuition. Therefore, we might reconsider our seemingly simple question and ask instead, "What is the total amount of income earned in the most recently completed tax year by you and any other adults in your household, including all sources of income?" This measure puts the nonworking child of wealthy parents ahead of the student from the less-well-off family. And, for most social science purposes, this is the measure of "income" that we would find most theoretically useful.[8]

At this point, it is worth highlighting that the *best* measure of income – as well as that of most other concepts – depends on what our theoretical objectives are. The best measure of something as simple as a respondent's income depends on what we intend to relate that measure to in our hypothesis testing.

6.3.2 Reliability

An operational measure of a concept is said to be reliable to the extent that it is repeatable or consistent; that is, applying the same measurement rules to the same case or observation will produce identical results. An unreliable measure, by contrast, would produce inconsistent results for the same observation. For obvious reasons, all scientists want their measures to be reliable.

Perhaps the most simple example to help you understand this is your bathroom scale. Say you step up on the scale one morning and the scale tells you that you weigh 150 pounds. You step down off the scale and it returns to zero. But have you ever *not* trusted that scale reading, and thought to yourself, "Maybe if I hop back up on the scale, I'll get a number I like better"? That is a **reliability** check. If you (immediately) step back on the scale, and it tells you that you now weigh 146 pounds, your scale is unreliable, because repeated measures of the same case – your body at that particular point in time – produced different results.

[8] The same issues would arise in assessing the income of retired people who no longer participate in the workforce.

To take our bathroom scale example to the extreme, we should not confuse over-time variability with unreliability. If you wake up one week later and weigh 157 instead of 150 pounds, that does not necessarily mean that your scale is unreliable (though that might be true). Perhaps you substituted french fries for salads at dinner in the intervening week, and perhaps you exercised less vigorously or less often.

Reliability is often an important issue when scholars need to code events or text for quantitative analysis. For example, if a researcher was trying to code the text of news coverage that was favorable or unfavorable toward the legalization of medical marijuana, he would develop some specific coding rules to apply to the text – in effect, to count certain references as either "pro" or "con" with respect to legalization. Suppose that, for the coding, the researcher employs a group of students to code the text – a practice that is common in this kind of research. A *reliable* set of coding rules would imply that, when one student applies the rules to the text, the results would be the same as when another student takes the rules and applies them to the same text. An *unreliable* set of coding rules would imply the opposite, namely, that when two different coders try to apply the same rules to the same news articles, they reach different conclusions.[9] The same issues arise when one codes things such as events by using newspaper coverage.[10]

6.3.3 Measurement Bias and Reliability

One of the concerns that comes up with any measurement technique is **measurement bias**, which is the systematic over-reporting or under-reporting of values for a variable. Although measurement bias is a serious problem for anyone who wants to know the "true" values of variables for particular cases, it is less of a problem than you might think for theory-testing purposes. To better understand this, imagine that we have to choose between two different operationalizations of the same variable. Operationalization A is biased but reliable, and Operationalization B is unbiased but unreliable. For theory-testing purposes we would greatly prefer the biased but reliable Operationalization A!

You will be better able to see why this is the case once you have an understanding of statistical hypothesis testing from Chapter 9 and beyond. For now, though, keep in mind that as we test our theories we are looking for general patterns between two variables. For instance, with *higher* values

[9] Of course, it is possible that the coding *scheme* is perfectly reliable, but the *coders themselves* are not.

[10] There are a variety of tools for assessing reliability, many of which are beyond the scope of this discussion.

of X, do we tend to see *higher* values of Y, or with *higher* values of X, do we tend to see *lower* values of Y? If the measurement of X was biased upward, the same general pattern of association with Y would be visible. But if the measurement of X was unreliable, it would obscure the underlying relationship between X and Y.

6.3.4 Validity

The most important feature of a measure is that it is valid. A valid measure accurately represents the concept that it is supposed to measure, whereas an invalid measure measures something other than what was originally intended. All of this might sound a bit circular, we realize.

Perhaps it is useful to think of some important concepts that represent thorny measurement examples in the social sciences. In sociology, social psychology, and political science, the study of the concept of *prejudice* has been particularly important. Among individuals, the level of prejudice can vary, from vanishingly small amounts to very high levels. Measuring prejudice can be important in social-psychological terms, so we can try to determine what factors cause some people to be prejudiced whereas other factors do not. In sociology, in particular, we are often interested in what the attitudinal and behavioral consequences of prejudice might be. Assuming that some form of truth serum is unavailable, how can we obtain a quantitative measure of prejudice that can tell us who harbors large amounts of prejudice, who harbors some, and who harbors little or none? It would be easy enough to ask respondents to do a survey if they were prejudiced or not. For example, we could ask respondents: "With respect to people who have a different race or ethnicity than you, would you say that you are extremely prejudiced, somewhat prejudiced, mildly prejudiced, or not at all prejudiced toward them?" But we would have clear reasons to doubt the **validity** of their answers – whether their measured responses accurately reflected their true levels of prejudice.

There are a variety of ways to assess a measure's validity, though it is critical to note that all of them are theoretical and subject to large degrees of disagreement. There is no simple formula to check for a measure's validity on a scale of 0 to 100, unfortunately. Instead, we rely on several overlapping ways to determine a measure's validity. First, and most simply, we can examine a measure's **face validity**. When examining a measurement strategy, we can first ask whether or not, on its face, the measure appears to be measuring what it purports to be measuring. This is face validity. Second, and a bit more advanced, we can scrutinize a measure's **content validity**. What is the concept to be measured? What are all of the essential elements to that concept and the features that define it? And have you excluded all of the things that are not it? For example, the concept of prejudice surely contains the element of "a sense of group position" (Blumer, 1958), but it also must incorporate more than mere group position, because group position is also a component of the racial thinking of minority group members. What else must be in a valid measure of prejudice? (More on this notion later on.) Basically, content validation is a rigorous process that forces the researcher to come up with a list of all of the critical elements that, as a group, define the concept we wish to measure.[11] Finally, we can examine a measure's **construct validity**: the degree to which the measure is related to other measures that theory requires them to be related to. That is, if we have a theory that connects prejudice and views about what causes racial inequality, then a measure of causal attributions of inequality that is related to a measure of prejudice (as our theory requires) serves simultaneously to confirm the theory and also to validate the measure of prejudice. Of course, one difficulty with this approach is what happens when the expected association is not present. Is it because our measure of prejudice is invalid or because the theory is misguided? There is no conclusive way to tell.

6.3.5 The Relationship between Validity and Reliability

What is the connection between validity and reliability? Is it possible to have a valid but unreliable measure? And is it possible to have a reliable but invalid measure? With respect to the second question, some scientific debate exists; there are some who believe that it is possible to have a reliable but invalid measure. In our view, that is possible in abstract terms. But because we are interested in measuring concepts in the interest of evaluating causal theories, we believe that, in all practical terms, any conceivable measures that are reliable but invalid will not be useful in evaluating causal theories.

Similarly, it is theoretically possible to have valid but unreliable measures. But those measures also will be problematic for evaluating causal theories, because we will have no confidence in the hypothesis tests that we conduct. We present the relationship between reliability and validity in Figure 6.1, where we show that, if a measure is unreliable, there is little point in evaluating its validity. Once we have established that a measure is reliable, we can assess its validity, and only reliable and valid measures are useful for evaluating causal theories.

[11] A further complication is that, in some instances, scholars disagree as to what content areas define a concept's domain.

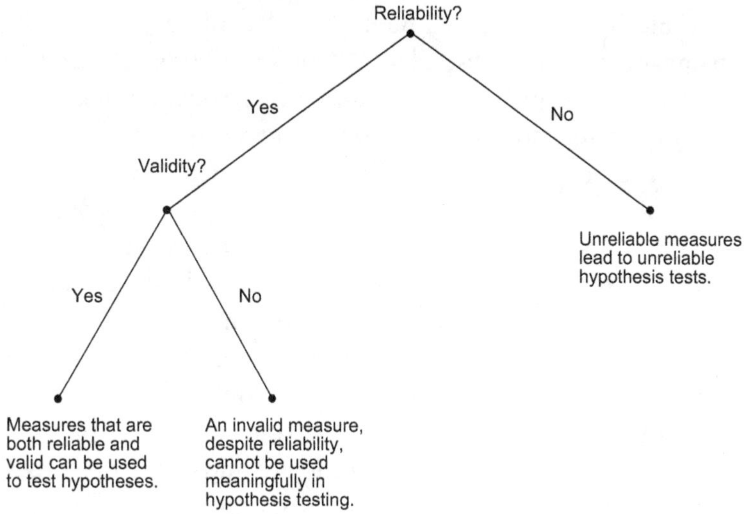

Figure 6.1 Reliability, validity, and hypothesis testing

6.4 CONTROVERSY: MEASURING RACIAL TOLERANCE

We know that some continuum exists in which, on the one end, some individuals are extremely "tolerant" and, on the other end, other individuals are extremely "intolerant." In other words, racial tolerance and intolerance, at the conceptual level, are real things. Some individuals have more tolerance and others have less. It is easy to imagine why sociologists and other social scientists would be interested in racial tolerance and intolerance. Are there systematic factors that cause some people to be tolerant and others to be intolerant?

Measuring racial tolerance, on the other hand, is far from easy. Tolerance is not like cholesterol, for which a simple blood test can tell us how much of the good and how much of the bad we have inside of us. The naive approach to measuring political tolerance – conducting a survey and asking people directly "Are you tolerant or intolerant?" – seems silly right off the bat. Any such survey question would surely produce extremely high rates of "tolerance," because presumably very few people – even intolerant people – think of themselves as intolerant. Even those who are aware of their own intolerance are unlikely to admit that fact to a pollster. Given this situation, how have social scientists tackled this problem?

A topic of long-standing interest among sociologists, political scientists, and others who study racial attitudes is the gap between whites' support for principles of racial equality, on the one hand, and their intransigence on policies designed to reduce inequality, on the other. Much has been written on possible explanations of this "principle–policy gap" and what the gap reveals about the state of race relations today. If, as many have argued, President Obama's election as our nation's first African American president is evidence that racial animus is waning, we would expect to find a decrease over time in opposition to policies that are intended to reduce racial disadvantage, from preferences in hiring and promotion of blacks to spending on programs to improve African Americans' social and economic conditions to ensuring racial fairness in jobs. In fact, however, no such trend has occurred. The question is why.

Several explanations of the sources of the principle–policy gap have been proposed in the social science literature. One explanation that has received considerable attention is referred to as "racial resentment." Proponents of this explanation argue that "old-fashioned" biological racism has been replaced by a "modern" version of anti-black affect that is rooted in early racial socialization experiences and in the beliefs of many whites that African Americans violate such traditional values as self-reliance, hard work, and individualism. According to this account, racial resentment is the principal factor shaping whites' racial policy views; in other words, whites are not in favor of racial policies because they believe that blacks are undeserving of them (Kinder and Sanders, 1996; Hughes, 1997).

Others, however, have argued that the measure of racial resentment is so flawed as to render the concept suspect at best (Carmines, Sniderman, and Easter, 2011; Schuman, 2000). As we discussed earlier in this chapter, in order for our theories to do a good job of explaining social phenomena, there must be reliable and valid measures of the concepts that constitute the theories. The questions typically used as measures of racial resentment are the following:

1. "Irish, Italians, Jews, and many other minorities overcame prejudice and worked their way up. Blacks should do the same without any special favors."
2. "Over the past few years blacks have gotten less than they deserve."
3. "Generations of slavery and discrimination have created conditions that make it difficult for blacks to work their way out of the lower class."
4. "It's really a matter of some people not trying hard enough; if blacks would only try harder they could be just as well off as whites."

In their review of the racial resentment literature, Huddy and Feldman (2009, page 426) summarize the criticisms of these measures as follows: "From a measurement perspective, [racial resentment] questions remain ambiguous indicators of racial prejudice because they ask white Americans to agree with complex statements that could garner support for reasons *other than racial prejudice*" [emphasis added]. In the language of social science measurement, these authors are questioning the validity of the racial resentment measures.

Our goal in relating this controversy is to highlight the critical importance of measurement in sociology and other social sciences. Like all theories in the social sciences, the racial resentment theoretical framework is only as good as the quality of the measures that we employ to represent it.

6.5 ARE THERE CONSEQUENCES TO POOR MEASUREMENT?

What happens when we fail to measure the key concepts in our theory in a way that is both valid and reliable? Refer back to Figure 1.2, which highlights the distinction between the abstract concepts of theoretical interest and the variables we observe in the real world. If the variables that we observe in the real world do not do a good job of mirroring the abstract concepts, then that affects our ability to evaluate conclusively a theory's empirical support. That is, how can we know if our theory is supported if we have done a poor job measuring the key concepts that we observe? If our empirical analysis is based on measures that do not capture the essence of the abstract concepts in our theory, then we are unlikely to have any confidence in the findings themselves.

6.6 CONCLUSIONS

How we measure the concepts that we care about matters. As we can see from the preceding examples, different measurement strategies can and sometimes do produce different conclusions about causal relationships.

One of the take-home points of this chapter should be that measurement cannot take place in a theoretical vacuum. The *theoretical purpose* of the scholarly enterprise must inform the process of how we measure what we measure. For example, recall our previous discussion about the various ways to measure poverty. How we want to measure this concept depends on what our objective is. In the process of measuring poverty, if our theoretical aim is to evaluate the effectiveness of different policies at combating poverty, we would have different measurement issues than would scholars whose theoretical aim is to study how being poor influences a person's political attitudes. In the former case, we would give strong consideration to pretransfer measures of poverty, whereas in the latter example, posttransfer measures would likely be more applicable. In the next chapter, we demonstrate how to describe a single variable, in terms of its typical values and its spread.

CONCEPTS INTRODUCED IN THIS CHAPTER

- construct validity – the degree to which the measure is related to other measures that theory requires them to be related to
- content validity – the degree to which a measure contains all of the critical elements that, as a group, define the concept we wish to measure
- face validity – whether or not, on its face, the measure appears to be measuring what it purports to be measuring
- measurement bias – the systematic over-reporting or under-reporting of values for a variable
- reliability – the extent to which applying the same measurement rules to the same case or observation will produce identical results
- validity – the degree to which a measure accurately represents the concept that it is supposed to measure

EXERCISES

1. Suppose that a researcher wanted to measure the federal government's efforts to make the education of its citizenry a priority. The researcher proposed to count the government's budget for education as a percentage of the total GDP and use that as the measure of the government's commitment to education. In terms of validity, what are the strengths and weaknesses of such a measure?
2. Suppose that a researcher wanted to create a measure of media coverage of a protest rally, and therefore created a set of coding rules to code words in newspaper articles as either "pro" or "con" toward the protest. Instead of hiring students to implement these rules, however, the researcher used a computer to code the text, by counting the frequency with which certain words were mentioned in a series of articles. What would be the reliability of such a computer-driven measurement strategy, and why?
3. For each of the following concepts, identify whether there would, in measuring the concept, likely be a problem of measurement bias, invalidity, unreliability, or none of the above. Explain your answer.

   (a) Measuring the concept of the public's approval of the President by using a series of survey results asking respondents whether they approve or disapprove of the President's job performance.

   (b) Measuring the concept of the public's support for racial equality by asking respondents whether they live in a racially diverse neighborhood.

   (c) Measuring the concept of political corruption as the percentage of politicians in a country in a year who are convicted of corrupt practices.

4. Download a codebook for a social science data set in which you are interested.

    (a) Describe the data set and the purpose for which it was assembled.

    (b) What are the time and space dimensions of the data set? Read the details of how one of the variables in which you are interested was coded. Write your answers to the following questions:

        i. Does this seem like a reliable method of operationalizing this variable? How might the reliability of this operationalization be improved?

        ii. Assess the various elements of the validity for this variable operationalization. How might the validity of this operationalization be improved?

5. If you have not yet done Exercise 5 in Chapter 3, do so now. For the theory that you developed, evaluate the measurement of both the independent and dependent variables. Write about the reliability, and the various aspects of validity for each measure. Can you think of a better way to operationalize these variables to test your theory?

7 Getting to Know Your Data

OVERVIEW

Descriptive statistics and descriptive graphs are what they sound like – they are tools that describe variables. These tools are valuable, because they can summarize a tremendous amount of information in a succinct fashion. In this chapter we discuss some of the most commonly used descriptive statistics and graphs, how we should interpret them, how we should use them, and their limitations.

These go to eleven

—Nigel Tufnel (played by Christopher Guest), describing the volume knob on his amplifier, in the movie *This Is Spinal Tap*

7.1 GETTING TO KNOW YOUR DATA STATISTICALLY

In the previous chapter, we discussed details of the measurement of variables. A lot of thought and effort goes into the measurement of individual variables. But once a researcher has collected data and become familiar and satisfied with how they were measured, it is important for her to get a good idea of the types of values that the individual variables take on before moving to testing for causal connections between two or more variables. What do "typical" values for a variable look like? How tightly clustered (or widely dispersed) are these values?

Before proceeding to test for theorized relationships *between* two or more variables, it is essential to understand the properties and characteristics of each variable. To put it differently, we want to learn something about what the values of each variable "look like." How do we accomplish this? One possibility is to list all of the observed values of a measured variable. For example, the following are the percentages of African Americans in the 1985–2014 General Social Surveys who reported owning a home in survey years that the question was asked: 40.0, 41.5, 42.2, 36.1, 46.0, 54.9, 50.0, 43.9, 43.4, 45.5, 46.3, 40.9, 33.8, 44.8, 48.2, 45.7, 38.4, 45.0, 41.4. We can see from this example that, once we get beyond a small number of observations, a listing of values becomes unwieldy. We will get lost in the trees and have no idea of the overall shape of the forest. For this reason, we turn to descriptive statistics and descriptive graphs, to take what would be a large amount of information and reduce it to bite-size chunks that summarize that information.

Descriptive statistics and graphs are useful tools for helping researchers to get to know their data before they move to testing causal hypotheses. They are also sometimes helpful when writing about one's research. You have to make the decision of whether or not to present descriptive statistics and/or graphs in the body of a paper on a case-by-case basis. It is scientifically important, however, that this information be made available to consumers of your research in some way.[1]

One major way to distinguish among variables is the **measurement metric.** A variable's measurement metric is the type of values that the variable takes on, and we discuss this in detail in the next section by describing three different variable types. We then explain that, despite the imperfect nature of the distinctions among these three variable types, we are forced to choose between two broad classifications of variables – categorical or continuous – when we describe them. The rest of this chapter discusses strategies for describing **categorical variables** and **continuous variables.**

7.2 WHAT IS THE VARIABLE'S MEASUREMENT METRIC?

There are no hard-and-fast rules for describing variables, but a major initial juncture that we encounter involves the metric in which we measure each variable. Remember from Chapter 1 that we can think of each variable in terms of its label and its values. The label is the description of the variable – such as "Gender of survey respondent" – and its values are the denominations in which the variable occurs – such as "Male" or "Female." For treatment in most statistical analyses, we are forced to divide our variables into two types according to the metric in which the values of the variable occur: categorical or continuous. In reality, variables come in at least three different metric types, and there are a lot of variables that do not neatly fit into just one of these classifications. To help you to better understand each of these variable types, we will go through each with an

[1] Many researchers will present this information in an appendix unless there is something particularly noteworthy about the characteristics of one or more of their variables.

example. All of the examples that we are using in these initial descriptions come from survey research, but the same basic principles of measurement metric hold regardless of the type of data being analyzed.

7.2.1 Categorical Variables

Categorical variables are variables for which cases have values that are either qualitatively different or the same as the values for other cases, but about which we cannot make any ranking distinctions.[2] If we consider a variable that we might label "Religious Identification," some values for this variable are "Catholic," "Muslim," "nonreligious," and so on. Although these values are clearly different from each other, we cannot make ranking distinctions across them. More casually, with categorical variables like this one, it is not possible to rank order the categories from least to greatest: The value "Muslim" is neither greater nor less than "nonreligious" (and so on), for example. Instead, we are left knowing that cases with the same value for this variable are the same, whereas those cases with different values are different. The term "categorical" expresses the essence of this variable type; we can put individual cases into categories based on their values, but we cannot go any further in terms of ranking or otherwise ordering these values.

7.2.2 Ordinal Variables

Like categorical variables, **ordinal variables** are also variables for which cases have values that are either different or the same as the values for other cases. The distinction between ordinal and categorical variables is that we *can* make ranking distinctions across the variable values for ordinal variables. For instance, consider the variable labeled "Satisfaction with Financial Situation" that has commonly been used in individual-level studies as one indicator of overall life satisfaction. In the 2014 GSS, this variable was measured by asking respondents to answer the following question: "We are interested in how people are getting along financially these days. So far as you and your family are concerned, would you say that you are pretty well satisfied with your present financial situation, more or less satisfied, or not satisfied at all?" The resulting variable was then coded as follows:

1. pretty well satisfied
2. more or less satisfied
3. not satisfied at all

[2] We sometimes refer to these variables as "nominal variables."

This variable is pretty clearly an ordinal variable because as we go from the top to the bottom of the list we are moving from better to worse evaluations of how individuals (and their families) have been faring financially.

As another example, consider the variable labeled "Party Identification." In the 2014 GSS, researchers created this variable by using each respondent's answer to the question, "Generally speaking, do you usually think of yourself as a Republican, a Democrat, an independent, or what?"[3] which we can code as taking on the following values:

1. Republican
2. Independent
3. Democrat

If all cases that take on the value "Independent" represent individuals whose views lie somewhere between "Republican" and "Democrat," we can call "Party Identification" an ordinal variable. If this is not the case, then this variable is a categorical variable.

7.2.3 Continuous Variables

An important characteristic that ordinal variables *do not* have is **equal unit differences.** A variable has equal unit differences if a one-unit increase in the value of that variable *always* means the same thing. If we return to the examples from the previous section, we can rank order the three categories of "Satisfaction with Financial Situation" from 1 for the most satisfied to 3 for the least satisfied. But we may not feel very confident working with these assigned values the way that we typically work with numbers. In other words, can we say that the difference between "not satisfied at all" and "more or less satisfied" (3 – 2) is the same as the difference between "more or less satisfied" and "pretty well satisfied" (2 – 1)? If the answer to this question is "yes," then satisfaction with financial situation is a continuous variable. However, the answer, very likely, is "no."

If we ask the same question about "Party Identification," we should be equally skeptical. We can rank order the three categories of "Party Identification," but we cannot with great confidence assign "Republican" a value of 1, "Independent" a value of 2, and "Democrat" a value of 3, and work with these values in the way that we typically work with

[3] Almost all U.S. respondents put themselves into one of these three categories. For instance, in 2014, 2450 of the 2538 respondents (96.5 percent) responded that they were a Republican, a Democrat, or an independent. For our purposes, we will ignore the "or what" cases. Note that researchers usually present partisan identification across seven values ranging from "Strong Republican" to "Strong Democrat" based on follow-up questions that ask respondents to further characterize their positions.

numbers. We cannot say that the difference between an "Independent" and a "Republican" (2 – 1) is the same as the difference between a "Democrat" and an "Independent" (3 – 2), despite the fact that both 3 – 2 and 2 – 1 = 1. Certainly, we cannot say that the difference between a "Democrat" and a "Republican" (3 – 1) is twice the difference between an "Independent" and a "Republican" (2 – 1), despite the fact that 2 is twice as big as 1.

The metric in which we measure a variable has equal unit differences if a one-unit increase in the value of that variable indicates the same amount of change across *all values* of that variable. Continuous variables are variables that *do* have equal unit differences.[4] Imagine, for instance, a variable labeled "Age in Years." A one-unit increase in this variable *always* indicates an individual who is one year older; this is true when we are talking about a case with a value of 21 just as it is when we are talking about a case with a value of 55.

7.2.4 Variable Types and Statistical Analyses

As we saw in the preceding subsections, variables do not always neatly fit into the three categories. When we move to the vast majority of statistical analyses, we must decide between treating each of our variables as though it is categorical or as though it is continuous. For some variables, this is a very straightforward choice. However, for others, this is a very difficult choice. If we treat an ordinal variable as though it is categorical, we are acting as though we know less about the values of this variable than we really know. On the other hand, treating an ordinal variable as though it is a continuous variable means that we are assuming that it has equal unit differences. Either way, it is critical that we be aware of our decisions. We can always repeat our analyses under a different assumption and see how robust our conclusions are to our choices.

With all of this in mind, we present separate discussions of the process of describing a variable's **variation** for categorical and continuous variables. A variable's variation is the distribution of values that it takes across the cases for which it is measured. It is important that we have a strong knowledge of the variation in each of our variables before we can translate our theory into hypotheses, assess whether there is covariation between two variables (causal hurdle 3 from Chapter 3), and think about whether or not there might exist a third variable that makes any observed covariation between our independent and dependent variables spurious (hurdle 4). As we just outlined, descriptive statistics and graphs are useful

[4] We sometimes call these variables "interval variables." A further distinction you will encounter with continuous variables is whether they have a substantively meaningful zero point. We usually describe variables that have this characteristic as "ratio" variables.

summaries of the variation for individual variables. Another way in which we describe distributions of variables is through measures of **central tendency**. Measures of central tendency tell us about typical values for a particular variable at the center of its distribution.

7.3 DESCRIBING CATEGORICAL VARIABLES

With categorical variables, we want to understand the frequency with which each value of the variable occurs in our data. The simplest way of seeing this is to produce a frequency table in which the values of the categorical variable are displayed down one column and the frequency with which it occurs (in absolute number of cases and/or in percentage terms) is displayed in (an)other column(s). Table 7.1 shows such a table for the variable "Religious Identification" from the 2014 GSS survey.

Table 7.1 Frequency table for "Religious Identification" in the 2014 GSS

Category	Number of cases	Percent
Protestant	1126	44.7
Catholic	606	24.0
Jewish	40	1.6
Other	227	9.0
None	522	20.7

The only measure of central tendency that is appropriate for a categorical variable is the **mode**, which is defined as the most frequently occurring value. In Table 7.1, the mode of the distribution is "Protestant," because there are more Protestants than there are members of any other single category.

A typical way in which nonstatisticians present frequency data is in a pie graph such as Figure 7.1. Pie graphs are one way for visualizing the percentage of cases that fall into particular categories. Many statisticians argue strongly against their use and, instead, advocate the use of bar graphs. Bar graphs, such as Figure 7.2, are another graphical way to illustrate frequencies of categorical variables. It is worth noting, however, that most of the information that we are able to gather from these two figures is very clearly and precisely presented in the columns of frequencies and percentages displayed in Table 7.1.

7.4 DESCRIBING CONTINUOUS VARIABLES

The statistics and graphs for describing continuous variables are considerably more complicated than those for categorical variables. This is because continuous variables are more mathematically complex than categorical variables. With continuous variables, we want to know about

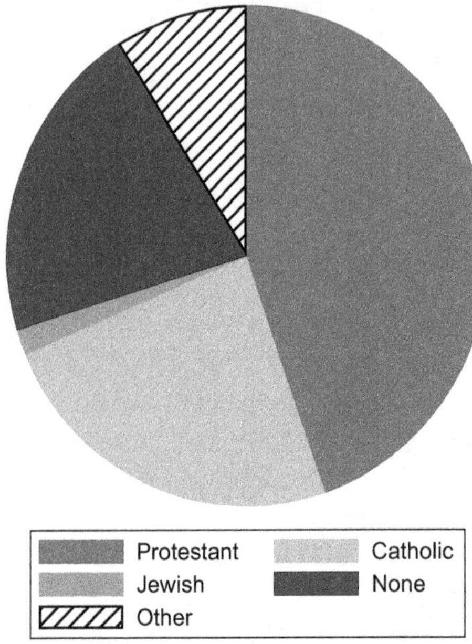

Figure 7.1 Pie graph of "Religious Identification," GSS 2014

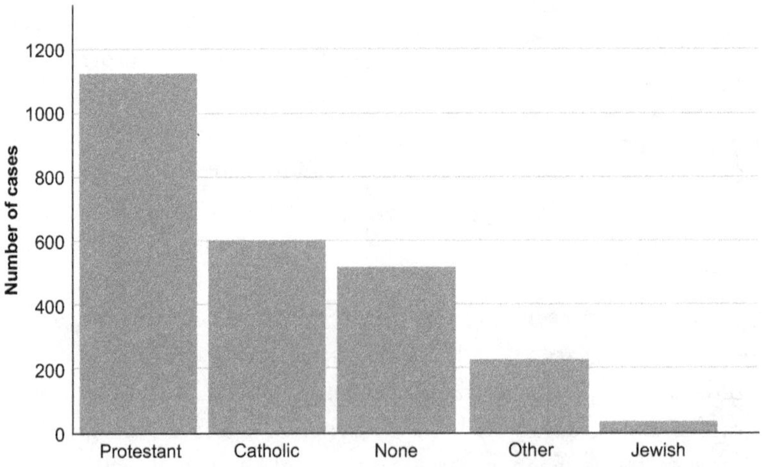

Figure 7.2 Bar graph of "Religious Identification," GSS 2014

the central tendency and the spread or variation of the values around the central tendency. With continuous variables we also want to be on the lookout for **outliers.** Outliers are cases for which the value of the variable is extremely high or low relative to the rest of the values for that variable. When we encounter an outlier, we want to make sure that such a case is real and not created by some kind of error.

Most statistical software programs have a command for getting a battery of descriptive statistics on continuous variables. Figure 7.3 shows

	Percentiles	Smallest		
1%	33.8	33.8		
10%	36.1	36.1		
25%	40.9	38.4	Obs	19
		40.0	Sum of Wgt.	19
50%	43.9		Mean	43.58
			Std. Dev.	4.86
		Largest		
75%	46.0	46.3	Variance	23.62
90%	50.0	48.2	Skewness	.157
99%	54.9	50.0	Kurtosis	.873
		54.9		

Figure 7.3 Rank statistics and statistical moments from SPSS's "frequencies" procedure

several such statistics from an SPSS "frequencies" procedure for the percentage of African American respondents who reported owning a home in the 1985–2014 GSS surveys. The statistics on the left-hand side (the first three columns on the left) of the figure are what we call **rank statistics**, and the statistics on the right-hand side (the two columns on the right) are known as the **statistical moments.** Although both rank statistics and statistical moments are intended to describe the variation of continuous variables, they do so in slightly different ways and are thus quite useful together for getting a complete picture of the variation for a single variable.

7.4.1 Rank Statistics

The calculation of rank statistics begins with the ranking of the values of a continuous variable from smallest to largest, followed by the identification of crucial junctures along the way. Once we have our cases ranked, the midpoint as we count through our cases is known as the median case. Remember that earlier in the chapter we defined the variable in Figure 7.3 as the percentage of African Americans in the 1985–2014 GSS surveys who identified themselves as homeowners. We will call this variable "African American Homeownership" for short. To calculate rank statistics for this variable, we need to first put the cases in order from the smallest to the largest observed value. This ordering is shown in Table 7.2. With rank statistics, we measure the central tendency as the **median value** of the variable. The median value is the value of the case that sits at the exact center of our cases when we rank them from the smallest to the largest observed values. In our example the median is 43.9.[5] This is also known as the value of the variable at the 50% rank. In a similar way, we can talk

[5] When we have an even number of cases, we average the values of the two centermost ranked cases to obtain the median value.

about the value of the variable at any other percentage rank in which we have an interest. Other ranks that are often of interest are the 25% and 75% ranks, which are also known as the first and third "quartile ranks" for a distribution. The difference between the variable value at the 25% and the 75% ranks is known as the "interquartile range" or "IQR" of the variable. In our example variable, the 25% value is 40.9 and the 75% value is 46.0. This makes the IQR = 46.0 – 40.9 = 5.1. In the language of rank statistics, the median value for a variable is a measure of its central tendency, whereas the IQR is a measure of the **dispersion**, or spread, of values.

Table 7.2 Values of African American homeownership ranked from smallest to largest

Rank	Year	Value
1	2002	33.80
2	1988	36.10
3	2010	38.40
4	1985	40.00
5	2000	40.90
6	2014	41.40
7	1986	41.50
8	1987	42.20
9	1994	43.40
10	1993	43.90
11	2004	44.80
12	2012	45.00
13	1996	45.50
14	2008	45.70
15	1989	46.00
16	1998	46.30
17	2006	48.20
18	1991	50.00
19	1990	54.90

With rank statistics, we also want to look at the smallest and largest values to identify outliers. Remember that we defined outliers at the beginning of this section as "cases for which the value of the variable is extremely high or low relative to the rest of the values for that variable." If we look at the highest values in Table 7.2, we can see that there is only one case that fits this description, 54.90 in 1990. Otherwise, there seems to be a fairly even progression from the 75% value up to the highest value. The story at the other range of values in Table 7.2 is similar. The value of 33.80 in 2002 seems to meet our definition of an outlier. Whenever we see outliers, we should begin by checking whether we have measured the values for these cases accurately. Sometimes we find that outliers are the result of errors when entering data. In this case, a check of our data set reveals that the outlier cases occurred in 1990 and 2002 when the percentages of black homeownership were 54.90 and 33.80, respectively. A further check of our data indicates that there were no errors in entering these variables.

Figure 7.4 presents a box–whisker plot of the rank statistics for our African American homeownership variable. This plot displays the distribution of the variable along the vertical dimension. If we start at the center of the box in Figure 7.4, we see the median value (or 50% rank value) of our variable represented as the slight gap in the center of the box.

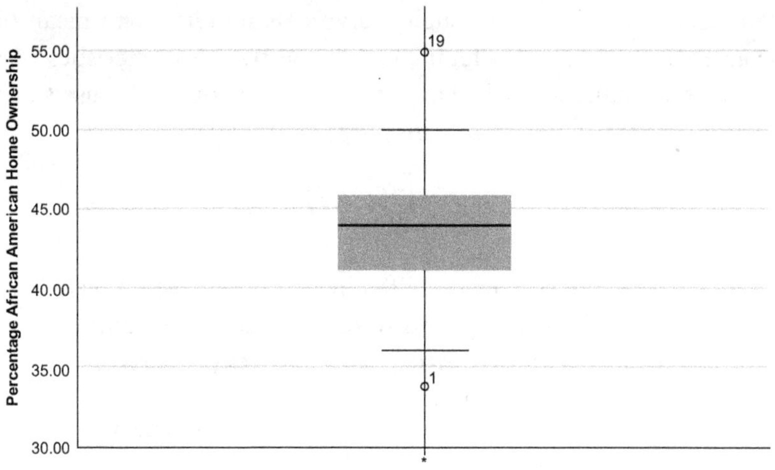

Figure 7.4 Box–whisker plot of African American homeownership, 1985–2014

The other two ends of the box show the values of the 25% rank and the 75% rank of our variable. The ends of the whiskers show the lowest and highest nonoutlier values of our variable. Each statistical program has its own rules for dealing with outliers, so it is important to know whether your box–whisker plot is or is not set up to display outliers. These settings are usually adjustable within the statistical program. The calculation of whether an individual case is or is not an outlier in this box–whisker plot is fairly standard. This calculation starts with the IQR for the variable. Any case is defined as an outlier if its value is either 1.5 times the IQR higher than the 75% value or if its value is 1.5 times the IQR lower than the 25% value. For Figure 7.4 we have set things up so that the plot displays the outliers, and we can see one such value at the top and one at the bottom of our figure. As we already know from Table 7.2, these are the values of 54.90 and 33.80 from the 1990 and 2002 surveys, respectively.

7.4.2 Moments

The statistical moments of a variable are a set of statistics that describe the central tendency for a single variable and the distribution of values around it. The most familiar of these statistics is known as the **mean value** or "average" value for the variable. For a variable Y, the mean value is depicted and calculated as

$$\bar{Y} = \frac{\sum_{i=1}^{n} Y_i}{n},$$

where $\bar{Y}$, known as "Y-bar," indicates the mean of Y, which is equal to the sum of all values of Y across individual cases of Y, Y_i, divided by the total number of cases n.[6] Although everyone is familiar with mean or average values, not everyone is familiar with the two characteristics of the mean value that make it particularly attractive to people who use statistics. The first is known as the "**zero-sum property**":

$$\sum_{i=1}^{n}(Y_i - \bar{Y}) = 0,$$

which means the sum of the difference between each Y value, Y_i, and the mean value of Y, $\bar{Y}$, is equal to zero. The second desirable characteristic of the mean value is known as the "**least-squares property**":

$$\sum_{i=1}^{n}(Y_i - \bar{Y})^2 < \sum_{i=1}^{n}(Y_i - c)^2 \quad \forall\, c \neq \bar{Y},$$

which means that the sum of the squared differences between each Y value, Y_i, and the mean value of Y, $\bar{Y}$, is less than the sum of the squared differences between each Y value, Y_i, and some value c, for all ($\forall$) c values not equal to ($\neq$) $\bar{Y}$. Because of these two properties, the mean value is also referred to as the **expected value** of a variable. Think of it this way: If someone were to ask you to guess what the value for an individual case is without giving you any more information than the mean value, based on these two properties of the mean, the mean value would be the best guess.

The next statistical moment for a variable is the **variance.** We represent and calculate the variance as follows:

$$\text{var}(Y) = \text{var}_Y = s_Y^2 = \frac{\sum_{i=1}^{n}(Y_i - \bar{Y})^2}{n-1},$$

which means that the variance of Y is equal to the sum of the squared differences between each Y value, Y_i, and its mean divided by the number of cases minus one.[7] If we look through this formula, what would happen if we had no variation on Y at all ($Y_i = \bar{Y}\ \forall\ i$)? In this case, the variance would be equal to zero. But as individual cases are spread further and further from the mean, this calculation would increase. This is the logic of variance: It conveys the spread of the data around the mean. A more intuitive measure of variance is the **standard deviation:**

$$\text{sd}(Y) = \text{sd}_Y = s_Y = \sqrt{\text{var}(Y)} = \sqrt{\frac{\sum_{i=1}^{n}(Y_i - \bar{Y})^2}{n-1}}.$$

[6] To understand formulae like this, it is helpful to read through each of the pieces of the formula and translate them into words, as we have done here.

[7] The "minus one" in this equation is an adjustment that is made to account for the number of "degrees of freedom" with which this calculation was made. We will discuss degrees of freedom in Chapter 9.

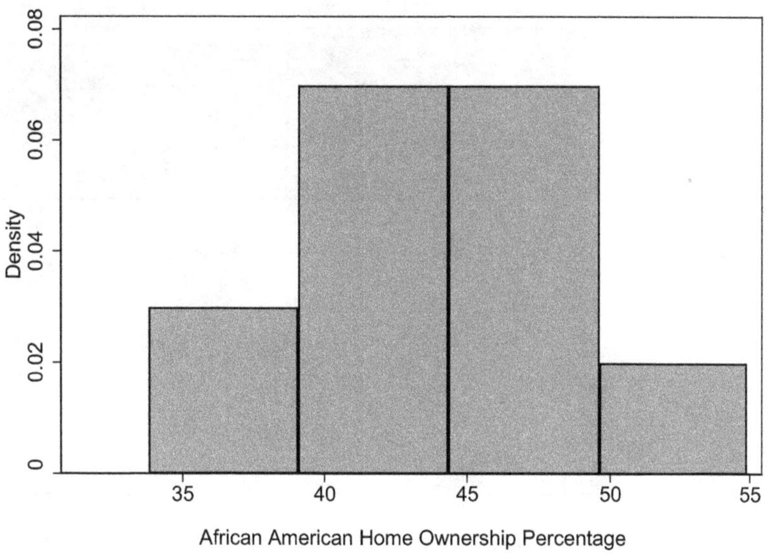

Figure 7.5 Histogram of African American homeownership, 1985–2014

Roughly speaking, this is the average difference between values of Y (Y_i) and the mean of Y ($\bar{Y}$). At first glance, this may not be apparent. But the important thing to understand about this formula is that the purpose of squaring each difference from the mean and then taking the square root of the resulting sum of squared deviations is to keep the negative and positive deviations from canceling each other out.[8]

The variance and the standard deviation give us a numerical summary of the distribution of cases around the mean value for a variable.[9] We can also visually depict distributions. The idea of visually depicting distributions is to produce a two-dimensional figure in which the horizontal dimension (x axis) displays the values of the variable and the vertical dimension (y axis) displays the relative frequency of cases. One of the most popular visual depictions of a variable's distribution is the **histogram**, such as Figure 7.5. One problem with histograms is that we (or the computer

[8] An alternative method that would produce a very similar calculation would be to calculate the average value of the absolute value of each difference from the mean: $(\sum_{i=1}^{n} |Y_i - \bar{Y}|)/n$.

[9] The **skewness** and the **kurtosis** of a variable convey further aspects of the distribution of a variable. The skewness calculation indicates the symmetry of the distribution around the mean. If the data are symmetrically distributed around the mean, then this statistic will equal zero. If skewness is negative, this indicates that there are more values below the mean than there are above; if skewness is positive, this indicates that there are more values above the mean than there are below. The kurtosis indicates the steepness of the statistical distribution. Positive kurtosis values indicate very steep distributions, or a concentration of values close to the mean value, whereas negative kurtosis values indicate a flatter distribution, or more cases further from the mean value. For the normal distribution, which we will discuss in Chapter 8, skewness equals zero and kurtosis equals three.

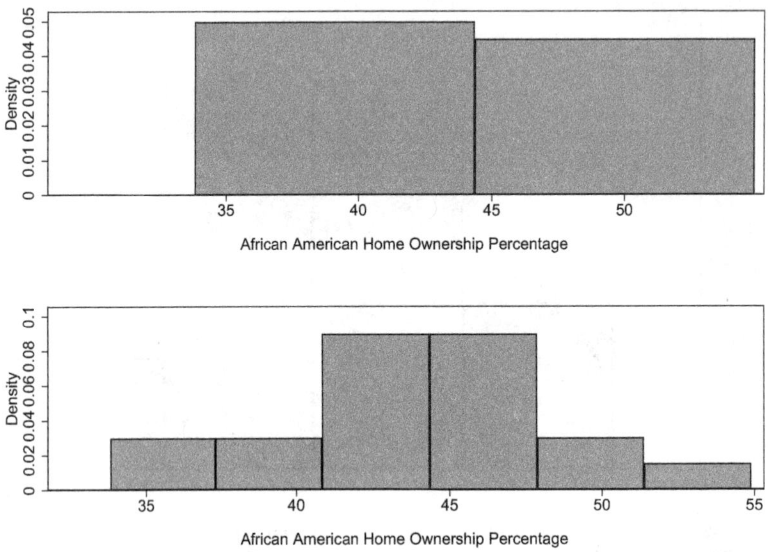

Figure 7.6 Histograms of African American homeownership, 1985–2014, depicted with two and six blocks

program with which we are working) must choose how many rectangular blocks (called "bins") are depicted in our histogram. Changing the number of blocks in a histogram can change our impression of the distribution of the variable being depicted. Figure 7.6 shows the same variable as in Figure 7.5 with two and then six blocks. Although we generate both of the graphs in Figure 7.6 from the same data, they are fairly different from each other.

Another option is the **kernel density plot**, as in Figure 7.7, which is based on a smoothed calculation of the density of cases across the range of values.

When students are learning about histograms and kernel density plots, a frequent question that they have is, "Which is better?" We don't have a definitive answer to this question. Both histograms and kernel densities are graphical ways for summarizing the distribution of values for one variable in a sample data set. As such, they both simplify reality. The histogram does this by dividing the different values for the variable being depicted into ranges called "bins" that look like the bars in a bar graph and then displaying the density of the number of cases within each of these ranges or bins. Kernel density plots, on the other hand, produce a more smoothed depiction of the contours of the forest of values for the variable being summarized. To go back to the metaphor that we started with, both histograms and kernel density plots are trying to summarize the broad shape of the forest and thus miss some of the details of individual trees. If you're having difficulty choosing which one you like better, one option is to put them both in the same figure. Figure 7.8 is an example of this.

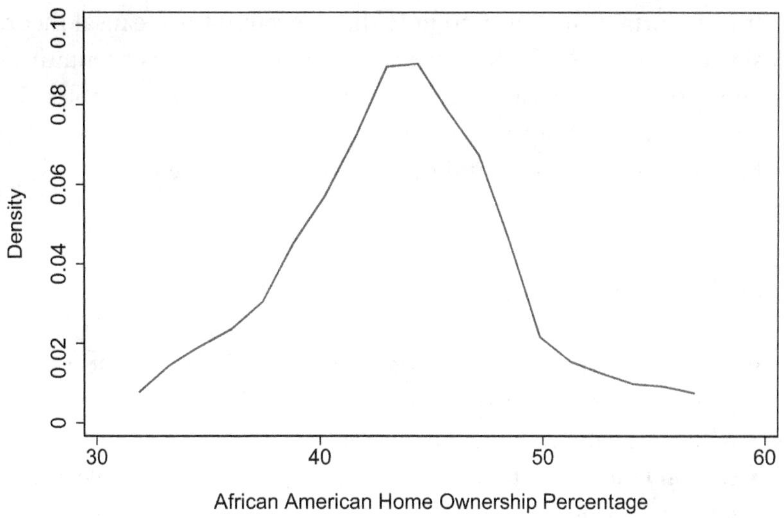

Figure 7.7 Kernel density plot of African American homeownership, 1985–2014

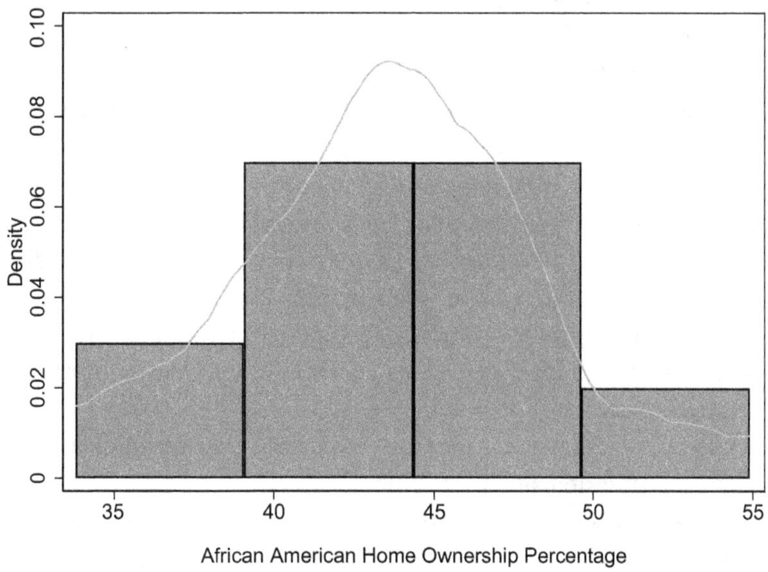

Figure 7.8 Combination histogram and kernel density plot of African American homeownership, 1985–2014

7.5 LIMITATIONS OF DESCRIPTIVE STATISTICS AND GRAPHS

The tools that we have presented in this chapter for describing a variable's central tendency and variation are helpful for providing a first look at data, one variable at a time. Taking a look at your data with these tools will help you to better know your data and make fewer mistakes in the long run.

It is important, however, to note that we cannot test causal theories with a single variable. After all, as we have noted, a theory is a tentative statement about the possible causal relationship between two variables. Because we have discussed how to describe only a single variable, we have not yet begun to subject our causal theories to appropriate tests.

CONCEPTS INTRODUCED IN THIS CHAPTER

- categorical variable – a variable for which cases have values that are either different from or the same as the values for other cases, but about which we cannot make any universally holding ranking distinctions
- central tendency – typical values for a particular variable at the center of its distribution
- continuous variable – a variable whose metric has equal unit differences such that a one-unit increase in the value of the variable indicates the same amount of change across all values of that variable
- dispersion – the spread or range of values of a variable
- equal unit differences – a variable has equal unit differences if a one-unit increase in the value of that variable always means the same thing
- expected value – a synonym for "mean value"
- histogram – a visual depiction of the distribution of a single variable that produces a two-dimensional figure in which the horizontal dimension (x axis) displays the values of the variable and the vertical dimension (y axis) displays the relative frequency of cases
- kernel density plot – a visual depiction of the distribution of a single variable based on a smooth calculation of the density of cases across the range of values
- kurtosis – a statistical measure indicating the steepness of the statistical distribution of a single variable
- least-squares property – a property of the mean value for a single variable Y, which means that the sum of the squared differences between each Y value, Y_i, and the mean value of Y, $\bar{Y}$, is less than the sum of the squared differences between each Y value, Y_i, and some value c, for all ($\forall$) c values not equal to ($\neq$)$\bar{Y}$
- mean value – the arithmetical average of a variable equal to the sum of all values of Y across individual cases of Y, Y_i, divided by the total number of cases
- measurement metric – the type of values that the variable takes on
- median value – the value of the case that sits at the exact center of our cases when we rank the values of a single variable from the smallest to the largest observed values

- mode – the most frequently occurring value of a variable
- ordinal variable – a variable for which we can make universally holding ranking distinctions across the variable values, but whose metric does not have equal unit differences
- outlier – a case for which the value of the variable is extremely high or low relative to the rest of the values for that variable
- rank statistics – a class of statistics used to describe the variation of continuous variables based on their ranking from lowest to highest observed values
- skewness – a statistical measure indicating the symmetry of the distribution around the mean
- standard deviation – a statistical measure of the dispersion of a variable around its mean
- statistical moments – a class of statistics used to describe the variation of continuous variables based on numerical calculations
- variance – a statistical measure of the dispersion of a variable around its mean
- variation – the distribution of values that a variable takes across the cases for which it is measured
- zero-sum property – a property of the mean value for a single variable Y, which means that the sum of the difference between each Y value, Y_i, and the mean value of Y, $\bar{Y}$, is equal to zero

EXERCISES

1. *Collecting and describing a categorical variable.* Find data for a categorical variable in which you are interested. Get those data into a format that can be read by the statistical software that you are using. Produce a frequency table and describe what you see.
2. *Collecting and describing a continuous variable.* Find data for a continuous variable in which you are interested. Get those data into a format that can be read by the statistical software that you are using. Produce a table of descriptive statistics and a histogram. Describe what you have found out from doing this.
3. In Table 7.1, why would it be problematic to calculate the mean value of the variable "Religious Identification"?
4. *Moving from mathematical formulae to textual statements.* Write a sentence that conveys what is going on in each of the following equations:

   (a) $Y = 3 \ \forall \ X_i = 2$;

   (b) $Y_{\text{total}} = \sum_{i=1}^{n} Y_i = n\bar{Y}$.

Table 7.3 Median incomes of the fifty states, 2004–05

State	Income	State	Income
Alabama	37,502	Montana	36,202
Alaska	56,398	Nebraska	46,587
Arizona	45,279	Nevada	48,496
Arkansas	36,406	New Hampshire	57,850
California	51,312	New Jersey	60,246
Colorado	51,518	New Mexico	39,916
Connecticut	56,889	New York	46,659
Delaware	50,445	North Carolina	41,820
Florida	42,440	North Dakota	41,362
Georgia	44,140	Ohio	44,349
Hawaii	58,854	Oklahoma	39,292
Idaho	45,009	Oregon	43,262
Illinois	48,008	Pennsylvania	45,941
Indiana	43,091	Rhode Island	49,511
Iowa	45,671	South Carolina	40,107
Kansas	42,233	South Dakota	42,816
Kentucky	36,750	Tennessee	39,376
Louisiana	37,442	Texas	42,102
Maine	43,317	Utah	53,693
Maryland	59,762	Vermont	49,808
Massachusetts	54,888	Virginia	52,383
Michigan	44,801	Washington	51,119
Minnesota	56,098	West Virginia	35,467
Mississippi	34,396	Wisconsin	45,956
Missouri	43,266	Wyoming	45,817

Source: www.census.gov/library/working-papers/2007/acs/2007_Webster_01.html. Accessed January 11, 2007.

5. *Computing means and standard deviations*. Table 7.3 contains the median income for each of the fifty U.S. states for the years 2004–05. What is the mean of this distribution, and what is its standard deviation? Show all of your work.

8 Probability and Statistical Inference

OVERVIEW

Researchers aspire to draw conclusions about the entire population of cases that are relevant to a particular research question. However, in most cases, they must rely on data from only a sample of those cases to do so. In this chapter, we lay the foundation for how researchers make inferences about a population of cases while only observing a sample of data. This foundation rests on probability theory, which we introduce here with extensive references to examples. We conclude the chapter with an example familiar to many of you – namely, the "plus-or-minus" error figures in polls, showing where such figures come from, and how they illustrate the principles of building bridges from samples we know about with certainty to the underlying population of interest.

How dare we speak of the laws of chance? Is not chance the antithesis of all law?

—Bertrand Russell

8.1 POPULATIONS AND SAMPLES

In Chapter 6, we learned how to measure our key concepts of interest, and then, in Chapter 7, how to use descriptive statistics to summarize large amounts of information about a single variable. In particular, you discovered how to characterize a distribution by computing measures of central tendency (like the mean or median) and measures of dispersion (like the standard deviation or IQR). For example, you can implement these formulae to characterize the distribution of income in the United States, or, for that matter, the scores of a midterm examination your professor may have just handed back.

But it is time to draw a critical distinction between two types of data sets that social scientists might use. The first type is data about the **population** – that is, data for every possible relevant case. In your experience, the example of population data that might come to mind first is that of the U.S. Census, an attempt by the U.S. government to gather some critical bits of data about the entire U.S. population once every ten years.[1] It is a relatively rare occurrence that social scientists will make use of data pertaining to the entire population.[2]

The second type of data is drawn from a **sample** – a subset of cases that is drawn from an underlying population. Because of the proliferation of public opinion polls today, many of you might assume that the word "sample" implies a **random sample.**[3] It does not. Researchers *may* draw a sample of data on the basis of randomness – meaning that each member of the population has an equal probability of being selected in the sample. But samples may also be nonrandom, which we refer to as samples of convenience.

The vast majority of analyses undertaken by social scientists are done on sample data, not population data. Why make this distinction? Even though the overwhelming majority of social science data sets are comprised of a sample, not the population, it is critical to note that we are not interested in the properties of the sample *per se*; we are interested in the sample only insofar as it helps us to learn about the underlying population. In effect, we try to build a bridge from what we know about the sample to what we believe, probabilistically, to be true about the broader population. That process is called **statistical inference**, because we use what we *know* to be true about one thing (the sample) to *infer* what is likely to be true about another thing (the population).

There are implications for using sample data to learn about a population. First and foremost is that this process of statistical inference involves, by definition, some degree of uncertainty. That notion is relatively straightforward: Any time that we wish to learn something general based on something specific, we are going to encounter some degree of uncertainty.

[1] The Bureau of the Census's website is www.census.gov.

[2] But we try to make inferences about some population of interest, and it is up to the researcher to define explicitly what that population of interest is. Sometimes, as in the case of the U.S. Census, the relevant population – all U.S. residents – is easy to understand. Other times, it is a bit less obvious. Consider a pre-election survey, in which the researcher needs to decide whether the population of interest is all adult citizens, or likely voters, or something else.

[3] When we discussed research design in Chapter 4, we distinguished between the experimental notion of random assignment to treatment groups, on the one hand, and random sampling, on the other. See Chapter 4 if you need a refresher on this difference. Revisit Chapter 5 for a review of types of random sampling.

In this chapter, we discuss this process of statistical inference, including the tools that social scientists use to learn about the population that they are interested in by using samples of data. Our first step in this process is to discuss the basics of probability theory, which, in turn, forms the basis for all of statistical inference.

8.2 SOME BASICS OF PROBABILITY THEORY

Let's start with an example.

Suppose that you take an empty pillowcase, and that, without anyone else looking, you meticulously count out 550 small blue beads, and 450 small red beads, and place all 1000 of them into the pillowcase. You twist the pillowcase opening a few times to close it up, and then give it a robust shake to mix up the beads. Next, you have a friend reach her hand into the pillowcase – no peeking! – and have her draw out 100 beads, and then count the red and blue beads.

Obviously, your friend knows that she is taking just a small sample of beads from the population that is in the pillowcase. And because you shook that pillowcase vigorously, and forbade your friend from looking into the pillowcase while selecting the 100 beads, her selection of 100 (more or less) represents a random sample of that population. Your friend doesn't know, of course, how many red and blue beads are in the pillowcase. She only knows how many red and blue beads she observed in the sample that she plucked out of it.

Next, you ask her to count the number of red and blue beads. Let's imagine that she happened to draw 46 red beads and 54 blue ones. Once she does this, you then ask her the key question: Based on her count, what is her best guess about the percentage of red beads versus blue beads in the entire pillowcase? The only way for your friend to know for sure how many red and blue beads are in the pillowcase, of course, is to dump out the entire pillowcase and count all 1000 beads. But, on the other hand, you're not exactly asking your friend to make some wild guess. She has some information, after all, and she can use that information to make a better guess than simply randomly picking a number between 0 percent and 100 percent.

Sensibly, given the results of her sample, she guesses that 46 percent of the beads in the entire pillowcase are red, and 54 percent are blue. (Think about it: Even though you know that her guess is wrong, it's the best guess she could have made given what she observed, right?)

Before telling her the true answer, you have her dump all 100 beads back into the pillowcase, remix the 1000 beads, and have her repeat the process: reach into the pillowcase again, redraw 100 beads, and count the number of reds and blues drawn again. This time, she draws 43 red beads and 57 blue ones.

You ask your friend if she'd like to revise her guess, and, based on some new information and some quick averaging on her part, she revises her guess to say that she thinks that 44.5 percent of the beads are red, and 55.5 percent of the beads are blue. (She does this by simply averaging the 46 percent of red beads from the first sample and 43 percent of red beads from the second sample.)

The laws of probability are useful in many ways – in calculating gambling odds, for example – but in the above example, they are useful for taking particular information about a characteristic of an observed sample of data and attempting to generalize that information to the underlying and unobserved population. The observed samples above, of course, are the two samples of 100 that your friend drew from the pillowcase. The underlying population is represented by the 1000 beads in the bag.

Of course, the example above has some limitations. In particular, in the example, you knew the actual population characteristic – there were 450 red and 550 blue beads. In social reality, there is usually no comparable knowledge of the value of the true characteristic of the underlying population.

Now, some definitions.

An **outcome** is the result of a random observation. Two or more outcomes can be said to be **independent outcomes** if the realization of one of the outcomes does not affect the realization of the other outcome. For example, the roll of two dice represents independent outcomes, because the outcome of the first die does not affect the outcome of the second die.

Probability has several key properties. First, all outcomes have some probability ranging from 0 to 1. A probability value of 0 for an outcome means that the outcome is impossible, and a probability value of 1 for an outcome means that the outcome is absolutely certain to happen. For example, taking two fair dice, rolling them, and adding up the sides facing up, and calculating the probability that the sum will equal 13 is 0, since the highest possible roll is 12.

Second, the sum of all possible outcomes must be exactly 1. A different way of putting this is that, once you undertake a random observation, you must observe something. If you flip a fair coin, the probability of it landing heads is 1/2, and the probability of it landing tails is 1/2, and the probability of landing either a head or a tail is 1, because $1/2 + 1/2 = 1$.

Third, if (but only if!) two outcomes are independent, then the probability of those events both occurring is equal to the product of them individually. So, if we have our fair coin, and toss it three times – and be mindful that each toss is an independent outcome – the probability of tossing three tails is $1/2 \times 1/2 \times 1/2 = 1/8$.

Of course, many of the outcomes in which we are interested are not independent. And in these circumstances, more complex rules of probability are required that are beyond the scope of this discussion.

Why is probability relevant for scientific investigations, and in particular, for social science? For several reasons. First, because social scientists typically work with samples (not populations) of data, the rules of probability tell us how we can generalize from our sample to the broader population. Second, and relatedly, the rules of probability are the key to identifying which relationships are "statistically significant" (a concept that we define in the next chapter). Put differently, we use probability theory to decide whether the patterns of relationships we observe in a sample could have occurred simply by chance.

8.3 LEARNING ABOUT THE POPULATION FROM A SAMPLE: THE CENTRAL LIMIT THEOREM

The reasons that social scientists rely on sample data instead of on population data – in spite of the fact that we care about the results in the population instead of in the sample – are easy to understand. Consider an election campaign, in which the media, the public, and the politicians involved all want a sense of which candidates the public favors and by how much. Is it practicable to take a census in such circumstances? Of course not. The adult population in the United States is approximately 255 million people, and it is an understatement to say that we can't interview each and every one of these individuals. We simply don't have the time or the money to do that. There is a reason why the U.S. government conducts a **census** only once every ten years.[4]

Of course, anyone familiar with the ubiquitous public opinion polls knows that scholars and news organizations conduct surveys on a sample of Americans routinely and use the results of these surveys to generalize about the people as a whole. When you think about it, it seems a little audacious to think that you can interview perhaps as few as 1000 people and then use the results of those interviews to generalize to the beliefs and opinions of the entire 255 million. How is that possible?

The answer lies in a fundamental result from statistics called the **central limit theorem**, which Dutch statistician Henk Tijms (2004) calls "the unofficial sovereign of probability theory." Before diving into what the theorem demonstrates, and how it applies to social science research, we

[4] You might not be aware that, even though the federal government conducts only one census per ten years, it conducts sample surveys with great frequency in an attempt to measure population characteristics such as economic activity.

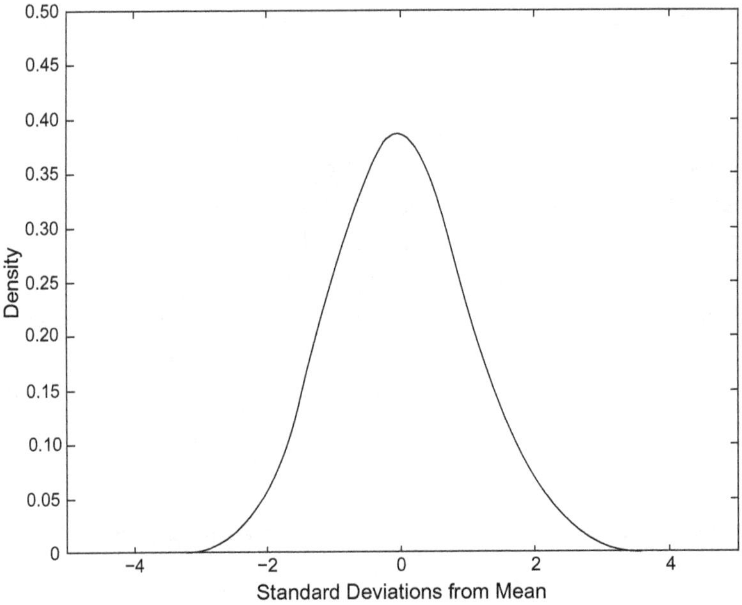

Figure 8.1 The normal probability distribution

need to explore one of the most useful probability distributions in statistics, the **normal distribution.**

8.3.1 The Normal Distribution

To say that a particular distribution is "normal" is *not* to say that it is "typical" or "desirable" or "good." A distribution that is not "normal" is not something odd like the "deviant" or "abnormal" distribution. It is worth emphasizing, as well, that normal distributions are not necessarily common in the real world. Yet, as we will see, they are incredibly useful in the world of statistics.

The normal distribution is often called a "bell curve" in common language. It is shown in Figure 8.1 and has several special properties. First, it is symmetrical about its mean,[5] such that the mode, median, and mean are the same. Second, the normal distribution has a predictable area under the curve within specified distances of the mean. Starting from the mean and going one standard deviation in each direction will capture

[5] Equivalently, but a bit more formally, we can characterize the distribution by its mean and variance (or standard deviation). The skewness and the kurtosis of a variable convey the further aspects of the distribution of a variable – see footnote 9 in Chapter 7.

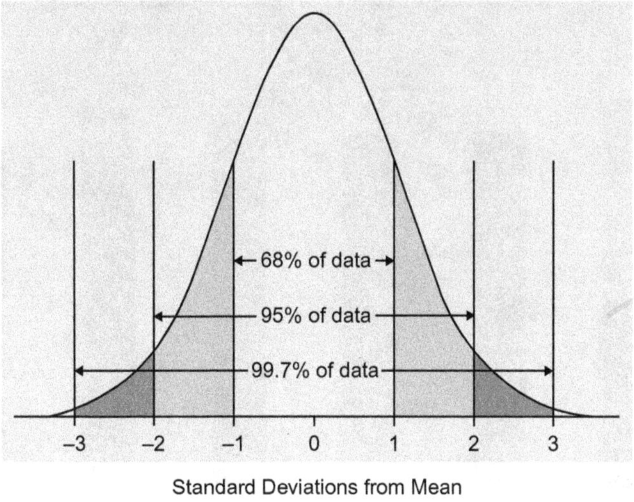

Figure 8.2 The 68–95–99 rule

68 percent of the area under the curve. Going one additional standard deviation in each direction will capture a shade over 95 percent of the total area under the curve.[6] And going a third standard deviation in each direction will capture more than 99 percent of the total area under the curve. This is commonly referred to as the **68–95–99 rule** and is illustrated in Figure 8.2. You should bear in mind that this is a special feature of the normal distribution and does not apply to any other-shaped distribution. What do the normal distribution and the 68–95–99 rule have to do with the process of learning about population characteristics based on a sample?

The distribution of actual scores in a sample – called a **frequency distribution**, to represent the frequency of each value of a particular variable – on any variable might be shaped normally, or it might not be. Consider the frequency distribution of 600 rolls of a six-sided (and unbiased) die, presented in Figure 8.3. Note something about Figure 8.3 right off the bat: That frequency distribution does not even remotely resemble a normal distribution.[7] If we roll a fair six-sided die 600 times, how many 1's, 2's, etc., should we see? On average, 100 of each, right?

[6] To get exactly 95 percent of the area under the curve, we would actually go 1.96, not 2, standard deviations in each direction from the mean. Nevertheless, the rule of two is a handy rule of thumb for many statistical calculations.

[7] In fact, the distribution in the figure very closely resembles a uniform or flat distribution.

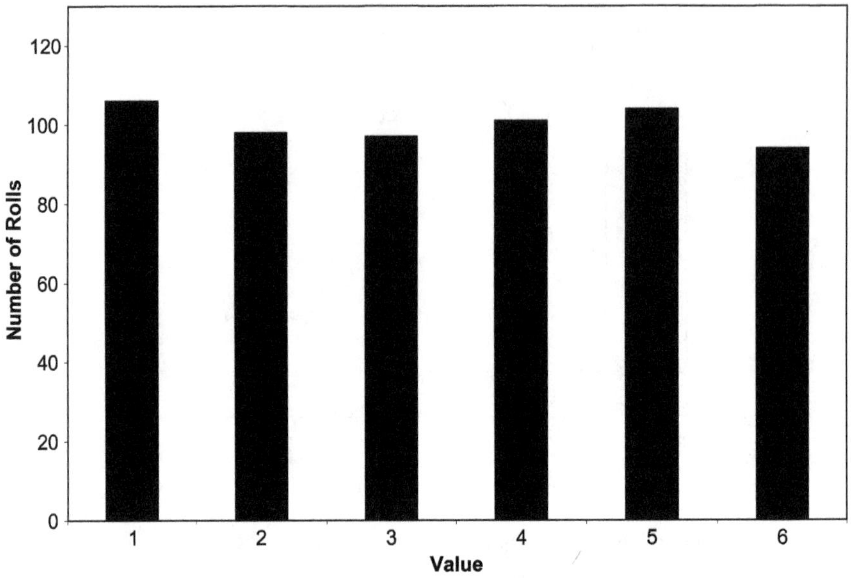

Figure 8.3 Frequency distribution of 600 rolls of a die

That's *pretty close* to what we see in the figure, but only pretty close. Purely because of chance, we rolled a couple too many 1's, for example, and a couple too few 6's.

What can we say about this sample of 600 rolls of the die? And, more to the point, from these 600 rolls of the die, what can we say about the underlying population of all rolls of a fair six-sided die? Before we answer the second question, which will require some inference, let's answer the first, which we can answer with certainty. We can calculate the mean of these rolls of dice in the straightforward way that we learned in Chapter 7: Add up all of the "scores" – that is, the 1's, 2's, and so on – and divide by the total number of rolls, which in this case is 600. That will lead to the following calculation:

$$\begin{aligned}\bar{Y} &= \frac{\sum_{i=1}^{n} Y_i}{n} \\ &= \frac{\sum(1 \times 106) + (2 \times 98) + (3 \times 97) + (4 \times 101) + (5 \times 104) + (6 \times 94)}{600} \\ &= 3.47.\end{aligned}$$

Following the formula for the mean, for our 600 rolls of the die, in the numerator we must add up all of the 1's (106 of them), all of the 2's (98 of them), and so on, and then divide by 600 to produce our result of 3.47.

We can also calculate the standard deviation of this distribution:

$$s_Y = \sqrt{\frac{\sum_{i=1}^{n}(Y_i - \bar{Y})^2}{n-1}} = \sqrt{\frac{1753.40}{599}} = 1.71.$$

Looking at the numerator for the formula for the standard deviation that we learned in Chapter 7, we see that $\sum(Y_i - \bar{Y})^2$ indicates that, for each observation (a 1, 2, 3, 4, 5, or 6), we subtract its value from the mean (3.47), then square that difference, then add up all 600 squared deviations from the mean, which produces a numerator of 1753.40 beneath the square-root sign. Dividing that amount by 599 (that is, $n - 1$), then taking the square root, produces a standard deviation of 1.71.

As we noted, the sample mean is 3.47, but what should we have *expected* the mean to be? If we had exactly 100 rolls of each side of the die, the mean would have been 3.50, so our sample mean is a bit lower than we would have expected. But then again, we can see that we rolled a few "too many" 1's and a few "too few" 6's, so the fact that our mean is a bit below 3.50 makes sense.

What would happen, though, if we rolled that same die another 600 times? What would the mean value of those rolls be? We can't say for certain, of course. Perhaps we would come up with another sample mean of 3.47, or perhaps it would be a bit above 3.50, or perhaps the mean would hit 3.50 on the nose. Suppose that we rolled the die 600 times like this not once, and not twice, but an infinite number of times. Let's be clear: We do not mean *an infinite number of rolls*, we mean *rolling the die 600 times for an infinite number of times*. That distinction is critical. We are imagining that we are taking a sample of 600, not once, but an infinite number of times. We can refer to a hypothetical distribution of sample means, such as this, as a **sampling distribution**. It is hypothetical because scientists almost never actually draw more than one sample from an underlying population at one given point in time.

If we followed this procedure, we could take those sample means and plot them. Some would be above 3.50, some below, some right on it. Here is the key outcome, though: The sampling distribution would be normally shaped, even though the underlying frequency distribution is clearly not normally shaped.

That is the insight of the central limit theorem. If we can envision an infinite number of random samples and plot our sample means to each of these random samples, those sample means would be distributed normally. Furthermore, the mean of the sampling distribution would be equal to the true population mean. The standard deviation of the sampling distribution is

$$\sigma_{\bar{Y}} = \frac{s_Y}{\sqrt{n}},$$

where n is the sample size. The standard deviation of the sampling distribution of sample means, which is known as the **standard error of the mean** (or simply "standard error"), is simply equal to the sample standard deviation divided by the square root of the sample size. In the preceding die-rolling example, the standard error of the mean is

$$\sigma_{\bar{Y}} = \frac{1.71}{\sqrt{600}} = 0.07.$$

Recall that our goal here is to learn what we can about the underlying population based on what we know with certainty about our sample. We know that the mean of our sample of 600 rolls of the die is 3.47 and its standard deviation is 1.71. From those characteristics, we can imagine that, if we rolled that die 600 times an infinite number of times, the resulting sampling distribution would have a standard deviation of 0.07. Our best approximation of the population mean is 3.47, because that is the result that our sample generated.[8] But we realize that our sample of 600 might be different from the true population mean by a little bit, either too high or too low. What we can do, then, is use our knowledge that the sampling distribution is shaped normally and invoke the 68–95–99 rule to create a **confidence interval** about the likely location of the population mean.

How do we do that? First, we choose a degree of confidence that we want to have in our estimate. Although we can choose any confidence range up from just above 0 to just below 100, social scientists traditionally rely on the 95 percent confidence level. If we follow this tradition – and because our sampling distribution is normal – we would merely start at our mean (3.47) and move *two* standard errors of the mean in each direction to produce the interval within which we are approximately 95 percent confident that the population mean lies. Why *two* standard errors? Because just over 95 percent of the area under a normal curve lies within two standard errors of the mean. Again, to be precisely 95 percent confident, we would move 1.96, not 2, standard errors in each direction. But the rule of thumb of two is commonly used in practice. In other words,

$$\bar{Y} \pm (2 \times \sigma_{\bar{Y}}) = 3.47 \pm (2 \times 0.07) = 3.47 \pm 0.14.$$

That means, from our sample, we are 95 percent confident that the population mean for our rolls of the die lies somewhere in the interval between 3.33 and 3.61.

Is it possible that we're wrong and that the population mean lies outside that interval? Absolutely. Moreover, we know exactly *how* likely. There is a 2.5 percent chance that the population mean is less than 3.33,

[8] One might imagine that our best guess should be 3.50 because, in theory, a fair die ought to produce such a result.

and a 2.5 percent chance that the population mean is greater than 3.61, for a total of a 5 percent chance that the population mean is not in the interval from 3.33 to 3.61. For a variety of reasons, we might like to have more confidence in our estimate. Say that, instead of being 95 percent confident, we would be more comfortable with a 99 percent level of confidence. In that case, we would simply move *three* (instead of two) standard errors in each direction from our sample mean of 3.47, yielding an interval of 3.26 to 3.68.

Throughout this example we have been helped along by the fact that we knew the underlying characteristics of the data-generating process (a fair die). In the real world, social scientists almost never have this advantage. In the next section we consider such a case.

8.4 EXAMPLE: PRESIDENTIAL APPROVAL RATINGS

Between March 11 and 13, 2020, NBC News and *The Wall Street Journal* sponsored a survey in which 900 randomly selected registered voters were interviewed about their political beliefs. Among the questions they were asked was the following item intended to tap into a respondent's evaluation of the President's job performance:

> In general, do you approve or disapprove of the job Donald Trump is doing as president?

This question wording is the industry standard, used for over a half-century by almost all polling organizations.[9] In March, 2020, 46 percent of the sample approved of Trump's job performance, 51 percent disapproved, and 3 percent were unsure.[10]

These news organizations, of course, are not inherently interested in the opinions of those 900 Americans who happened to be in the sample, except insofar as they tell us something about the adult population as a whole. But we can use these 900 responses to do precisely that, using the logic of the central limit theorem and the tools previously described.

To reiterate, we know the properties of our randomly drawn sample of 900 people with absolute certainty. If we consider the 414 approving

[9] The only changes, of course, are for the name of the current President.

[10] The source for the survey was www.pollingreport.com/djt_job2.htm, accessed April 15, 2020.

responses to be 1's and the remaining 486 responses to be 0's, then we calculate our sample mean, $\bar{Y}$, as follows:[11]

$$\bar{Y} = \frac{\sum_{i=1}^{n} Y_i}{n} = \frac{\sum(414 \times 1) + (486 \times 0)}{900} = 0.46.$$

We calculate the sample standard deviation, s_Y, in the following way:

$$s_Y = \sqrt{\frac{\sum_{i=1}^{n}(Y_i - \bar{Y})^2}{n-1}} = \sqrt{\frac{414(1-0.46)^2 + 486(0-0.46)^2}{900-1}}$$

$$= \sqrt{\frac{223.6}{899}} = 0.50.$$

But what can we say about the population as a whole? Obviously, unlike the sample mean, the population mean cannot be known with certainty. But if we imagine that, instead of one sample of 900 respondents, we had an infinite number of samples of 900, then the central limit theorem tells us that those sample means would be distributed normally. Our best guess of the population mean, of course, is 0.46, because it is our sample mean. The standard error of the mean is

$$\sigma_{\bar{Y}} = \frac{0.50}{\sqrt{900}} = 0.017,$$

which is our measure of uncertainty about the population mean. If we use the rule of thumb and calculate the 95 percent confidence interval by using two standard errors in either direction from the sample mean, we are left with the following interval:

$$\bar{Y} \pm (2 \times \sigma_{\bar{Y}}) = 0.46 \pm (2 \times 0.017) = 0.46 \pm 0.034,$$

or between 0.426 and 0.494, which translates into being 95 percent confident that the population value of Trump approval is between 42.6 percent and 49.4 percent.

And this is where the "plus-or-minus" figures that we always see in public opinion polls come from.[12] The best guess for the population mean value is the sample mean value, plus or minus two standard errors. So the plus-or-minus figures we are accustomed to seeing are built, typically, on the 95 percent interval.

[11] There are a variety of different ways in which to handle mathematically the 3 percent of "unsure" responses. In this case, because we are interested in calculating the "approval" rating for this example, it is reasonable to lump the disapproving and unsure answers together. When we make decisions like this in our statistical work, it is very important to communicate exactly what we have done so that the scientific audience can make a reasoned evaluation of our work.

[12] In practice, most polling firms have their own additional adjustments that they make to these calculations, but they start with this basic logic.

8.4.1 What Kind of Sample Was That?

If you read the preceding example carefully, you will have noted that the NBC–*Wall Street Journal* poll we described used a *random* sample of 900 individuals. That means that they used some mechanism (like random-digit telephone dialing) to ensure that all members of the population had an equal probability of being selected for the survey. We want to reiterate the importance of using random samples. The central limit theorem applies *only* to samples that are selected randomly. With a sample of convenience, by contrast, we cannot invoke the central limit theorem to construct a sampling distribution and create a confidence interval.

This lesson is critical: A nonrandomly selected sample of convenience does very little to help us build bridges between the sample and the population about which we want to learn. This has all sorts of implications about "polls" that news organizations conduct on their websites. What do such "surveys" say about the population as a whole? Because their samples are clearly not random samples of the underlying population, the answer is "nothing."

8.4.2 A Note on the Effects of Sample Size

As the formula for the confidence interval indicates, the smaller the standard errors, the "tighter" our resulting confidence intervals will be; larger standard errors will produce "wider" confidence intervals. If we are interested in estimating population values, based on our samples, with as much precision as possible, then it is desirable to have tighter instead of wider confidence intervals.

How can we achieve this? From the formula for the standard error of the mean, it is clear through simple algebra that we can get a smaller quotient by having either a smaller numerator or a larger denominator. Because obtaining a smaller numerator – the sample standard deviation – is not something we can do in practice, we can consider whether it is possible to have a larger denominator – a larger sample size.

Larger sample sizes will reduce the size of the standard errors, and smaller sample sizes will increase the size of the standard errors. This, we hope, makes intuitive sense. If we have a large sample, then it should be easier to make inferences about the population of interest; smaller samples should produce less confidence about the population estimate.

In the preceding example, if instead of having our sample of 900, we had a much larger sample – say, 2500 – our standard error would have been

$$\sigma_{\bar{Y}} = \frac{0.50}{\sqrt{2500}} = 0.010,$$

which is less than two-thirds the size of our actual standard error of 0.017. You can do the math to see that going two standard errors of 0.010 in either direction produces a narrower interval than going two standard errors of 0.017. But note that the cost of reducing our error by about 1.2 percent in either direction is the addition of nearly another 1500 respondents, and in many cases that reduction in error will not be worth the financial and time costs involved in obtaining all of those extra interviews.

Consider the opposite case. If, instead of interviewing 900 individuals, we interviewed only 400, then our standard error would have been

$$\sigma_{\bar{Y}} = \frac{0.50}{\sqrt{400}} = 0.025,$$

which, when doubled to get our 95 percent confidence interval, would leave a plus-or-minus 0.050 (or 5 percent) in each direction.

We could be downright silly and obtain a random sample of only 64 people if we liked. That would generate some rather wide confidence intervals. The standard error would be

$$\sigma_{\bar{Y}} = \frac{0.50}{\sqrt{64}} = 0.062,$$

which, when doubled to get the 95 percent confidence interval, would leave a rather hefty plus-or-minus 0.124 (or 12.4 percent) in each direction. In this circumstance, we would guess that Trump approval in the population was 46 percent, but we would be 95 percent confident that it was between 33.6 percent and 58.4 percent – and that alarmingly wide interval would be just too wide to be particularly informative.

In short, the answer to the question, "How big does my sample need to be?" is another question: "How tight do you want your confidence intervals to be?"

8.5 A LOOK AHEAD: EXAMINING RELATIONSHIPS BETWEEN VARIABLES

Let's take stock for a moment. In this book, we have emphasized that social science research involves evaluating causal explanations, which entails examining the relationships between two or more variables. Yet, in this chapter, all we have done is talk about the process of statistical inference with a *single* variable. This was a necessary tangent, because we had to teach you the logic of statistical inference – that is, how we use samples to learn something about an underlying population.

In Chapter 9, you will learn four different ways to move into the world of bivariate hypothesis testing. We will examine relationships between two variables, typically in a sample, and then make probabilistic assessments of the likelihood that those relationships exist in the population. The logic is identical to what you have just learned; we merely extend it to cover relationships between two variables. After that, in Chapter 10, you will learn one other way to conduct hypothesis tests involving two variables – the two-variable (bivariate) regression model.

CONCEPTS INTRODUCED IN THIS CHAPTER

- 68–95–99 rule – a useful characteristic of the normal distribution which states that moving ± 1, ± 2, and ± 3 standard deviations from the mean will leave 68, 95, and 99 percent of the distribution's area under the curve
- census – an accounting of a population
- central limit theorem – a fundamental result from statistics indicating that if one were to collect an infinite number of random samples and plot the resulting sample means, those sample means would be distributed normally around the true population mean
- confidence interval – a probabilistic statement about the likely value of a population characteristic based on the observations in a sample
- frequency distribution – a distribution of actual scores in a sample
- independent outcomes – two or more outcomes such that the realization of one of the outcomes does not affect the realization of the other outcomes
- normal distribution – a bell-shaped statistical distribution that can be entirely characterized by its mean and standard deviation
- outcome – the result of a random observation
- population – data for every possible relevant case
- random sample – a sample such that each member of the underlying population has an equal probability of being selected
- sample – a subset of cases that is drawn from an underlying population
- sampling distribution – a hypothetical distribution of sample means
- standard error of the mean – the standard deviation of the sampling distribution of sample means
- statistical inference – the process of using what we know about a sample to make probabilistic statements about the broader population

EXERCISES

1. Go to www.pollingreport.com and find a polling statistic that interests you most. Be sure to note the sample size for the survey you choose. Then calculate

the 95 percent and 99 percent confidence intervals for the population value of the statistic you have in mind, showing all of your work. Print the page from the website and turn it in with your homework.

2. For the same survey item, what would happen to the confidence interval if the sample size were cut in half? What would happen instead if it were doubled? Assume that the sample standard deviation does not change and show your work.
3. Are larger sample sizes always better than smaller sample sizes? Explain your answer.
4. Refer back to Table 7.2, which shows the percentage of African American homeownership between 1985 and 2014. Calculate the standard error of the mean for that distribution, and then construct the 95 percent confidence interval for the population mean. Show your work. What does the 95 percent confidence interval tell us in this particular case?
5. If we take a representative sample of 1000 respondents from the population of the United States for a particular survey question and obtain a 95 percent confidence interval, how many respondents would you need to sample from the population of Maine to obtain the same interval, assuming that the distribution of responses is the same for both populations? Explain your answer.

9 Bivariate Hypothesis Testing

OVERVIEW

Once we have set up a hypothesis test and collected data, how do we evaluate what we have found? In this chapter we provide hands-on discussions of the basic building blocks used to make statistical inferences about the relationship between two variables. We deal with the often-misunderstood topic of "statistical significance" – focusing both on what it is and what it is not – as well as the nature of statistical uncertainty. We introduce four ways to examine relationships between two variables: tabular analysis, difference of means tests, correlation coefficients, and analysis of variance.[1] (We will introduce a fifth technique, two-variable (or bivariate) regression analysis, in Chapter 10.)

9.1 BIVARIATE HYPOTHESIS TESTS AND ESTABLISHING CAUSAL RELATIONSHIPS

In the preceding chapters we introduced the core concepts of hypothesis testing. In this chapter we discuss the basic mechanics of hypothesis testing with four different examples of bivariate hypothesis testing. It is worth noting that, although this type of analysis remains a part of social scientists' methodological toolkits, it is seldom used as the *primary* means of hypothesis testing in the professional journals today.[2] This is the case because these techniques are good at helping us with only the first principle

[1] Analysis of variance models can also include multiple independent variables, but in this chapter we focus on the bivariate, i.e., single independent variable and single dependent variable, case.

[2] By definition, researchers conducting bivariate hypothesis tests are making one of two assumptions about the state of the world. They are assuming either that there are no other variables that are causally related to the dependent variable in question, or that, if there are such omitted variables, they are unrelated to the independent variable in the model. We will have much more to say about omitting independent variables from causal models in

for establishing causal relationships. Namely, bivariate hypothesis tests help us to answer the question, "Are X and Y related?" By definition – "bivariate" means "two variables" – these tests cannot help us with the important question, "Have we controlled for all confounding variables Z that might make the observed association between X and Y spurious?"

Despite their limitations, the techniques covered in this chapter are important starting points for understanding the underlying logic of statistical hypothesis testing. In the sections that follow, we discuss how one chooses which bivariate test to conduct and then provide detailed discussions of four such tests. Throughout this chapter, try to keep in mind the main purpose of this exercise: We are attempting to apply the lessons of the previous chapters to real-world data. We will eventually do this with more appropriate and more sophisticated tools, but the lessons that we learn in this chapter will be crucial to our understanding of these more advanced methods. Put simply, we are trying to get up and walk in the complicated world of hypothesis testing with real-world data. Once we have mastered walking, we will then begin to work on running with more advanced techniques.

9.2 CHOOSING THE RIGHT BIVARIATE HYPOTHESIS TEST

As we discussed in previous chapters, and especially in Chapters 6 and 7, researchers make a number of critical decisions before they test their hypotheses. Once they have collected their data and want to conduct a bivariate hypothesis test, they need to consider the nature of their dependent and independent variables. As we discussed in Chapter 7, we can classify variables in terms of the types of values that cases take on. Table 9.1 shows four different scenarios for testing a bivariate hypothesis; which one is most appropriate depends on the variable type of the independent variable and the dependent variable. For each case, we have listed one or more appropriate types of bivariate hypothesis tests. In cases in which we can describe both the independent and dependent variables as categorical, we use a form of analysis referred to as **tabular analysis** to test our hypothesis. When the dependent variable is continuous and the independent variable is categorical, we use a **difference of means test** or **analysis of variance model.** When the independent variable is continuous and the dependent variable is categorical, analysts typically use either a probit or logit model. (These types of statistical models are discussed in Chapter 11.) Finally, when both the dependent and independent variables

Chapter 11. For now, bear in mind that, as we have discussed in previous chapters, these assumptions rarely hold when we are describing the social world.

Table 9.1 Variable types and appropriate bivariate hypothesis tests

		Independent variable type	
		Categorical	**Continuous**
Dependent variable type	**Categorical**	*tabular analysis*	probit/logit (Ch. 11)
	Continuous	*difference of means* *analysis of variance*	*correlation coefficient* bivariate regression model (Ch. 10)

Note: Tests in *italics* are discussed in this chapter.

are continuous, we use a **correlation coefficient** in this chapter, and, in Chapter 10, we will discuss the two-variable (or bivariate) regression model.

9.3 ALL ROADS LEAD TO *p*

One common element across a wide range of statistical hypothesis tests is the *p*-value (the *p* stands for "probability"). This value, ranging between 0 and 1, is the closest thing that we have to a bottom line in statistics. But it is often misunderstood and misused. In this section we discuss the basic logic of the *p*-value and relate it back to our discussion in Chapter 8 of using sample data to make inferences about an underlying population.

9.3.1 The Logic of *p*-Values

If we think back to the four principles for establishing causal relationships that were discussed in Chapter 3, the third hurdle is the question "Is there covariation between X and Y?" To answer this question, we need to apply standards to real-world data for determining whether there appears to be a relationship between our two variables, the independent variable X and the dependent variable Y. The tests listed in the cells in Table 9.1 are commonly accepted tests for each possible combination of data type. In each of these tests, we follow a common logic: We compare the actual relationship between X and Y in sample data with what we would expect to find if X and Y *were not* related in the underlying population. The *more different* the empirically observed relationship is from what we would expect to find if there were *not* a relationship, the more confidence we have that X and Y are related in the population. The logic of this inference from sample to population is the same as what we used in Chapter 8 to make inferences about the population mean from sample data.

The statistic that is most commonly associated with this type of logical exercise is the **p-value**. The p-value, which ranges between 0 and 1, is the probability that we would see the relationship that we are finding because of random chance. Put another way, the p-value tells us the probability that we would see the observed relationship between the two variables in our sample data if there were truly no relationship between them in the unobserved population. Thus, the lower the p-value, the greater confidence we have that there *is* a systematic relationship between the two variables for which we estimated the particular p-value.

One common characteristic across most statistical techniques is that, for a particular measured relationship, the more data on which the measurement is based, the lower our p-value will be. This is consistent with one of the lessons of Chapter 8 about sample size: The larger the sample size, the more confident we can be that our sample will more accurately represent the population.[3] (See Section 8.4.2 for a reminder.)

9.3.2 The Limitations of p-Values

Although p-values are powerful indicators of whether or not two variables are related, they are limited. In this section we review those limitations. It is important that we also understand what a p-value is not: The logic of a p-value is not reversible. In other words, $p = 0.001$ does not mean that there is a 0.999 chance that something systematic is going on. Also, it is important to realize that, although a p-value tells us something about our confidence that there is a relationship between two variables, it does not tell us whether that relationship is causal.

In addition, it might be tempting to assume that, when a p-value is very close to zero, this indicates that the relationship between X and Y is very *strong*. This is not necessarily true (though it might be true). As we previously noted, p-values represent our degree of confidence that there is a relationship in the underlying population. So we should naturally expect smaller p-values as our sample sizes increase. But a larger sample size does not magically make a relationship stronger; it *does* increase our confidence that the observed relationship in our sample accurately represents the underlying population. We saw a similar type of relationship in Chapter 8 when we calculated standard errors. Because the number of cases is in the denominator of the formula for the standard error of the mean, an increased number of cases leads to a smaller standard error and a more narrow confidence interval for our inferences about the population.

[3] Also, the smaller the sample size, the more likely it is that we will get a result that is not very representative of the population.

Another limitation of p-values is that they do not directly reflect the quality of the measurement procedure for our variables. Thus, if we are more confident in our measurement, we should be more confident in a particular p-value. The flip side of this is that, if we are not very confident in our measurement of one or both of our variables, we should be less confident in a particular p-value.

Finally, we should keep in mind that p-values are always based on the assumption that you are drawing a perfectly random sample from the underlying population. Mathematically, this is expressed as

$$p_i = P \quad \forall\, i.$$

This translates into "the probability of an individual case from our population ending up in our sample, p_i, is assumed to equal P for all of the individual cases i." If this assumption were valid, we would have a truly random sample. Because this is a standard that is almost never met, we should use this in our assessment of a particular p-value. The further we are from a truly random sample, the less confidence we should have in our p-value.

9.3.3 From p-Values to Statistical Significance

As we outlined in the preceding section, lower p-values increase our confidence that there is indeed a relationship between the two variables in question. A common way of referring to such a situation is to state that the relationship between the two variables is **statistically significant**. Although this type of statement has a ring of authoritative finality, it is always a qualified statement. In other words, an assertion of statistical significance depends on a number of other factors. One of these factors is the set of assumptions from the previous section. "Statistical significance" is achieved only to the extent that the assumptions underlying the calculation of the p-value hold. In addition, there are a variety of different standards for what is a statistically significant p-value. Most social scientists use the standard of a p-value of 0.05. If p is less than 0.05, they consider a relationship to be statistically significant. Others use a more stringent standard of 0.01, or a more loose standard of 0.1.[4]

We cannot emphasize strongly enough that finding that X and Y have a statistically significant relationship does *not* necessarily mean that the relationship between X and Y is strong, or especially that the relationship is causal. To evaluate whether or not a relationship is strong, we need to

[4] More recently, there has been a trend toward reporting the estimated p-value and letting readers make their own assessments of statistical significance.

use our substantive knowledge about what it means for the value of Y to change by a particular amount. We will discuss assessments of the strength of relationships in greater detail in Chapter 11. To evaluate the case for a causal relationship, we need to evaluate how well our theory has performed in terms of all four of the causal hurdles from Chapter 3.

9.3.4 The Null Hypothesis and *p*-Values

In Chapter 1, we introduced the concept of the null hypothesis. Our definition was "A null hypothesis is also a theory-based statement but it is about what we would observe if there were no relationship between an independent variable and the dependent variable." Thus, following the logic that we previously outlined, if our theory-driven hypothesis is that there is covariation between X and Y, then the corresponding null hypothesis is that there is no covariation between X and Y. In this context, another interpretation of the p-value is that it conveys the level of confidence with which we can reject the null hypothesis.

9.4 FOUR BIVARIATE HYPOTHESIS TESTS

We now turn to four specific bivariate hypothesis tests. In each case, we are testing for whether there is a relationship between X and Y. We are doing this with sample data, and then, based on what we find, making inferences about what is likely to be true in the underlying population.

9.4.1 Example 1: Tabular Analysis

Tabular presentations of data on two variables are still used quite widely. In the more recent social science literature, scholars use them as stepping stones on the way to multivariate analyses. It is worth noting at this point in the process that, in tables, most of the time the dependent variable is displayed in the rows, whereas the independent variable is displayed in the columns. Any time that you see a table, it is very important to take some time to make sure that you understand what is being conveyed. We can break this into the following three-step process:

1. Figure out what the variables are that define the rows and columns of the table.
2. Figure out what the individual cell values represent. Sometimes they will be the number of cases that take on the particular row and column values; other times the cell values will be proportions (ranging from 0 to 1.0) or percentages (ranging from 0 to 100). If this is the case, it is critical

Table 9.2 Union households and political party affiliation, 2014 GSS

Party	Not from a union household	From a union household	Total
Democrat	59.0	64.7	59.8
Republican	41.0	35.3	40.2
Total	100.0	100.0	100.0

Note: Cell entries are column percentages.

that you figure out whether the researcher calculated the percentages or proportions for the entire table or for each column or row.

3. Figure out what, if any, general patterns you see in the table.

Let's go through these steps with Table 9.2.[5] In this table we are testing the theory that affiliation with trade unions makes people more likely to identify with a left-of-center political party than with a right-of-center political party.[6] We can tell from the title and the column and row headings that this table is comparing people from union households with those not from union households using data from the 2014 General Social Survey. We can use the information in this table to test the hypothesis that respondents from union households are more likely to identify with the Democratic Party rather than the Republican.[7]

As the first step in reading this table, we determine that the columns indicate values for the independent variable (whether or not the individual was from a union household) and that the rows indicate values for the dependent variable (party affiliation). The second step is fairly straightforward; the table contains a footnote that tells us that the "cell entries are column percentages." This is the easiest format for pursuing step 3, because the column percentages correspond to the comparison that we want to make. We want to compare the political party affiliation

[5] The party identification variable was recoded into two categories by combining "strong Democrat," "not strong Democrat," and "independent, near Democrat" into "Democrat," and "strong Republican," "not strong Republican," and "independent, near Republican" into "Republican." Respondents who identified as "Independent" or "Other party" were excluded from the table.

[6] Take a moment to assess this theory in terms of the first two of the four hurdles that we discussed in Chapter 3. The causal mechanism is that left-leaning political parties tend to support policies favored by trade unions. Is this credible? What about hurdle 2? Can we rule out the possibility that being a member of a left-leaning party makes one more likely to be affiliated with a trade union?

[7] What do you think about the operationalization of these two variables? How well does it stand up to what we discussed in Chapter 6?

of people from union households with that of people not from union households. The pattern is fairly clear: People from the union households overwhelmingly identify as Democrats (64.7 percent Democrats versus 35.3 percent Republicans), whereas people from the nonunion households, though still majority Democrat, are somewhat less likely to do so (59.0 percent Democrat versus 41.0 percent Republican). If we think in terms of independent (X) and dependent (Y) variables, the comparison that we have made is between the distribution of the dependent variable ($Y =$ Party Affiliation) across values of the independent variable ($X =$ Type of Household).

In Table 9.2, we follow the simple convention of placing the values of the independent variable in the columns and the values of the dependent variable in the rows. Then, by calculating column percentages for the cell values, this makes comparing across the columns straightforward. It is wise to adhere to these norms, because it is the easiest way to make the comparison that we want, and because it is the way many readers will expect to see the information.

In our next example we are going to go step-by-step through a bivariate test of the hypothesis that gender (X) is related to empathy (Y). To test this hypothesis about gender and empathy, we are going to use data from the 2012 and 2014 General Social Surveys. Before we look at results obtained by using actual data, think briefly about the measurement of the variables of interest and what we would expect to find if there was no relationship between the two variables.

Table 9.3 shows partial information for the gender and empathy example. Empathy is measured using the following GSS question: "Please tell me whether you strongly agree, agree, neither agree nor disagree, disagree, or disagree strongly with the following statement. These days people need to look after themselves and not overly worry about others." We combined responses of strongly agree and agree into a "non-empathetic" category, and responses of disagree and disagree strongly into an "empathetic" category. Since the response "neither agree nor disagree" does not allow for placement into either the non-empathetic or empathetic category, we

Table 9.3 Gender and empathy, 2012 and 2014 GSS

Empathy	Male	Female	Row total
Empathetic	?	?	58.6
Not empathetic	?	?	41.4
Column total	100.0	100.0	100.0

Note: Cell entries are column percentages.

examine only respondents who did not choose this response option. Using our measure of empathy, 58.6 percent of our sample respondents are empathetic and 41.4 percent are not empathetic. But, as the question marks inside this table indicate, we do not know how empathy breaks down in terms of gender. If there were no relationship between gender and empathy, consider what we would expect to see given what we know from Table 9.3. In other words, what values should replace the question marks in Table 9.3 if there were no relationship between our independent variable (X) and dependent variable (Y)?

If there is not a relationship between gender and empathy, then we should expect to see no major differences between males and females in terms of how they respond to our measure of empathy. Because we know that 58.6 percent of our respondents are empathetic and 41.4 percent are not empathetic, what should we expect to see for males and for females? We should expect to see the same proportions of males and females who are empathetic and not empathetic. In other words, we should expect to see the question marks replaced with the values in Table 9.4. This table displays the expected cell values for the null hypothesis that there is no relationship between gender and empathy.

Table 9.5 shows the total number of respondents who fit into each column and row from the 2012 and 2014 GSS. If we do the calculations, we can see that the numbers in the rightmost column of Table 9.5 correspond with the percentages from Table 9.3. We can now combine the information

Table 9.4 Gender and empathy: expectations for hypothetical scenario if there were no relationship

Empathy	Male	Female	Row total
Empathetic	58.6	58.6	58.6
Not empathetic	41.4	41.4	41.4
Column total	100.0	100.0	100.0

Note: Cell entries are column percentages.

Table 9.5 Gender and empathy: raw number of respondents in marginal cells

Empathy	Male	Female	Row total
Empathetic	?	?	1158
Not empathetic	?	?	817
Column total	882	1093	1975

Note: Cell entries are number of respondents.

from Table 9.5 with our expectations from Table 9.4 to calculate the number of respondents that we would expect to see in each cell if gender and empathy were unrelated. We display these calculations in Table 9.6. In Table 9.7, we see the actual number of respondents that fell into each of the four cells.

Finally, in Table 9.8, we compare the observed number of cases in each cell (O) with the number of cases that we would expect to see if there were no relationship between our independent and dependent variables (E).

We can see a pattern. Among males, the proportion who are empathetic is lower than what we would expect if there were no relationship between the two variables. Also, among men, the proportion who are not empathetic is higher than what we would expect if there were no

Table 9.6 Gender and empathy: calculating the expected cell values if gender and empathy are unrelated

Empathy	Male	Female
Empathetic	(58.6% of 882) $= 0.586 \times 882 = 516.85$	(58.6% of 1093) $= 0.586 \times 1093 = 640.5$
Not empathetic	(41.4% of 882) $= 0.414 \times 882 = 365.15$	(41.4% of 1093) $= 0.414 \times 1093 = 452.5$

Note: Cell entries are expectation calculations if these two variables are unrelated.

Table 9.7 Gender and empathy: actual number of respondents

Empathy	Male	Female	Row total
Empathetic	472	686	1158
Not empathetic	410	407	817
Column total	882	1093	1975

Note: Cell entries are number of respondents.

Table 9.8 Gender and empathy: observed and expected cell frequencies

Empathy	Male	Female
Empathetic	$O = 472; E = 516.85$	$O = 686; E = 640.5$
Not empathetic	$O = 410; E = 365.15$	$O = 407; E = 452.5$

Note: Cell entries are the number observed (O) and the number expected if there were no relationship (E).

relationship. For females this pattern is reversed – the proportion who are empathetic is higher, and the proportion who are not empathetic is lower, than we would expect if there were no relationship between gender and empathy. The pattern of these differences is in line with the theory that women are more empathetic than men are. Although these differences are present, we have not yet determined that they are of such a magnitude that we should now have increased confidence in our theory. In other words, we want to know whether or not these differences are statistically significant.

To answer this question, we turn to the **chi-squared (χ^2) test for tabular association.** Karl Pearson originally developed this test when he was testing theories about the influence of nature versus nurture at the beginning of the twentieth century. His formula for the χ^2 statistic is

$$\chi^2 = \sum \frac{(O - E)^2}{E}.$$

The summation sign in this formula signifies that we sum over each cell in the table; so a 2×2 table would have four cells to add up. If we think about an individual cell's contribution to this formula, we can see the underlying logic of the χ^2 test. If the value observed, O, is exactly equal to the expected value if there were no relationship between the two variables, E, then we would get a contribution of zero from that cell to the overall formula (because $O - E$ would be zero). Thus, if all observed values were exactly equal to the values that we expect if there were no relationship between the two variables, then $\chi^2 = 0$. The more the O values differ from the E values, the greater the value will be for χ^2. Because the numerator on the right-hand side of the χ^2 formula $(O - E)$ is squared, any difference between O and E will contribute positively to the overall χ^2 value.

Here are the calculations for χ^2 made with the values in Table 9.8:

$$\begin{aligned}
\chi^2 &= \sum \frac{(O - E)^2}{E} \\
&= \frac{(472 - 516.85)^2}{516.85} + \frac{(686 - 640.50)^2}{640.50} + \frac{(410 - 365.15)^2}{365.15} \\
&\quad + \frac{(407 - 452.50)^2}{452.50} \\
&= \frac{2011.52}{516.85} + \frac{2070.25}{640.50} + \frac{2011.52}{365.15} + \frac{2070.25}{452.50} \\
&= 3.89 + 3.23 + 5.51 + 4.58 = 17.21.
\end{aligned}$$

So our calculated value of χ^2 is 17.21 based on the observed data. What do we do with this? We need to compare that 17.21 with some predetermined standard, called a **critical value,** of χ^2. If our calculated value is greater than the critical value, then we conclude that there is a relationship between the two variables; and if the calculated value is less than the critical value, we cannot make such a conclusion.

How do we obtain this critical value? First, we need a piece of information known as the degrees of freedom (df) for our test.[8] In this case, the df calculation is very simple: $\text{df} = (r - 1)(c - 1)$, where r is the number of rows in the table, and c is the number of columns in the table. In the example in Table 9.8, there are two rows and two columns, so $(2 - 1)(2 - 1) = 1$.

You can find a table with critical values of χ^2 in Appendix A. If we adopt the standard p-value of 0.05, we see that the critical value of χ^2 for $\text{df} = 1$ is 3.841. Therefore a calculated χ^2 value of 17.21 is well over the minimum value needed to achieve a p-value of 0.05. In fact, continuing out in this table, we can see that we have exceeded the critical value needed to achieve a p-value of 0.001.

At this point, we have established that the relationship between our two variables meets a conventionally accepted standard of statistical significance (i.e., $p < 0.05$). Although this result is supportive of our hypothesis, we have not yet established a causal relationship between gender and empathy. To see this, think back to the four hurdles along the route to establishing causal relationships that we discussed in Chapter 3. Thus far, we have cleared the third hurdle, by demonstrating that X (gender) and Y (empathy) covary. From what we know about gender differences in orientation toward others, we can easily cross hurdle 1, "Is there a credible causal mechanism that links X to Y?" Women might be more likely than men to display empathy toward others because, among other things, women may be socialized to have prosocial values (Beutel and Marini, 1995). If we turn to hurdle 2, "Can we rule out the possibility that Y could cause X?", we can pretty easily see that we have met this standard through basic logic. We know with confidence that changing one's level of empathy could not lead to a change in one's gender. We hit the most serious bump in the road to establishing causality for this relationship when we encounter hurdle 4, "Have we controlled for all confounding variables Z that might make the association between X and Y spurious?" Unfortunately, our answer here is that we do not yet know. In fact, with a bivariate analysis, we cannot know whether some other variable Z is relevant because, by definition, there are only two variables in such an analysis. So, until we see evidence that Z variables have been controlled for, our scorecard for this causal claim is [*y y y n*].

[8] We define degrees of freedom in the next subsection.

9.4.2 Example 2: Difference of Means

In our second example, we examine a situation in which we have a continuous dependent variable and a categorical independent variable. In this type of bivariate hypothesis test, we are looking to see if the means are different across the values of the independent variable. We follow the basic logic of hypothesis testing: comparing our real-world data with what we would expect to find if there were no relationship between our independent and dependent variables. We use the sample means and standard deviations to make inferences about the unobserved population.

To illustrate a difference of means test, we use years of education as our continuous dependent variable and race (for present purposes, non-Hispanic blacks and non-Hispanic whites only) as our categorical independent variable.

The 2000 to 2014 GSS surveys are our database. To get a better idea of the data we are comparing, we can turn to a graph that we introduced in Chapter 7 for viewing the distribution of continuous variables. Figure 9.1 presents box–whisker plots of years of education for non-Hispanic whites and non-Hispanic blacks, respectively. On the basis of this figure it appears that whites have slightly higher education than blacks.

To determine whether the differences in the figures are statistically significant, we turn to a difference of means test. In this test we compare what we have seen in the figures with what we would expect if there were

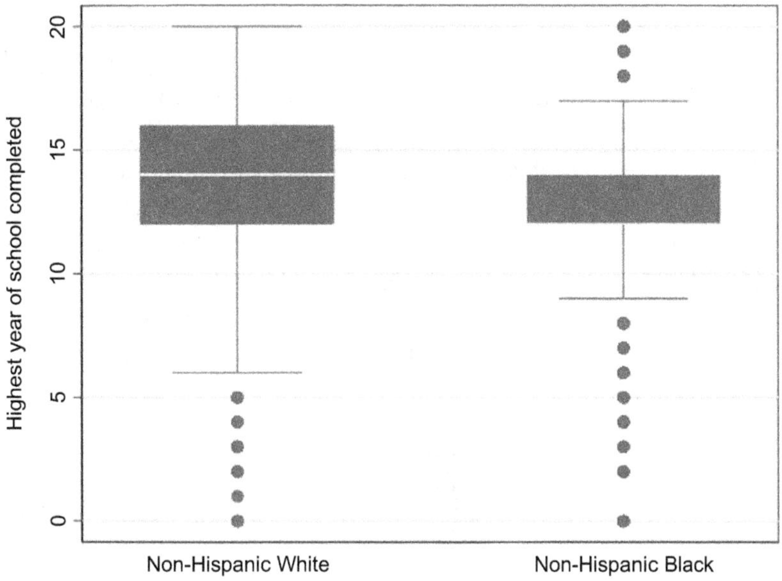

Figure 9.1 Box–whisker plot of highest year of school completed for non-Hispanic whites and non-Hispanic blacks

no relationship between race and education. If these two variables are not related, then education for both blacks and whites was drawn from the same underlying distribution. If this were the case, the average educational attainment would be the same for both groups.

To test the hypothesis that these means are drawn from the same underlying distribution, we use another test developed by Karl Pearson for these purposes. The test statistic for this is known as a *t*-test because it follows the *t*-distribution. The formula for this particular *t*-test is

$$t = \frac{\bar{Y}_1 - \bar{Y}_2}{\text{se}(\bar{Y}_1 - \bar{Y}_2)},$$

where $\bar{Y}_1$ is the mean of the dependent variable for the first value of the independent variable, $\bar{Y}_2$ is the mean of the dependent variable for the second value of the independent variable, and $\text{se}(\bar{Y}_1 - \bar{Y}_2)$ is the standard error of the difference between the two means. We can see from this formula that the greater the difference between the mean value of the dependent variable across the two values of the independent variable, the further the value of t will be from zero.

In Chapter 8 we introduced the notion of a standard error, which is a measure of uncertainty about a statistical estimate. The basic logic of a standard error is that the larger it is, the more uncertainty (or less confidence) we have in our ability to make precise statements. Similarly, the smaller the standard error, the greater our confidence about our ability to make precise statements.

To better understand the contribution of the numerator and denominator of the *t*-calculation for a difference of means, look again at Figure 9.1. The further apart the two means are and the less dispersed the distributions (as measured by the standard deviations s_1 and s_2), the greater confidence we have that $\bar{Y}_1$ and $\bar{Y}_2$ are different from each other.

Table 9.9 presents the descriptive statistics for educational attainment by race. From the values displayed in this table, we can calculate the *t*-test statistic for our hypothesis test. The standard error of the difference between two means ($\bar{Y}_1$ and $\bar{Y}_2$), $\text{se}(\bar{Y}_1 - \bar{Y}_2)$, is calculated from the following formula:

$$\text{se}(\bar{Y}_1 - \bar{Y}_2) = \sqrt{\left(\frac{(n_1 - 1)s_1^2 + (n_2 - 1)s_2^2}{n_1 + n_2 - 2}\right)} \times \sqrt{\left(\frac{1}{n_1} + \frac{1}{n_2}\right)},$$

where n_1 and n_2 are the sample sizes, and s_1^2 and s_2^2 are the sample variances. If we label the years of education of whites Y_1 and the years

Table 9.9 Race and educational attainment

Race	Number of observations	Mean	Standard deviation
White	14,083	13.82	2.83
Black	2,788	12.89	2.80

of education of blacks Y_2, then we can calculate the standard error as

$$\begin{aligned} se(\bar{Y}_1 - \bar{Y}_2) &= \sqrt{\left(\frac{(14\,083-1)(2.83)^2 + (2788-1)(2.80)^2}{14\,083+2788-2}\right)} \\ &\quad \times \sqrt{\left(\frac{1}{14\,083} + \frac{1}{2788}\right)} \\ &= 0.06 \end{aligned}$$

Now that we have the standard error, we can calculate the t-statistic:

$$t = \frac{\bar{Y}_1 - \bar{Y}_2}{se(\bar{Y}_1 - \bar{Y}_2)} = \frac{13.82 - 12.89}{0.06} = \frac{0.93}{0.06} = 15.50.$$

Now that we have calculated this t-statistic, we need one more piece of information before we can get to our p-value. This is called the **degrees of freedom** (df). Degrees of freedom reflect the basic idea that we will gain confidence in an observed pattern as the amount of data on which that pattern is based increases. In other words, as our sample size increases, we become more confident about our ability to say things about the underlying population. If we turn to Appendix B, which is a table of critical values for t, we can see that it reflects this logic. This table also follows the same basic logic as the χ^2 table. The way to read such a table is that the columns are defined by targeted p-values, and, to achieve a particular target p-value, you need to obtain a particular value of t. The rows in the t-table indicate the number of degrees of freedom. As the number of degrees of freedom goes up, the t-statistic we need to obtain a particular p-value goes down. We calculate the degrees of freedom for a difference of means t-statistic based on the sum of total sample size minus two. Thus our degrees of freedom is

$$n_1 + n_2 - 2 = 14\,083 + 2788 - 2 = 16\,871.$$

From the p-value, we can look across the row for which df $= \alpha$ and see the minimum t-value needed to achieve each targeted value of p. In the second column of the t-table, we can see that, to have a p-value of 0.10 (meaning that there is a 10 percent, or one in ten, chance that we would see this relationship randomly in our sample if there were no relationship between

X and Y in the underlying population), we must have a t-statistic greater than or equal to 1.282. Because $15.50 > 1.282$, we can proceed to the next column for $p = 0.05$ and see that 15.50 is also greater than 1.645. In fact, if we go all the way to the end of the row for df $= \infty$, we can see that our t-statistic is greater than 3.090, which is the t-value needed to achieve $p = 0.001$ (meaning that there is a 0.1 percent, or one in 1000, chance that we would see this relationship randomly in our sample if there were no relationship between X and Y in the underlying population). This indicates that we have very confidently cleared the third hurdle in our assessment of whether or not there is a causal relationship between race and educational attainment.

9.4.3 Example 3: Correlation Coefficient

In our next example of bivariate hypothesis testing we look at a situation in which both the independent variable and the dependent variable are continuous. We test the hypothesis that there is a positive relationship between the unemployment rate and citizen support for government assistance to the poor. The theory is that in periods when the economy is struggling, as indicated by increasing unemployment rates, citizen support for government assistance to the poor will be higher than in periods when the economy is functioning better and unemployment rates are declining.

In Chapter 7 we discussed the variation (or variance) of a single variable, and in Chapter 1 we introduced the concept of covariation. In the examples that we have looked at so far, we have found there to be covariation between being from a union household and party affiliation, between gender and empathy, and between race and years of schooling. All of these examples used at least one categorical variable. When we have an independent variable and a dependent variable that are both continuous, we can visually detect covariation pretty easily in graphs. Consider the graph in Figure 9.2, which shows a scatter plot of annual unemployment rates and citizen support for government assistance to the poor in selected years between 1975 and 2014.[9] Scatter plots are useful for getting an initial look at the relationship between two continuous variables. Any time that you examine a scatter plot, you should figure out what are the axes and then what each point in the scatter plot represents. In these plots,

[9] The wording for the government assistance question is: "Some people think that the government in Washington should do everything possible to improve the standard of living of all poor Americans; they are at point 1 on this card. Other people think it is not the government's responsibility, and that each person should take care of himself; they are at point 5. Where would you place yourself on this scale, or haven't you made up your mind on this?"

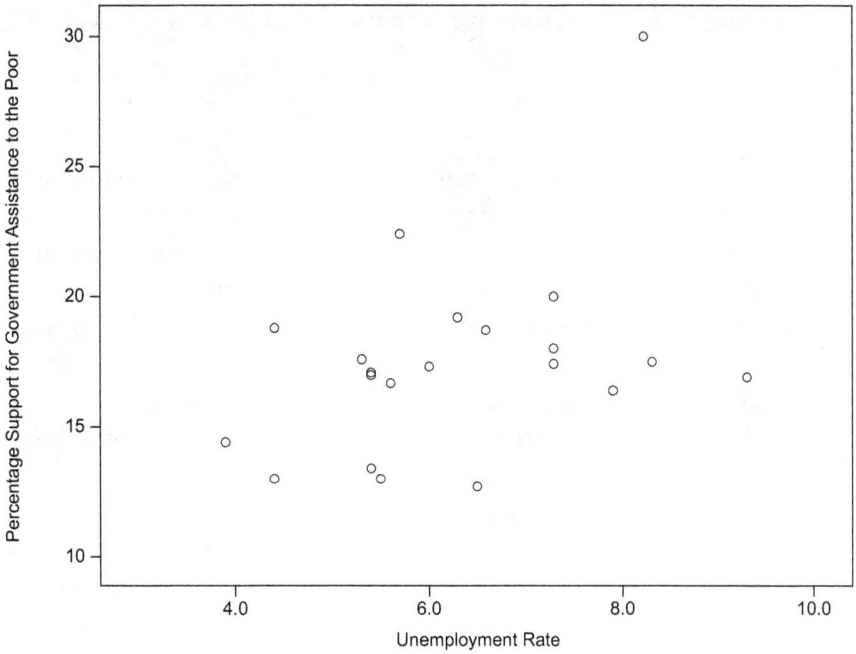

Figure 9.2 Scatter plot of unemployment rate and percentage of support for government assistance to the poor, selected years 1975–2014

the dependent variable (in this case support for government assistance to the poor) should be displayed on the vertical axis, while the independent variable (in this case unemployment rates) should be displayed on the horizontal axis. Each point in the scatter plot should represent the values for the two variables for an individual case. So, in Figure 9.2, we are looking at the values of support for government assistance to the poor and unemployment rates for every year between 1975 and 2014 in which we have data for both variables.

When we look at this graph, we want to assess whether or not we see a pattern. Since our theory implies that the independent variable causes the dependent variable, we should move from left to right on the horizontal axis (representing increasing values of the independent variable) and see whether there is a corresponding increase or decrease in the values of the dependent variable. In the case of Figure 9.2, as we move from left to right, we generally see a pattern of increasing values on the vertical axis. This indicates that, as expected by our hypothesis, when unemployment rates increase (more rightward values on the horizontal axis), we also tend to see higher percentages in favor of government assistance to the poor (higher values on the vertical axis).

Covariance is a statistical way of summarizing the general pattern of association (or the lack thereof) between two continuous variables. The formula for covariance between two variables X and Y is

$$\text{cov}_{XY} = \frac{\sum_{i=1}^{n}(X_i - \bar{X})(Y_i - \bar{Y})}{n-1}.$$

To better understand the intuition behind the covariance formula, it is helpful to think of individual cases in terms of their values relative to the mean of X ($\bar{X}$) and the mean of Y ($\bar{Y}$). If an individual case has a value for the independent variable that is greater than the mean of X ($X_i - \bar{X} > 0$) and its value for the dependent variable is greater than the mean of Y ($Y_i - \bar{Y} > 0$), that case's contribution to the numerator in the covariance equation will be positive. If an individual case has a value for the independent variable that is less than the mean of X ($X_i - \bar{X} < 0$) and a value of the dependent variable that is less than the mean of Y ($Y_i - \bar{Y} < 0$), that case's contribution to the numerator in the covariance equation will also be positive, because multiplying two negative numbers yields a positive product. If a case has a combination of one value greater than the mean and one value less than the mean, its contribution to the numerator in the covariance equation will be negative, because multiplying a positive number by a negative number yields a negative product.

Figure 9.3 illustrates this; we see the same plot of unemployment versus support for government assistance to the poor, but with the addition of lines showing the mean value of each variable. In each of these mean-delimited quadrants, we can see the contribution of the cases to the numerator. If a plot contains cases in mostly the upper-right and lower-left quadrants, the covariance will tend to be positive. On the other hand, if a plot contains cases in mostly the lower-right and upper-left quadrants, the covariance will tend to be negative. If a plot contains a balance of cases in all four quadrants, the covariance calculation will be close to zero because the positive and negative values will cancel out each other. When the covariance between two variables is positive, we describe this situation as a positive relationship between the variables, and when the covariation between two variables is negative, we describe this situation as a negative relationship.

Table 9.10 presents the calculations for each year in the covariance formula for the data that we presented in Figure 9.3. For each year, we have started out by calculating the difference between each X and $\bar{X}$, and the difference between each Y and $\bar{Y}$. If we begin with the year 1975, we can see that the value for unemployment (X_{1975}) was 8.2 and the value for government assistance (Y_{1975}) was 30.0. The value for unemployment is greater than the mean and the value for government assistance is greater than the mean, $X_{1975} - \bar{X} = 8.2 - 6.29 = 1.91$ and $Y_{1975} - \bar{Y} = 30.0 - 17.5 = 12.5$. In Figure 9.3, the dot for 1975 is in the upper-right quadrant.

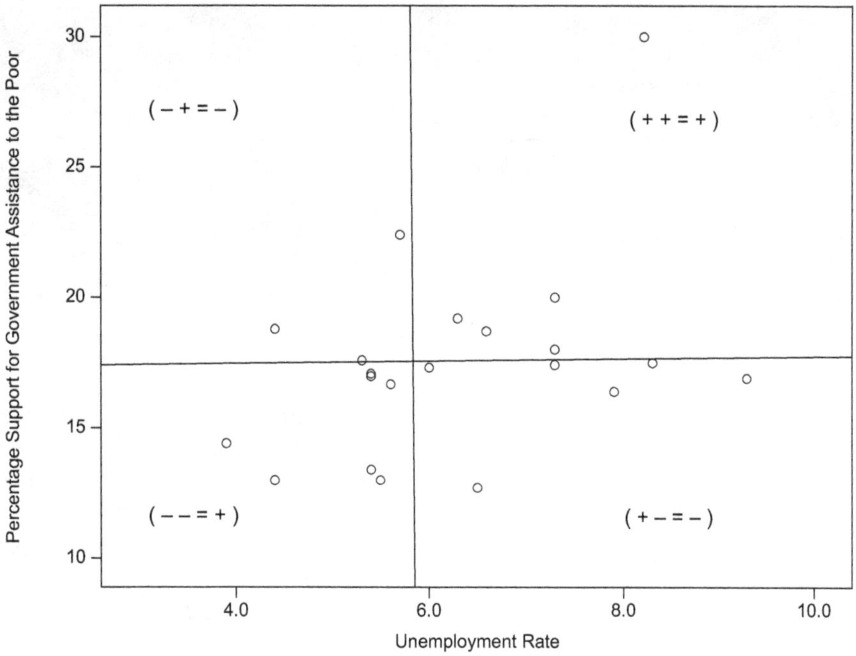

Figure 9.3 Scatter plot of unemployment rate and percentage support for government assistance to the poor with mean-delimited quadrants, selected years 1975–2014

When we multiply these two mean deviations together, we get $(X_{1975} - \bar{X})(Y_{1975} - \bar{Y}) = 23.87$.

We repeat this same calculation for every case (year). Each negative calculation contributes evidence that the overall relationship between X and Y is negative, whereas each positive calculation contributes evidence that the overall relationship between X and Y is positive. The sum across all 21 years of data in Table 9.10 is 41.69, indicating that the positive values have outweighed the negative values. When we divide this by 20, we have the sample covariance, which equals 2.085. This tells us that we have a positive relationship, but it does not tell us how confident we can be that this relationship is different from what we would see if our independent and dependent variables were not related in our underlying population of interest. To see this, we turn to a third test developed by Karl Pearson, Pearson's correlation coefficient. This is also known as **Pearson's *r***, the formula for which is

$$r = \frac{\text{cov}_{XY}}{\sqrt{\text{var}_X \, \text{var}_Y}}.$$

Table 9.10 Contributions of individual election years to the covariance calculation

Year	Unemployment (X_i)	Government Assistance (Y_i)	$X_i - \bar{X}$	$Y_i - \bar{Y}$	$(X_i - \bar{X})(Y_i - \bar{Y})$
1975	8.2	30.0	1.91	12.5	23.87
1983	8.3	17.5	2.01	0.0	0.0
1984	7.3	18.0	1.01	0.5	0.50
1986	6.6	18.7	0.31	1.2	0.37
1987	5.7	22.4	−0.59	4.9	−2.89
1988	5.3	17.6	−0.99	0.1	−0.10
1989	5.4	17.0	−0.89	−0.5	0.44
1990	6.3	19.2	0.01	1.7	0.02
1991	7.3	17.4	1.01	−0.1	−0.10
1993	6.5	12.7	0.21	−4.8	−1.01
1994	5.5	13.0	−0.79	−4.5	3.56
1996	5.4	13.4	−0.89	−4.1	3.65
1998	4.4	13.0	−1.89	−4.5	8.50
2000	3.9	14.4	−2.39	−3.1	7.41
2002	6.0	17.3	0.29	−0.2	0.06
2004	5.4	17.1	−0.89	−0.4	0.36
2006	4.4	18.8	−1.89	1.3	−2.46
2008	7.3	20.0	1.01	2.5	2.52
2010	9.3	16.9	3.01	−0.6	−1.81
2012	7.9	16.4	1.61	−1.1	−1.76
2014	5.6	16.7	−0.69	−0.8	0.55
	$\bar{X} = 6.29$	$\bar{Y} = 17.5$			$\sum(X_i - \bar{X})(Y_i - \bar{Y}) = 41.69$

Table 9.11 Covariance table for unemployment and support for government assistance to the poor, 1975–2014

	Unemployment	Assistance
Unemployment	2.014	
Assistance	2.085	14.271

Table 9.11 is a covariance table. In a covariance table, the cells across the main diagonal (from upper left to lower right) are cells for which the column and the row reference the same variable. In this case the cell entry is the variance for the referenced variable. Each of the cells off of the main diagonal displays the covariance for a pair of variables. In covariance tables, the cells above the main diagonal are often left blank, because the values in these cells are a mirror image of the values in the corresponding cells below the main diagonal. For instance, in Table 9.11 the covariance between assistance and unemployment is the same as the

covariance between unemployment and assistance, so the upper-right cell in this table is left blank.

Using the entries in Table 9.11, we can calculate the correlation coefficient:

$$\begin{aligned} r &= \frac{\text{cov}_{XY}}{\sqrt{\text{var}_X \, \text{var}_Y}} \\ &= \frac{2.085}{\sqrt{2.014 \times 14.271}} \\ &= \frac{2.085}{\sqrt{28.742}} \\ &= \frac{2.085}{5.361} \\ &= 0.389. \end{aligned}$$

There are a couple of points worth noting about the correlation coefficient. If all of the points in the plot line up perfectly on a straight, positively sloping line, the correlation coefficient will equal +1.0. If all of the points in the plot line up perfectly on a straight, negatively sloping line, the correlation coefficient will equal −1.0. Otherwise, the values will lie between +1.0 and −1.0. This standardization of correlation coefficient values is a particularly useful improvement over the covariance calculation. Additionally, we can calculate a *t*-statistic for a correlation coefficient as

$$t_r = \frac{r\sqrt{n-2}}{\sqrt{1-r^2}},$$

with $n - 2$ degrees of freedom, where n is the number of cases. In this case, our degrees of freedom equal $21 - 2 = 19$.

For the current example,

$$\begin{aligned} t_r &= \frac{r\sqrt{n-2}}{\sqrt{1-r^2}} \\ &= \frac{0.389\sqrt{21-2}}{\sqrt{1-(0.389)^2}} \\ &= \frac{0.389 \times 4.359}{\sqrt{1-0.1512}} \\ &= \frac{1.696}{\sqrt{0.849}} \\ &= \frac{1.696}{0.921} \\ &= 1.840. \end{aligned}$$

With the degrees of freedom equal to 21 ($n = 21$) minus two, or 19, we can now turn to the *t*-table in Appendix B. Looking down the column labeled “df” for 19, we see that there is no row corresponding to 19 df. In such cases we can use an online tool that calculates exact values of

t for us. Visit www.danielsoper.com/statcalc/calculator.aspx?id=10. Scroll down to "t-Distribution," and click on "Student t-Value Calculator." Enter the degrees of freedom (19 in our case) and the probability level (0.05 in our case), then click "Calculate!". The "t-value (right tail)" gives us the information we need – the t-value of 1.729.[10] This tells us that the probability of seeing this relationship due to random chance is less than 0.05, or five in 100. When we estimate our correlation coefficient with a computer program, we get a more precise p-value of 0.041.[11] Thus we can be quite confident that there is covariation between the unemployment rate and support for government assistance to the poor and that our theory has successfully cleared our third causal hurdle.[12]

9.4.4 Example 4: Analysis of Variance

In our final example of bivariate hypothesis testing, we examine a situation in which the dependent variable is continuous and the independent variable is categorical. Unlike the difference of means test discussed in Section 9.4.2, however, the independent variable now has three categories instead of two. In order to determine if the means on the dependent variable differ across the three categories of the independent variable, we use a test of significance referred to as analysis of variance, or ANOVA for short. You can think of the two-sample difference of means test as a special case of ANOVA, which analyzes three or more groups simultaneously.[13] As we did in the two-group case, we use the sample means and standard deviations to make inferences about the unobserved population. If there is no relationship between the independent and dependent variables in our sample, we conclude that the group means were drawn from the same underlying distribution – in other words, that they are all equal.

10 A one-tailed test is appropriate in this instance because our theory predicts that support will be higher when unemployment increases. We discuss both one- and two-tailed tests in detail in Chapter 10.

11 Most computer programs report the p-value from a two-tailed t-test, which in this example is $p = 0.0815$

12 The first causal hurdle is pretty well cleared if we refer back to the discussion of the theory of how the state of the economy might affect support for government assistance to the poor in earlier chapters. The second causal hurdle also can be pretty well cleared logically. It is difficult to imagine that views toward government assistance Y cause the unemployment rate X.

13 We limit our discussion of ANOVA to models with a single independent variable, referred to as one-way analysis of variance.

In discussing ANOVA we will extend the race and education example from Section 9.4.2 to include Latinos in addition to African Americans and whites. To test whether or not the educational attainments of these three groups differ, we pose the following null and alternative hypotheses:

$$H_0: \quad \mu_1 = \mu_2 = \mu_3,$$

$$H_1: \quad \mu_1 \neq \mu_2 \neq \mu_3,$$

where μ_1, μ_2, and μ_3 refer to the population means of whites, African Americans, and Latinos, respectively. In words, the null hypothesis states that, in the population from which the sample data were drawn, the means on education do not differ by racial group; the alternative hypothesis states that at least one of these group means differs from at least one of the other group means. As we did in the difference of means test in Section 9.4.2, we will use sample means to make inferences about the unknown population means.

Using the same GSS 2000 to 2014 survey years as we did in Section 9.4.2, we have a total of 19,249 respondents with no missing data on either the independent or dependent variables – 14,083 whites, 2788 African Americans, and 2378 Latinos. The mean educational attainment for all respondents, regardless of race or ethnicity, is 13.42; the mean for whites is 13.82, the mean for blacks is 12.89, and the mean for Latinos is 11.71. The question we address is whether the sample data reflect a difference in the population from which the sample was drawn.

In order to answer this question, ANOVA first partitions the variation in the dependent variable into a component due to a respondent's membership in one or another of the race/ethnic groups and a component not due to group membership. The latter quantity is referred to as error because it is variation that is unexplained by the independent variable. In order to accomplish this partitioning, ANOVA calculates three measures of variation. The first is the total variation of the scores, or SS_{Total}:

$$SS_{Total} = \sum_{j=1}^{J} \sum_{i=1}^{n_j} (Y_{ij} - \bar{Y})^2,$$

where n_j is the sample size, J is the number of groups, Y_{ij} is the score of the ith case ($i = 1, \ldots, N$) in the jth group ($j = 1, \ldots, J$) and $\bar{Y}$ = the grand mean.

Next, ANOVA decomposes the total sum of squares into two parts: the sum of squares between groups, or $SS_{Between}$, and the sum of squares within groups, or SS_{Within}. $SS_{Between}$ is a measure of the variability in the dependent variable that is explained by the independent variable; SS_{Within} is a measure of variability that is not explained by the independent variable:

$$SS_{Between} = n\sum_{j=1}^{J}(\bar{Y}_j - \bar{Y})^2.$$

$$SS_{Within} = \sum_{j=1}^{J}\sum_{i=1}^{n_j}(Y_{ij} - \bar{Y}_j^{\,2}).$$

and, thus,

$$SS_{Total} = SS_{Between} + SS_{Within}.$$

Race and Education

Let's look at an example of ANOVA using our three-category race/ethnicity independent variable and the educational attainment dependent variable. Table 9.12 displays the results of the ANOVA.

The mean squares in the table are estimates of variance, one ($MS_{Between}$) due to the independent variable and the other (MS_{Within}) due to error. Mean squares are calculated by dividing the corresponding sum of squares by their degrees of freedom. Thus,

$$MS_{Between} = SS_{Between}/df_{Between} = 10\,035.66/2 = 5017.83$$

and

$$MS_{Within} = SS_{Within}/df_{Within} = 169\,141.64/19\,246 = 8.79.$$

The F-statistic reported in the table is the ratio of the two mean squares and is distributed on v_1 and v_2 degrees of freedom:

$$F_{J-1,N-J} = MS_{Between}/MS_{Within} = 5017.83/8.79 = 570.96.$$

The last column in Table 9.12 indicates that the F-ratio is significant at the 0.001 p-value level.

Table 9.12 ANOVA of educational attainment by racial identification

	Sum of squares	df	Mean squares	F	Sig.
Between groups	10,035.66	2	5017.83	570.96	0.001
Within groups	169,141.64	19,246	8.79		
Total	179,177.30	19,248			

Note: Total N = 19,248: 14,083 non-Hispanic whites; 2788 non-Hispanic blacks; and 2378 Hispanics.

Given these results, what do we conclude about the effect of race-ethnicity on educational attainment? Recall that our null hypothesis is that the individual group means are all equal. With the p-value < 0.001 we can clearly reject the null in favor of the alternative hypothesis that at least one of the group means differs from at least one of the other group means. The question now is, which mean (or means) is (are) significantly different from which other mean (or means)? The ANOVA results presented so far do not allow us to answer this question. Instead, we must conduct another, related test referred to as a **multiple comparison procedure**, a topic that we address next.

9.5 MULTIPLE COMPARISONS

The F-statistic in Table 9.12 allows us to conclude that not all of the population means are equal to each other. It does not, however, give us the information we need to determine which particular means differ significantly from which others. You might wonder (reasonably) why a series of pairwise t-tests like those we performed in Section 9.4.2, with every mean compared to every other mean, is not conducted. The answer is that such a procedure does not guarantee that the individual tests are independent of one another, with the result that one or more of the pairwise comparisons might exceed our alpha level. A common approach to resolving this problem is to conduct one of the several multiple comparison procedures that are available in most statistical software packages.

Table 9.13 presents the results of one commonly used multiple comparison procedure, the Scheffe test. The first row of the table compares means on education for non-Hispanic whites with the means for non-Hispanic blacks and Hispanics; the second row compares blacks with whites and Hispanics; and the third row compares Hispanics with whites and blacks.

Table 9.13 Scheffe multiple comparison test of race/ethnic differences in education

					95% Conf. int.	
Race/ethnicity	Race/ethnicity	Mean diff.	Std. er.	Sig.	Lo bound	Hi bound
Non-Hisp. wh.	Non-Hisp. bl.	0.934*	0.061	0.001	0.78	1.08
	Hispanic	2.114*	0.066	0.001	1.95	2.28
Non-Hisp. bl.	Non-Hisp. wh.	−0.934*	0.061	0.001	−1.08	−0.78
	Hispanic	1.180*	0.083	0.001	0.98	1.38
Hispanic	Non-Hisp. wh.	−2.114*	0.066	0.001	−2.28	−1.95
	Non-Hisp. bl.	−1.180*	0.083	0.001	−1.38	−0.98

Note: *Indicates $p < 0.05$.

The column labeled "Mean diff." displays the absolute magnitude of the difference in means between the groups being compared. Thus, the mean for whites (13.82) minus the mean for blacks (12.89) = 0.93. Also displayed for each comparison is the standard error of the difference in means, the significance levels of the difference, and 95 percent confidence intervals for the estimates. The most important finding in Table 9.13 is that the mean on education for every race/ethnic group is significantly different from every other mean. Thus, we can conclude with a high degree of confidence that in the population from which the GSS samples were drawn, the mean educational attainment for whites is higher than the mean for blacks and is higher than the mean for Hispanics, and that the mean for blacks is higher than the mean for Hispanics. Together with the ANOVA results reported in Table 9.12, the multiple comparison test provides strong evidence of continuing racial and ethnic differences in educational attainment between 2000 and 2014.

9.6 WRAPPING UP

We have introduced four methods to conduct bivariate hypothesis tests – tabular analysis, difference of means tests, correlation coefficients, and analysis of variance. Which test is most appropriate in any given situation depends on the measurement metric of your independent and dependent variables. Table 9.1 should serve as a helpful reference for you on this front.

We have yet to introduce the final method for conducting bivariate hypothesis tests covered in this book, namely bivariate regression analysis. That is the topic of our next chapter, and it serves as the initial building block for multiple regression (which we will cover in Chapter 11).

CONCEPTS INTRODUCED IN THIS CHAPTER

- analysis of variance – a method of hypothesis testing that is appropriate for a categorical independent variable with three or more categories and a continuous dependent variable
- chi-squared (χ^2) test for tabular association – a statistical test for a relationship between two categorical variables
- correlation coefficient – a measure of linear association between two continuous variables
- covariance – an unstandardized statistical measure summarizing the general pattern of association (or the lack thereof) between two continuous variables

- critical value – a predetermined standard for a statistical test such that if the calculated value is greater than the critical value, then we conclude that there is a relationship between the two variables; and if the calculated value is less than the critical value, we cannot make such a conclusion
- degrees of freedom – the number of pieces of information we have beyond the minimum that we would need to make a particular inference
- difference of means test – a method of bivariate hypothesis testing that is appropriate for a categorical independent variable with two categories and a continuous dependent variable
- multiple comparisons – a statistical procedure used if the null hypothesis of equality of population means in an ANOVA model is rejected; multiple comparisons allow us to determine which mean(s) is(are) significantly different from which other mean(s)
- Pearson's r – the most commonly employed correlation coefficient
- p-value – the probability that we would see the relationship that we are finding because of random chance
- statistically significant relationship – a conclusion, based on the observed data, that the relationship between two variables is not due to random chance, and therefore exists in the broader population
- tabular analysis – a type of bivariate analysis that is appropriate for two categorical variables

EXERCISES

1. What form of bivariate hypothesis test would be appropriate for the following research questions:

   (a) You want to test the theory that being female causes lower salaries.

   (b) You want to test the theory that a state's percentage of college graduates is positively related to its turnout percentage.

   (c) You want to test the theory that individuals with higher incomes are more likely than those with lower incomes to vote in national elections.

2. Explain why each of the following statements is either true or false:

   (a) The computer program gave me a p-value of 0.000, so I know that my theory has been verified.

   (b) The computer program gave me a p-value of 0.02, so I know that I have found a very strong relationship.

MORAL VALUES – THE TRANSATLANTIC GULF

Q How often do you go to church?

	BRITAIN				US	
	All voters	Labour voters	Tory voters	Lib Dem voters	Bush voters	Kerry voters
More than weekly	2%	2%	3%	1%	63%	35%
Weekly	10%	10%	13%	7%	58%	41%
Monthly	5%	6%	4%	6%	50%	50%
A few times a year	36%	36%	38%	40%	44%	55%
Never	47%	46%	43%	44%	34%	64%

Q Which of the following is closest to your view of what the law should say about abortion?

	All voters	Labour voters	Tory voters	Lib Dem voters	Bush voters	Kerry voters
Always legal: absolute right to choose	38%	45%	34%	46%	24%	74%
Mostly legal: some restrictions	36%	35%	40%	32%	37%	62%
Mostly illegal: only in exceptional circumstances	19%	14%	18%	17%	72%	27%
Always illegal	4%	4%	3%	3%	77%	22%

Q Which of the following is closest to your view of what the law should be towards same-sex couples?

	All voters	Labour voters	Tory voters	Lib Dem voters	Bush voters	Kerry voters
Legal right to marry	28%	33%	18%	31%	22%	77%
Legally civil union but not marriage	37%	37%	39%	47%	51%	48%
No legal recognition of same sex couples	29%	23%	39%	20%	69%	30%

Figure 9.4 What is wrong with this table? (Table taken from "On God and sex there is a moral divide between Britain and US." *The Times*, London, November 10, 2004. See www.thetimes.co.uk/article/on-god-and-sex-there-is-a-moral-divide-between-britain-and-us-hsj2bpnvvj0. Sources: for British figures, Populus poll for *The Times* (November 5–7); for American figures, exit polls conducted by National Election Poll (November 2).)

(c) The computer program gave me a p-value of 0.07, so I know that this relationship is due to random chance.

(d) The computer program gave me a p-value of 0.50, so I know that there is only a 50 percent chance of this relationship being systematic.

3. Take a look at Figure 9.4. What is the dependent variable? What are the independent variables? What does this table tell us about the "transatlantic gulf"?

4. What makes the table in Figure 9.4 so confusing?

5. Conduct a tabular analysis from the information presented in the following hypothetical discussion of polling results: "We did a survey of 800 respondents and asked them about their views on gun control. Among these respondents, 45 percent favored tighter restrictions on the sale of guns and 55 percent opposed tighter restrictions. When we split the respondents in half at the median age of 40, we found some stark differences: Among the younger half of the sample respondents, we found that 72.2 percent opposed tighter restrictions and among the older sample respondents, we found that 68.2 percent favored restrictions."

6. For the example in Exercise 5, test the theory that age is related to views on gun control.

7. A lot of people in the United States think that the Watergate scandal in 1972 caused a sea change in terms of U.S. citizens' views toward incumbent politicians. Use the data in Table 9.14 to produce a difference of means test of the null hypothesis that average re-election rates were the same before and after the Watergate scandal. Because of the timing of the elections and the scandal, 1972 should be coded as a pre-scandal case. Do this test once each for the House and the Senate. Show all of your work.

8. Using the "GSS2018" dataset (which is available on the textbook's website at www.cambridge.org/fsr), produce a table that shows the cross-tabulation of the variables "Gunlaw" (Y) and "Xnorcsiz" (X). Read the descriptions of these two variables in the GSS2018 codebook (which is also available on the textbook's website) and write about what this table tells you about the relationship between size of place of residence and views on gun control in 2018. Dichotomize "Xnorcsiz" into urban (codes 1 through 6) and nonurban (codes 7 through 10) categories before doing your analysis.

9. Using the "GSS2018" dataset, test the hypothesis that values of "Educ" (Y) are different for African Americans (code 2 on "Racecen1") and Latinos (code 16 on "Racecen1") (X) in 2018. Read the descriptions of these two variables in the codebook and write about what this analysis tells you about the gap in educational attainment between the two largest minority groups in the U.S.

Table 9.14 Incumbent re-election rates in U.S. congressional elections, 1964–2006

Year	House	Senate
1964	87	85
1966	88	88
1968	97	71
1970	85	77
1972	94	74
1974	88	85
1976	96	64
1978	94	60
1980	91	55
1982	90	93
1984	95	90
1986	98	75
1988	98	85
1990	96	96
1992	88	83
1994	90	92
1996	94	91
1998	98	90
2000	98	79
2002	96	86
2004	98	96
2006	94	79

10. Using the "GSS2018" dataset, produce a scatter plot of the values for "Educ" (Y) and "Income16" (X). Calculate a correlation coefficient and p-value for the hypothesis that these two variables are related to each other. Read the descriptions of these two variables and write about what the scatter plot and table tell you about the relationship between education and income in 2018.

10 Two-Variable Regression Models

OVERVIEW

Regression models are the workhorses of data analysts in a wide range of fields in the social sciences. We begin this chapter with a discussion of fitting a line to a scatter plot of data, and then we discuss the additional inferences that can be made when we move from a correlation coefficient to a two-variable regression model. We include discussions of measures of goodness-of-fit and on the nature of hypothesis testing and statistical significance in regression models. Throughout this chapter, we present important concepts in text, mathematical formulae, and graphical illustrations. This chapter concludes with a discussion of the assumptions of the regression model and minimal mathematical requirements for estimation.

10.1 TWO-VARIABLE REGRESSION

In Chapter 9 we introduced four different bivariate hypothesis tests. In this chapter we add a fifth: two-variable regression. This is an important first step toward the multiple regression model – which is the topic of Chapter 11 – in which we are able to "control for" another variable (Z) as we measure the relationship between our independent variable of interest (X) and our dependent variable (Y). It is crucial to develop an in-depth understanding of two-variable regression before moving to multiple regression. In the sections that follow, we begin with an overview of the two-variable regression model, in which a line is fit to a scatter plot of data. We then discuss the uncertainty associated with the line and how we use various measures of this uncertainty to make inferences about the underlying population. This chapter concludes with a discussion of the assumptions of the regression model and the minimal mathematical requirements for model estimation.

10.2 FITTING A LINE: POPULATION ⇔ SAMPLE

The basic idea of two-variable regression is that we are fitting the "best" line through a scatter plot of data. This line, which is defined by its slope and y-intercept, serves as a **statistical model** of reality. In this sense, two-variable regression is very different from three of the four hypothesis-testing techniques that we introduced in Chapter 9; although those techniques allow hypothesis testing, only ANOVA produces a statistical model.

You may remember from a geometry course the formula for a line expressed as

$$Y = a + bx,$$

where a is the y-intercept and b is the slope – often explained as the "rise-over-run" component of the line formula. For a one-unit increase (run) in X, b is the corresponding amount of rise in Y (or fall in Y, if b is negative). Together, these two elements (a and b) are described as the line's **parameters**.[1] You may remember exercises from junior high or high-school math classes in which you were given the values of a and b and then asked to draw the resulting line on graph paper. Once we know these two parameters for a line, we can draw that line across any range of X values.[2]

In a two-variable regression model, we represent the y-intercept parameter by the Greek letter alpha (α) and the slope parameter by the Greek letter beta (β).[3] As foreshadowed by all of our other discussions of variables, Y is the dependent variable and X is the independent variable. Our theory about the underlying population in which we are interested is expressed in the **population regression model:**

$$Y_i = \alpha + \beta X_i + u_i.$$

Note that in this model there is one additional component, u_i, which does not correspond with what we are used to seeing in line formulae from geometry classes. This term is the **stochastic** (or "random") component of our dependent variable. We have this term because we do not expect all of our data points to line up perfectly on a straight line. This corresponds directly with our discussion in earlier chapters about the probabilistic (as opposed to deterministic) nature of causal theories about

1 The term "parameter" is a synonym for "boundary" with a more mathematical connotation. In the description of a line, the parameters (a and b in this case) are fixed whereas the variables (X and Y in this case) vary.

2 If this is not familiar to you, or if you merely want to refresh your memory, you may want to complete Exercise 1 at the end of this chapter before you continue reading.

3 Different textbooks on regression use slightly different notation for these parameters, so it is important not to assume that all textbooks use the same notation when comparing across them.

social phenomena. We are, after all, trying to explain processes that involve human behavior. Because human beings are complex, there is bound to be a fair amount of random noise in our measures of their behavior. Thus we think about the values of our dependent variable Y_i as having a systematic component, $\alpha + \beta X_i$, and a stochastic component, u_i.

As we have discussed, we rarely work with population data. Instead, we use sample data to make inferences about the underlying population of interest. In two-variable regression, we use information from the **sample regression model** to make inferences about the unseen population regression model. To distinguish between these two, we place hats ($\hat{}$) over terms in the sample regression model that are estimates of terms from the unseen population regression model. Because they have hats, we can describe $\hat{\alpha}$ and $\hat{\beta}$ as being **parameter estimates**. These terms are our best guesses of the unseen population parameters α and β:

$$\text{sample regression model} \quad Y_i = \hat{\alpha} + \hat{\beta} X_i + \hat{u}_i.$$

Note that, in the sample regression model, α, β, and u_i get hats, but Y_i and X_i do not. This is because Y_i and X_i are values for cases in the population that ended up in the sample. As such, Y_i and X_i are values that are *measured* rather than *estimated*. We use them to estimate α, β, and the u_i values. The values that define the line are the estimated systematic components of Y. For each X_i value, we use $\hat{\alpha}$ and $\hat{\beta}$ to calculate the predicted value of Y_i, which we call $\hat{Y}_i$, where

$$\hat{Y}_i = \hat{\alpha} + \hat{\beta} X_i.$$

This can also be written in terms of expectations,

$$E(Y|X_i) = \hat{Y}_i = \hat{\alpha} + \hat{\beta} X_i,$$

which means that the expected value of Y given X_i (or $\hat{Y}_i$) is equal to our formula for the two-variable regression line. So we can now talk about each Y_i as having an estimated systematic component, $\hat{Y}_i$, and an estimated stochastic component, $\hat{u}_i$. We can thus write our model as

$$Y_i = \hat{Y}_i + \hat{u}_i,$$

and we can rewrite this in terms of $\hat{u}_i$ to get a better understanding of the estimated stochastic component:

$$\hat{u}_i = Y_i - \hat{Y}_i.$$

From this formula, we can see that the estimated stochastic component ($\hat{u}_i$) is equal to the difference between the actual value of the dependent variable (Y_i) and the predicted value of the dependent variable from our two-variable regression model. Another name for the estimated stochastic

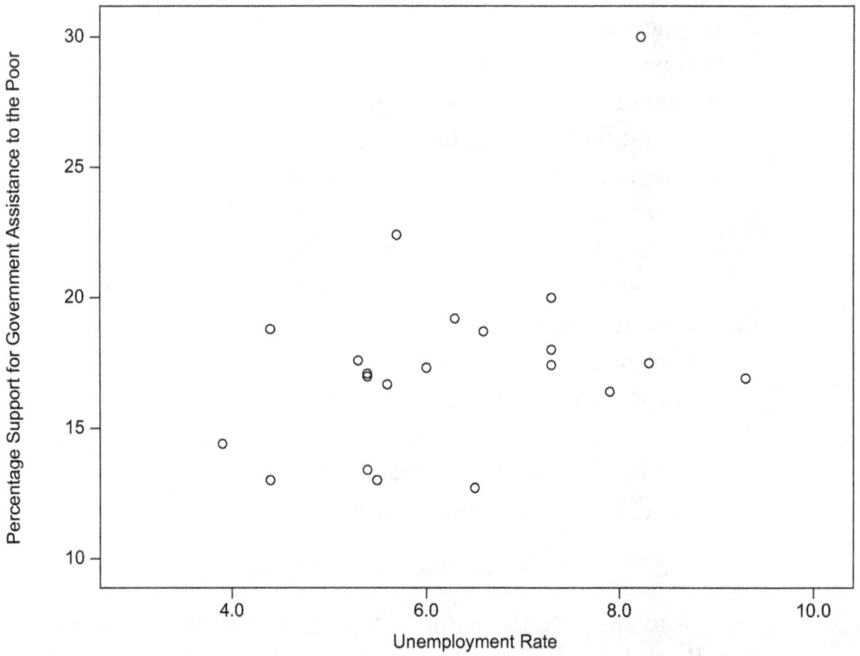

Figure 10.1 Scatter plot of unemployment rate and support for government assistance to the poor, selected years 1975–2014

component is the **residual.** "Residual" is another word for "leftover," and this is appropriate, because $\hat{u}_i$ is the leftover part of Y_i after we have drawn the line defined by $\hat{Y}_i = \hat{\alpha} + \hat{\beta}X_i$. Another way to refer to $\hat{u}_i$, which follows from the formula $\hat{u}_i = Y_i - \hat{Y}_i$, is to call it the **sample error term.** Because $\hat{u}_i$ is an estimate of u_i, a corresponding way of referring to u_i is to call it the **population error term.**

10.3 WHICH LINE FITS BEST? ESTIMATING THE REGRESSION LINE

Consider the scatter plot of data in Figure 10.1 (which reproduces our earlier Figure 9.2). Our task is to draw a straight line that describes the relationship between our independent variable X and our dependent variable Y.[4] How do we draw our line? We clearly want to draw a line that comes as close as possible to the cases in our scatter plot of data. Because the data have a general pattern from lower left to upper right, we know that our slope will be positive.

[4] By "straight line," we mean a line with a single slope that does not change as we move from left to right in our figure.

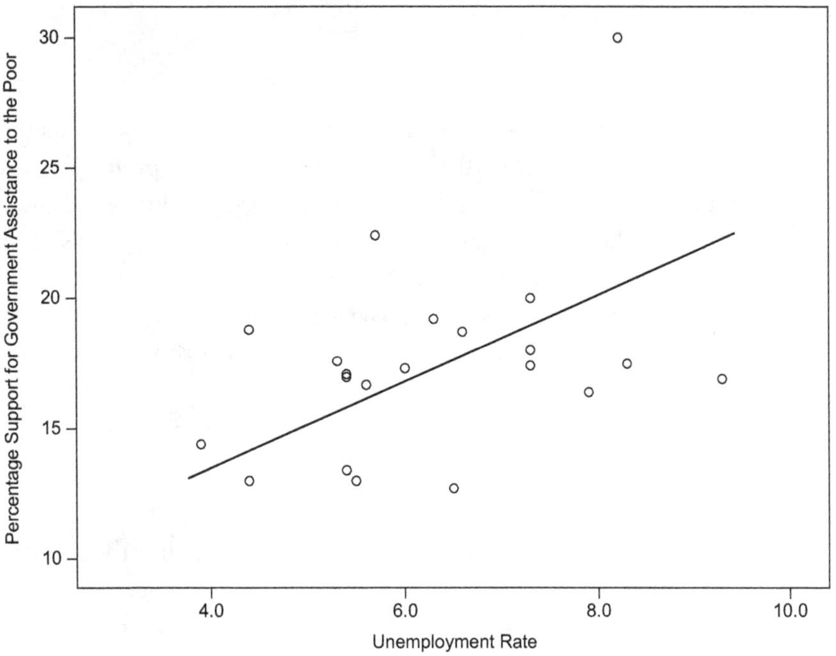

Figure 10.2 Freehand regression line

In Figure 10.2, we have drawn a freehand regression line with a positive slope through the scatter plot of unemployment rate and support for government assistance to the poor. So, how do we decide if the line fits the data that we see in our scatter plot of X_i and Y_i values? Because we are interested in explaining our dependent variable, we want our residual values, $\hat{u}_i$, which are vertical distances between each Y_i and the corresponding $\hat{Y}_i$, to be as small as possible. But, because these vertical distances come in both positive and negative values, we cannot just add them up and have a good summary of the "fit" between the line and our data.[5]

So we need a method of assessing the fit of the line in which the positive and negative residuals do not cancel each other out. One possibility is to add together the absolute value of the residuals:

$$\sum_{i=1}^{n} |\hat{u}_i|.$$

Another possibility is to add together the squared value of each of the residuals:

[5] Initially, we might think that we would want to minimize the sum of our residuals. But the line that minimizes the sum of the residuals is actually a flat line parallel to the x-axis. Such a line does not help us to explain the relationship between X and Y.

$$\sum_{i=1}^{n} \hat{u}_i^2.$$

Although the absolute-value calculation is just as valid as the squared-residual calculation, statisticians have tended to prefer the latter (both methods identify the same line as being "best"). Thus we draw a line that minimizes the sum of the *squared* residuals $\sum_{i=1}^{n} \hat{u}_i^2$. This technique for estimating the parameters of a regression model is known as **ordinary least-squares** (OLS) regression. For a two-variable OLS regression, the formulae for the parameter estimates of the line that meet this criterion are[6]

$$\hat{\beta} = \frac{\sum_{i=1}^{n}(X_i - \bar{X})(Y_i - \bar{Y})}{\sum_{i=1}^{n}(X_i - \bar{X})^2},$$

$$\hat{\alpha} = \bar{Y} - \hat{\beta}\bar{X}.$$

If we examine the formula for $\hat{\beta}$, we can see that the numerator is the same as the numerator for calculating the covariance between X and Y. Thus the logic of how each case contributes to this formula is the same. The denominator in the formula for $\hat{\beta}$ is the sum of squared deviations of the X_i values from the mean value of X ($\bar{X}$). Thus, for a given covariance between X and Y, the more (less) spread out X is, the less (more) steep the estimated slope of the regression line.

One of the mathematical properties of OLS regression is that the line produced by the parameter estimates goes through the sample mean values of X and Y. This makes the estimation of $\hat{\alpha}$ fairly simple. If we start out at the point defined by the mean value of X and the mean value of Y and then use the estimated slope ($\hat{\beta}$) to draw a line, the value of X where Y equals zero is $\hat{\alpha}$. Figure 10.3 shows the OLS regression line through the scatter plot of data. We can see from this figure that the OLS regression line passes through the point where the line depicting the mean value of X meets the line depicting the mean value of Y.

Using the data presented in Table 9.10 in the preceding formulae, we have calculated $\hat{\alpha} = 10.99$ and $\hat{\beta} = 1.04$, making our sample regression line formula $Y = 10.99 + 1.04X$. If we think about what this tells us, we first need to remember that X is the unemployment rate and Y is the percentage of respondents who support government assistance to the poor. So, if our measure of unemployment equals zero, we would expect percentage support for government assistance to the poor to be 10.99 percent. If unemployment is not equal to zero, we multiply the value of

[6] The formulae for OLS parameter estimates come from setting the sum of squared residuals equal to zero and using differential calculus to solve for the values of $\hat{\beta}$ and $\hat{\alpha}$.

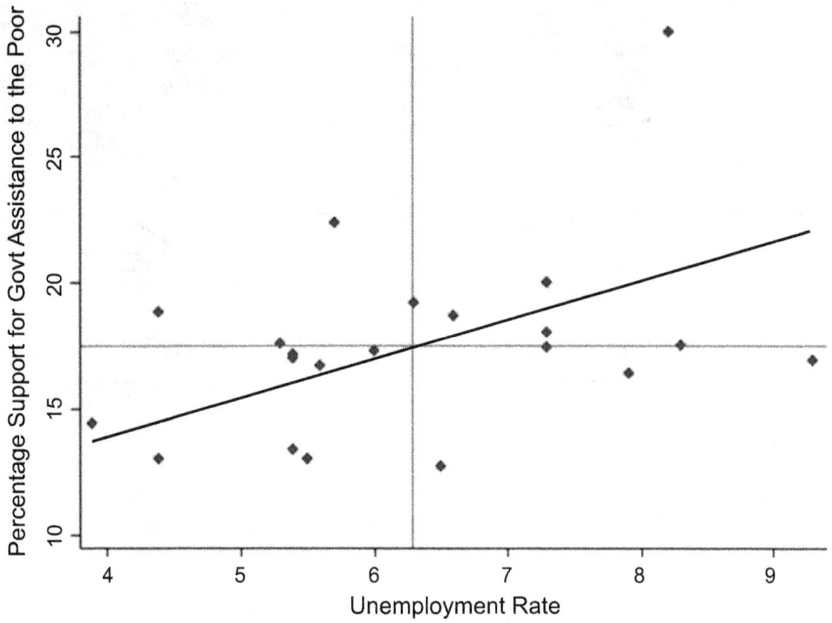

Figure 10.3 OLS regression line through scatter plot with mean-delimited quadrants

unemployment by 1.04 and add the result to 10.99 to obtain our best guess of the value of support for government assistance. Moving to the right or the left along our sample regression line in Figure 10.3 means that we are increasing or decreasing the value of unemployment. For each right–left movement, we see a corresponding rise or decline in the value of the expected level of support. If we go back to the logic of rise-over-run, our estimated slope parameter answers the question of how much change in Y we expect to see from a one-unit increase in X. In other words, a one-unit increase in our independent variable, unemployment, is expected to lead to a 1.04 increase in our dependent variable, support for government assistance.[7]

We can tell from Figure 10.3 that there are points that lie above and below our regression line. We therefore know that our model does not perfectly fit the real world. In the next section, we discuss a series of inferences that we can make about the uncertainty associated with our sample regression model.

[7] Be sure not to invert the independent and dependent variables in describing results. It is *not* correct to interpret these results to say "for every 1.04-point change in the unemployment rate, we should expect to see, on average, an extra 1 percent in the percentage of support for government assistance to the poor." Be sure that you can see the difference in those descriptions.

Source	SS	df	MS
Model	43.143	1	43.143
Residual	242.277	19	12.751
Total	285.42	20	14.271

Number of Obs = 21

F (1, 19) = 3.38

Prob > F = .082

R-squared = .151

Adj R-squared = .106

Root MSE = 3.571

Support	Coef.	Std. Err.	t	p> |t|	[95% Conf. Interval]
unemployment	1.035	0.563	1.839	.082	-0.143 2.212
_cons	10.995	3.621	3.036	.007	3.416 18.574

Figure 10.4 Results for two-variable regression model between support for government assistance and unemployment rate; support = $\alpha + \beta \times$ unemployment

10.4 MEASURING OUR UNCERTAINTY ABOUT THE OLS REGRESSION LINE

As we have seen in Chapters 8 and 9, inferences about the underlying population of interest from sample data are made with varying degrees of uncertainty. In Chapter 9 we discussed the role of *p*-values in expressing this uncertainty. With an OLS regression model, we have several different ways in which to measure our uncertainty. We discuss these measures in terms of the overall fit between X and Y first and then discuss the uncertainty about individual parameters. Our uncertainty about individual parameters is used in the testing of our hypotheses. Throughout this discussion, we refer to our example of fitting a regression line to our data on support for government assistance to the poor in order to test our theory that when the economy is struggling (as measured by rates of unemployment), citizen support for government assistance to the poor will be higher than in periods when the economy is functioning more efficiently and unemployment rates are lower. Numerical results for this model are displayed in Figure 10.4. These numerical results can be partitioned into three separate areas. The table in the upper-left corner of Figure 10.4 gives us measures of the variation in our model. The set of statistics listed in the upper-right corner of Figure 10.4 gives us a set of summary statistics about the entire model. Across the bottom of Figure 10.4 we get a table of statistics on the model's parameter estimates. The name of the dependent variable, "Support," is displayed at the top of this table. Underneath we see the name of our independent variable, "Unemployment," and "_cons," which is short for "constant" (another name for the *y*-intercept term), which we also know as $\hat{\alpha}$. Moving to the right in the table at the bottom of Figure 10.4, we see that the next column heading here is "Coef.," which is short for "coefficient," which is another name for parameter estimate. In this column we see the values of $\hat{\beta}$

and $\hat{\alpha}$, which are 1.04 and 10.99 when we round these results to the second decimal place.[8]

10.4.1 Goodness-of-Fit: Root Mean-Squared Error

Measures of the overall fit between a regression model and the dependent variable are called goodness-of-fit measures. One of the most intuitive of these measures (despite its name) is **root mean-squared error** (root MSE). This statistic is sometimes referred to as the standard error of the regression model. It provides a measure of the average accuracy of the model in the metric of the dependent variable. This statistic ("Root MSE" in Figure 10.4) is calculated as

$$\text{root MSE} = \sqrt{\frac{\sum_{i=1}^{n} \hat{u}_i^2}{n}}.$$

The squaring and then taking the square root of the quantities in this formula are done to adjust for the fact that some of our residuals will be positive (points for which Y_i is above the regression line) and some will be negative (points for which Y_i is below the regression line). Once we realize this, we can see that this statistic is basically the average distance between the data points and the regression line.

From the numeric results depicted in Figure 10.4, we can see that the root MSE for our two-variable model of support for government assistance to the poor is 3.57. This value is found on the sixth line of the column of results on the right-hand side of Figure 10.4. It indicates that, on average, our model is off by 3.57 points in predicting the percentage of respondents who support assistance. It is worth emphasizing that the root MSE is always expressed in terms of the metric in which the dependent variable is measured. The only reason why this particular value corresponds to a percentage is because the metric of the dependent variable is a percentage.

10.4.2 Goodness-of-Fit: *R*-Squared Statistic

Another popular indicator of the model's goodness-of-fit is the ***R*-squared statistic** (typically written as R^2). The R^2 statistic ranges between zero and one, indicating the proportion of the variation in the dependent variable that is accounted for by the model. The basic idea of the R^2 statistic is shown in Figure 10.5, which is a Venn diagram depiction of variations in X and Y as well as covariation between X and Y. The idea behind this diagram is that we are depicting variation in each variable with a circle.

[8] The choice of how many decimal places to report should be decided based on the value of the dependent variable. In this case, because our dependent variable is a percentage, we have chosen the second decimal place. Social scientists usually do not report results beyond the first two decimal places.

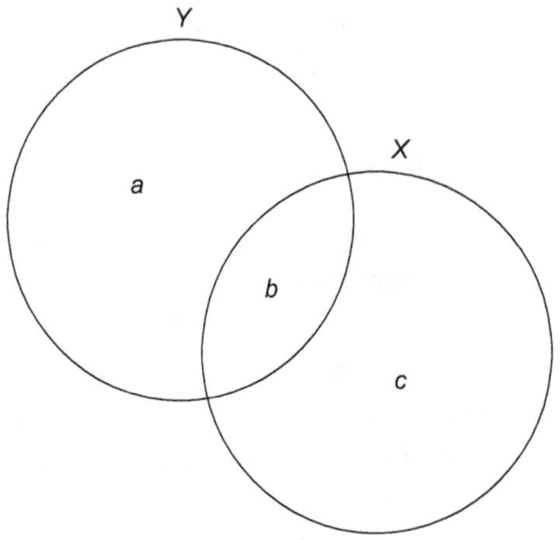

Figure 10.5 Venn diagram of variance and covariance for X and Y

The larger the circle, the larger the variation. In this figure, the variation in Y consists of two areas, a and b, and the variation in X consists of areas b and c. Area a represents variation in Y that is not related to variation in X, and area b represents covariation between X and Y. In a two-variable regression model, area a is the residual or stochastic variation in Y. The R^2 statistic is equal to area b over the total variation in Y, which is equal to the sum of areas a and b. Thus smaller values of area a and larger values of area b lead to a larger R^2 statistic. The formula for total variation in Y (areas a and b in Figure 10.5), also known as the total sum of squares (TSS), is

$$\text{TSS} = \sum_{i=1}^{n} (Y_i - \bar{Y})^2.$$

The formula for the residual variation in Y, area a that is not accounted for by X, called the residual sum of squares (RSS), is

$$\text{RSS} = \sum_{i=1}^{n} \hat{u}_i^2.$$

Once we have these two quantities, we can calculate the R^2 statistic as

$$R^2 = 1 - \frac{\text{RSS}}{\text{TSS}}.$$

The formula for the other part of the TSS that is not the RSS, called the model sum of squares (MSS), is

$$\text{MSS} = \sum_{i=1}^{n} (\hat{Y}_i - \bar{Y})^2.$$

This can also be used to calculate R^2 as

$$R^2 = \frac{\text{MSS}}{\text{TSS}}.$$

From the numeric results depicted in Figure 10.4, we can see that the R^2 statistic for our two-variable model of support for government assistance to the poor is 0.151. This number appears on the fourth line of the column of results on the right-hand side of Figure 10.4. It indicates that our model accounts for about 15 percent of the variation in the dependent variable. We can also see in Figure 10.4 the values for the MSS, RSS, and TSS under the column labeled "SS" in the table in the upper-left-hand corner.

10.4.3 Is That a "Good" Goodness-of-Fit?

A logical question to ask when we see a measure of a model's goodness-of-fit is "What is a good or bad value for the root MSE and/or R^2?" This is not an easy question to answer. In part, the answer depends on what you are trying to do with the model. If you are primarily interested in predicting values of the dependent variable, saying that you can predict public support for government assistance to the poor with a typical error of 3.57 percent may seem quite good. On the other hand, looking at this another way, in terms of R^2, explaining only 15 percent of the variation may seem inadequate. Actually, given the difficulty involved in accounting for variation in almost any outcome variable with a single predictor, explaining 15 percent of the variation is not unsubstantial. In fact, we would suggest that this tells us something pretty remarkable about the effect of the economy on citizens' values.

10.4.4 Uncertainty about Individual Components of the Sample Regression Model

Before we go through this section, we want to warn you that there are a lot of formulae in it. To use a familiar metaphor, as you go through the formulae in this section it is important to focus on the contours of the forest and not to get caught up in the details of the many trees that we will see along the way. Instead of memorizing each formula, concentrate on what makes the overall values generated by these equations larger or smaller.

A crucial part of the uncertainty in OLS regression models is the degree of uncertainty about individual estimates of population parameter values from the sample regression model. We can use the same logic that we discussed in Chapter 8 for making inferences from sample values about population values for each of the individual parameters in a sample regression model.

One estimate that factors into the calculations of our uncertainty about each of the population parameters is the estimated variance of the population stochastic component, u_i. This unseen variance, σ^2, is estimated from the residuals ($\hat{u}_i$) after the parameters for the sample regression model have been estimated by the following formula:

$$\hat{\sigma}^2 = \frac{\sum_{i=1}^{n} \hat{u}_i^2}{n-2}.$$

Looking at this formula, we can see two components that play a role in determining the magnitude of this estimate. The first component comes from the individual residual values ($\hat{u}_i$). Remember that these values (calculated as $\hat{u}_i = Y_i - \hat{Y}_i$) are the vertical distance between each observed Y_i value and the regression line. The larger these values are, the further the individual cases are from the regression line. The second component of this formula comes from n, the sample size. By now, you should be familiar with the idea that the larger the sample size, the smaller the variance of the estimate. This is the case with our formula for $\hat{\sigma}^2$.

Once we have estimated $\hat{\sigma}^2$, the variance and standard errors for the slope parameter estimate ($\hat{\beta}$) are then estimated from the following formulae:

$$\text{var}(\hat{\beta}) = \frac{\hat{\sigma}^2}{\sum_{i=1}^{n}(X_i - \bar{X})^2},$$

$$\text{se}(\hat{\beta}) = \sqrt{\text{var}(\hat{\beta})} = \frac{\hat{\sigma}}{\sqrt{\sum_{i=1}^{n}(X_i - \bar{X})^2}}.$$

Both of these formulae can be broken into two components that determine their magnitude. In the numerator, we find $\hat{\sigma}$ values. So the larger these values are, the larger will be the variance and standard error of the slope parameter estimate. This makes sense, because the farther the points representing our data are from the regression line, the less confidence we will have in the value of the slope. If we look at the denominator in this equation, we see the term $\sum_{i=1}^{n}(X_i - \bar{X})^2$, which is a measure of the variation of the X_i values around their mean ($\bar{X}$). The greater this variation, the smaller will be the variance and standard error of the slope parameter estimate. This is an important property; in real-world terms it means that the more variation we have in X, the more precisely we will be able to estimate the relationship between X and Y.

The variance and standard errors for the intercept parameter estimate ($\hat{\alpha}$) are then estimated from the following formulae:

$$\text{var}(\hat{\alpha}) = \frac{\hat{\sigma}^2 \sum_{i=1}^{n} X_i^2}{n \sum_{i=1}^{n}(X_i - \bar{X})^2},$$

$$\text{se}(\hat{\alpha}) = \sqrt{\text{var}(\hat{\alpha})} = \sqrt{\frac{\hat{\sigma}^2 \sum_{i=1}^{n} X_i^2}{n \sum_{i=1}^{n}(X_i - \bar{X})^2}}.$$

The logic for taking apart the components of these formulae is slightly more complicated because we can see that the sum of the X_i values squared appears in the numerator. We can see, however, that the denominator contains the measure of the variation of the X_i values around their mean ($\bar{X}$) multiplied by n, the number of cases. Thus the same basic logic holds for these terms: The larger the $\hat{u}_i$ values are, the larger will be the variance and standard error of the intercept parameter estimate; and the larger the variation of the X_i values around their mean, the smaller will be the variance and standard error of the intercept parameter estimate.

Less obvious – but nevertheless true – from the preceding formulae is the fact that larger sample sizes will also produce smaller standard errors.[9] So, just as we learned about the effects of sample size when calculating the standard error of the mean in Chapter 8, there is an identical effect here. Larger sample sizes will, other things being equal, produce smaller standard errors of our estimated regression coefficients.

10.4.5 Confidence Intervals about Parameter Estimates

In Chapter 8 we discussed how we use the normal distribution (supported by the central limit theorem) to estimate confidence intervals for the unseen population mean from sample data. We go through the same logical steps to estimate confidence intervals for the unseen parameters from the population regression model by using the results from the sample regression model. The formulae for estimating confidence intervals are

$$\hat{\beta} \pm [t \times \text{se}(\hat{\beta})],$$
$$\hat{\alpha} \pm [t \times \text{se}(\hat{\alpha})],$$

where the value for t is determined from the t-table in Appendix B. So, for instance, if we want to calculate a 95 percent confidence interval, this means that we are looking down the column for 0.025.[10] Once we have determined the appropriate column, we select our row based on the number of degrees of freedom. The number of degrees of freedom for this t-test is equal to the number of observations (n) minus the number of parameters estimated (k). In the case of the regression model presented in Figure 10.4, $n = 21$ and $k = 2$, so our degrees of freedom equal 19. Looking down the

[9] It is true because the numerator of the expression contains $\hat{\sigma}$, which, as seen previously, has the sample size n in its denominator.

[10] To understand this, think back to Chapter 8, where we introduced confidence intervals. A 95 percent confidence interval would mean that would leave a total of 5 percent in the tails. Because there are two tails, we are going to use the 0.025 column.

column for a two-tailed test at $\alpha = 0.05$ and across the row for 19 df, we can see that $t = 2.093$.[11] Thus our 95 percent confidence intervals are

$$\hat{\beta} \pm [t \times \text{se}(\hat{\beta})] = 1.035 \pm (2.093 \times 0.563) = -0.143 \text{ to } 2.212,$$
$$\hat{\alpha} \pm [t \times \text{se}(\hat{\alpha})] = 10.995 \pm (2.093 \times 3.621) = 3.416 \text{ to } 18.574.$$

These values are displayed in the lower right-hand corner of the table at the bottom of Figure 10.4.

The traditional approach to hypothesis testing with OLS regression is that we specify a null hypothesis and an **alternative hypothesis** and then compare the two. Although we can test hypotheses about either the slope or the intercept parameter, we are usually more concerned with tests about the slope parameter. In particular, we are usually concerned with testing the hypothesis that the population slope parameter is equal to zero. The logic of this hypothesis test corresponds closely with the logic of the bivariate hypothesis tests introduced in Chapter 9. We observe a sample slope parameter, which is an estimate of the population slope. Then, from the value of this parameter estimate, the confidence interval around it, and the size of our sample, we evaluate how likely it is that we observe this sample slope if the true but unobserved population slope is equal to zero. If the answer is "very likely," then we conclude that the population slope is equal to zero.

To understand why we so often focus on a slope value of zero, think about what this corresponds to in the formula for a line. Remember that the slope is the change in Y from a one-unit increase in X. If that change is equal to zero, then there is no covariation between X and Y, and we have failed to clear our third causal hurdle.

These types of tests are either one- or two-tailed. Most statistical computer programs report the results from two-tailed hypothesis tests that the parameter in question is not equal to zero. Despite this, many social science theories are more appropriately translated into one-tailed hypothesis tests, which are sometimes referred to as "directional" hypothesis tests. We review both types of hypothesis tests with the example regression from Figure 10.4.

10.4.6 Two-Tailed Hypothesis Tests

The most common form of statistical hypothesis tests about the parameters from an OLS regression model is a two-tailed hypothesis test that the slope parameter is equal to zero. It is expressed as

[11] The exact value of t is calculated automatically by statistical packages. For an online tool that gives exact values of t, visit www.danielsoper.com/statcalc/calculator.aspx?id=10.

$$H_0: \quad \beta = 0,$$
$$H_1: \quad \beta \neq 0,$$

where H_0 is the null hypothesis and H_1 is the alternative hypothesis. Note that these two rival hypotheses are expressed in terms of the slope parameter from the population regression model. To test which of these two hypotheses is supported, we calculate a ***t*-ratio** in which β is set equal to the value specified in the null hypothesis (in this case zero because H_0: $\beta = 0$), which we represent as β^*:

$$t_{n-k} = \frac{\hat{\beta} - \beta^*}{\text{se}(\hat{\beta})}.$$

For the slope parameter in the two-variable regression model presented in Figure 10.4, we can calculate this as

$$t_{19} = \frac{\hat{\beta} - \beta^*}{\text{se}(\hat{\beta})} = \frac{1.035 - 0}{0.563} = 1.839.$$

From what we have seen in previous chapters, we can tell that this t-ratio is not quite large enough to reject the null hypothesis that $\beta = 0$ at the 0.05 level of significance. Remember that a typical standard for statistical significance in the social sciences is when the p-value is less than 0.05. If we look across the row for degrees of freedom equal to 19 in Appendix B, we can see that, to have a p-value of less than 0.05, we would need a t-ratio of 2.093 or larger. Since our t-ratio is 1.839, we cannot reject the null hypothesis. However, if we adopt the slightly less stringent criterion of significance 0.10, we can reject the H_0 since $t = 1.729$. If we look at the table at the bottom of Figure 10.4, we can see that the t-ratio and resulting p-value for this hypothesis test are presented in the third and fourth columns of the "Unemployment" row ($t = 1.839, p = 0.082$).

The exact same logic is used to test hypotheses about the y-intercept parameter. The formula for this t-ratio is

$$t_{n-k} = \frac{\hat{\alpha} - \alpha^*}{\text{se}(\hat{\alpha})}.$$

In Figure 10.4 we see the calculation for the following null hypothesis and alternative:

$$H_0: \quad \alpha = 0,$$
$$H_1: \quad \alpha \neq 0.$$

The resulting t-ratio is 3.036. This makes sense when we think about this quantity in real-world terms. Remember that the y-intercept is the expected value of the dependent variable Y when the independent variable X is equal to zero. In our model, this means we want to know the expected value of support for government assistance to the poor when unemployment equals zero. Even when the economy is doing well, there are always going to be some who will support government assistance to the poor. Thus it makes sense that the null hypothesis H_0: $\alpha = 0$ would be pretty easy to reject.

10.4.7 The Relationship between Confidence Intervals and Two-Tailed Hypothesis Tests

In the previous three subsections, we introduced confidence intervals and hypothesis tests as two of the ways for making inferences about the parameters of the population regression model from our sample regression model. These two methods for making inferences are mathematically related to each other. We can tell this because they each rely on the *t*-table. The relationship between the two is such that, if the 95 percent confidence interval does not include a particular value, then the null hypothesis that the population parameter equals that value (a two-tailed hypothesis test) will have a *p*-value smaller than 0.05. We can see this for both of the hypothesis tests that we discussed in Section 10.4.6 on two-tailed hypothesis tests:

- Because the 95 percent confidence interval for our slope parameter includes 0, the *p*-value for the hypothesis test that $\beta = 0$ is greater than 0.05.
- Because the 95 percent confidence interval for our intercept parameter does not include 0, the *p*-value for the hypothesis test that $\alpha = 0$ is less than 0.05.

10.4.8 One-Tailed Hypothesis Tests

As we pointed out in previous sections, the most common form of statistical hypothesis test about the parameters from an OLS regression model is a two-tailed hypothesis test that the slope parameter is equal to zero. That this is the most common test is somewhat of a fluke. By default, most statistical computer programs report the results of this hypothesis test. In reality, though, most social science hypotheses are that a parameter is either positive or negative and not just that the parameter is different from zero. This is what we call a **directional hypothesis**. Consider, for instance, the theory of economic performance and how we would translate it into a hypothesis about the slope parameter in our current example. Our theory is that the *worse* the economy is performing, as measured by unemployment rates, the *higher* will be the percentage of respondents who support government assistance to the poor. In other words, we expect to see a positive relationship between unemployment and support for government assistance, meaning that we expect β to be greater than zero.

When our theory leads to such a directional hypothesis, it is expressed as

$$H_0: \quad \beta \leq 0,$$
$$H_1: \quad \beta > 0,$$

where H_0 is the null hypothesis and H_1 is the alternative hypothesis. As was the case with the two-tailed test, these two rival hypotheses are expressed in terms of the slope parameter from the population regression model. To test which of these two hypotheses is supported, we calculate a t-ratio where β is set equal to the value specified in the null hypothesis[12] (in this case zero because H_0: $\beta \leq 0$), which we represent as β^*:

$$t_{n-k} = \frac{\hat{\beta} - \beta^*}{\text{se}(\hat{\beta})}.$$

For the slope parameter in the two-variable regression model presented in Figure 10.4, we can calculate this as

$$t_{19} = \frac{\hat{\beta} - \beta^*}{\text{se}(\hat{\beta})} = \frac{1.035 - 0}{0.563} = 1.839.$$

Do these calculations look familiar to you? They should, because this t-ratio is calculated exactly the same way as the t-ratio for the two-sided hypothesis about this parameter was calculated. The difference comes in how we use the t-table in Appendix B to arrive at the appropriate p-value for this hypothesis test. Because this is a one-tailed hypothesis test, we use the column labeled "0.05" instead of the column labeled "0.025" to assess whether we have achieved a t-ratio such that $p < 0.05$. In other words, we would need a t-ratio of only 1.729 for 19 degrees of freedom to achieve this level of significance for a one-tailed hypothesis test. For a two-tailed hypothesis test, we needed a t-ratio of 2.093. In other words, this is a case where the formulation of our hypothesis test as one-tailed versus two-tailed makes a pretty major difference, especially since many scholars judge 0.05 to be the standard for statistical significance.

We can see from these examples and from the t-table that, when we have a directional hypothesis, we can more easily reject a null hypothesis. One of the quirks of social science research is that, even when they have directional hypotheses, researchers often report the results of two-tailed hypothesis tests. We'll discuss the issue of how to present regression results in greater detail in Chapter 12.

[12] We choose 0 when the null hypothesis is H_0: $\beta \leq 0$ because this is the critical value for the null hypothesis. Under this null hypothesis, zero is the threshold, and evidence that β is equal to any value less than or equal to zero is supportive of this null hypothesis.

10.5 ASSUMPTIONS, MORE ASSUMPTIONS, AND MINIMAL MATHEMATICAL REQUIREMENTS

If assumptions were water, you'd need an umbrella right now. Any time that you estimate a regression model, you are implicitly making a large set of assumptions about the unseen population model. In this section, we break these assumptions into assumptions about the population stochastic component and assumptions about our model specification. In addition, there are some minimal mathematical requirements that must be met before a regression model can be estimated. In this final section we list these assumptions and requirements and briefly discuss them as they apply to our working example of a two-variable regression model of the impact of economic performance on support for government assistance to the poor.

10.5.1 Assumptions about the Population Stochastic Component

The most important assumptions about the population stochastic component u_i are about its distribution. These can be summarized as

$$u_i \sim N(0, \sigma^2),$$

which means that we assume that u_i is distributed normally ($\sim N$) with the mean equal to zero and the variance equal to σ^2.[13] This compact mathematical statement contains three of the five assumptions that we make about the population stochastic component any time we estimate a regression model. We now go over each one separately.

u_i Is Normally Distributed

The assumption that u_i is normally distributed allows us to use the t-table to make probabilistic inferences about the population regression model from the sample regression model. The main justification for this assumption is the central limit theorem that we discussed in Chapter 8.

$E(u_i) = 0$: No Bias

The assumption that u_i has a mean or expected value equal to zero is also known as the assumption of zero bias. Consider what it would mean if there was a case for which $E(u_i) \neq 0$. In other words, this would be a case for which we would *expect* our regression model to be off. If we have cases like this, we would essentially be ignoring some theoretical insight that we

[13] Strictly speaking we do not need to make all of these assumptions to estimate the parameters of an OLS model. But we do need to make all of these assumptions to interpret the results from an OLS model in the standard fashion.

have about the underlying causes of Y. Remember, this term is supposed to be random. If $E(u_i) \neq 0$, then there must be some nonrandom component to this term. It is important to note here that we do not expect *all* of our u_i values to equal zero because we know that some of our cases will fall above and some below the regression line. But this assumption means that our best guess or expected value for each individual u_i value is zero.

If we think about the example in this chapter, this assumption means that we do not have any particular cases for which we expect our model, with unemployment as the independent variable, to overpredict or underpredict the value of government support for assistance to the poor in any particular year. If, on the other hand, we had some expectation along these lines, we would not be able to make this assumption. Say, for instance, that the proportion of citizens who steadfastly favor limited government under any circumstances, regardless of the health of the economy, was especially high during times of job growth. Under these circumstances, we would not be able to make this assumption. The solution to this problem would be to include another independent variable in our model that measured whether or not the economy was expanding at the time of each survey. Once we control for all such potential sources of bias, we can feel comfortable making this assumption. The inclusion of additional independent variables is the main subject covered in Chapter 11.

u_i Has Variance σ^2: Homoscedasticity

The assumption that u_i has variance equal to σ^2 seems pretty straightforward. But, because this notation for variance does not contain an i subscript, it means that the variance for every case in the underlying population is assumed to be the same. The word for describing this situation is "homoscedasticity," which means "uniform error variance." If this assumption does not hold, we have a situation in which the variance of u_i is σ_i^2, known as "heteroscedasticity," which means "unequal error variance." When we have heteroscedasticity, our regression model fits some of the cases in the population better than others. This can potentially cause us problems when we are estimating confidence intervals and testing hypotheses.

In our example for this chapter, this assumption would be violated if, for some reason, some survey years were harder than others for our model to predict support for government assistance. In this case, our model would be heteroscedastic. It could, for instance, be the case that presidential election years are harder to predict with our model in which the only independent variable is economic performance. Under these circumstances, the assumption of homoscedasticity would not be reasonable.

No Autocorrelation

We also assume that there is no autocorrelation. Autocorrelation occurs when the stochastic terms for any two or more cases are systematically related to each other. This clearly cuts against the grain of the idea that these terms are stochastic or random. Formally, we express this assumption as

$$\text{cov}_{u_i,u_j} = 0 \quad \forall\, i \neq j;$$

in words, this means that the covariance between the population error terms u_i and u_j is equal to zero for all i not equal to j (for any two unique cases).

The most common form of autocorrelation occurs in regression models of time-series data. As we discussed in Chapter 4, time-series data involve measurement of the relevant variables across time for a single spatial unit. In our example for this chapter, we are using measures of economic performance and support for government assistance to the poor measured every year (every other year since 1994) for the United States. If, for some reason, the error terms for adjacent pairs of years were correlated, we would have autocorrelation.

X Values Are Measured Without Error

At first, the assumption that X values are measured without error may seem to be out of place in a listing of assumptions about the population stochastic component. But this assumption is made to greatly simplify inferences that we make about our population regression model from our sample regression model. By assuming that X is measured without error, we are assuming that any variability from our regression line is due to the stochastic component u_i and not to measurement problems in X. To put it another way, if X also had a stochastic component, we would need to model X before we could model Y, and that would substantially complicate matters.

With just about any regression model that we estimate with real-world data, we will likely be pretty uncomfortable with this assumption. In the example for this chapter, we are assuming that we have exactly correct measures of the unemployment rate from 1975 to 2014. If we think a little more about this measure, we can think of all kinds of potential errors in measurement. For instance, the official unemployment rate does not include discouraged workers who have simply given up looking for jobs. How would including them change our results?

Despite the obvious problems with this assumption, we make it every time that we estimate an OLS model. Unless we move to considerably more complicated statistical techniques, this is an assumption that we have to live with and keep in the back of our minds as we evaluate our overall confidence in what our models tell us.

Recall from Chapter 6, when we discussed measuring our concepts of interest, that we argued that measurement is important because if we mismeasure our variables we may make incorrect causal inferences about the real world. This assumption should make the important lessons of that chapter crystal clear.

10.5.2 Assumptions about Our Model Specification

The assumptions about our model specification can be summarized as a single assumption that we have *the* correct model specification. We break this into two separate assumptions to highlight the range of ways in which this assumption might be violated.

No Causal Variables Left Out; No Noncausal Variables Included

This assumption means that, if we specify our two-variable regression model of the relationship between X and Y, there cannot be some other variable Z that also causes Y.[14] It also means that X must cause Y. In other words, this is just another way of saying that the sample regression model that we have specified *is* the true underlying population regression model.

As we have gone through the example in this chapter, we have already begun to come up with additional variables that we theorize to be causally related to our dependent variable. To comfortably make this assumption, we will need to include all such variables in our model. Adding additional independent variables to our model is the subject of Chapter 11.

Parametric Linearity

The assumption of parametric linearity is a fancy way of saying that our population parameter β for the relationship between X and Y does not vary. In other words, the relationship between X and Y is the same across all values of X.

In the context of our current example, this means that we are assuming that the impact of a one-unit increase in unemployment is always the same. So moving from a value of 3 to 4 has the same effect as moving from a value of 5 to 6. In Chapter 11 we discuss some techniques for relaxing this assumption.

[14] One exception to this is the very special case in which there is a Z variable that is causally related to Y but Z is uncorrelated with X and u_i. In this case, we would still be able to get a reasonable estimate of the relationship between X and Y despite leaving Z out of our model. More on this in Chapter 11.

10.5.3 Minimal Mathematical Requirements

For a two-variable regression model, we have two minimal requirements that must be met by our sample data before we can estimate our parameters. We will add to these requirements when we expand to multiple regression models.

X Must Vary

Think about what the scatter plot of our sample data would look like if X did not vary. Basically, we would have a stack of Y values at the same point on the x axis. The only reasonable line that we could draw through this set of points would be a straight line parallel to the y axis. Remember that our goal is to explain our dependent variable Y. Under these circumstances we would have failed miserably because any Y value would be just as good as any other, given our single value of X. Thus we need some variation in X in order to estimate an OLS regression model.

$n > k$

To estimate a regression model, the number of cases (n) must exceed the number of parameters to be estimated (k). Thus, as a minimum, when we estimate a two-variable regression model with two parameters (α and β) we must have *at least* three cases.

10.5.4 How Can We Make All of These Assumptions?

The mathematical requirements to estimate a regression model aren't too severe, but a sensible question to ask at this point is, "How can we reasonably make all of the assumptions just listed every time that we run a regression model?" To answer this question, we refer back to the discussion in Chapter 1 of the analogy between models and maps. We *know* that all of our assumptions cannot possibly be met. We also know that we are trying to simplify complex realities. The only way that we can do this is to make a large set of unrealistic assumptions about the world. It is crucial, though, that we never lose sight of the fact that we are making these assumptions. In the next chapter we relax one of these most unrealistic assumptions made in the two-variable regression model by controlling for a second variable, Z.

CONCEPTS INTRODUCED IN THIS CHAPTER

- alternative hypothesis – the theory-based expectation that is the opposite of the null hypothesis

- directional hypothesis – an alternative hypothesis in which the expected relationship is either positive or negative
- ordinary least-squares – also known as "OLS," the most popular method for computing sample regression models
- parameter – a synonym for "boundary" with a more mathematical connotation; in the context of statistics, the value of an unknown population characteristic
- parameter estimate – a sample-based calculation of a population characteristic
- population error term – in the population regression model, the difference between the model-based predicted value of the dependent variable and the true value of the dependent variable
- population regression model – a theoretical formulation of the proposed linear relationship between at least one independent variable and a dependent variable
- residual – same as population error term
- root mean-squared error (root MSE) – a calculation of goodness-of-fit made by squaring each sample error term, summing them up, dividing by the number of cases, and then taking the square root; also known as the "model standard error"
- R-squared statistic (R^2) – a goodness-of-fit measure that varies between 0 and 1 representing the proportion of variation in the dependent variable that is accounted for by the model
- sample error term – in the sample regression model, the sample-based estimate of the residual
- sample regression model – a sample-based estimate of the population regression model
- statistical model – a numerical representation of a relationship between at least one independent variable and a dependent variable
- stochastic – random
- t-ratio – the ratio of an estimated parameter to its estimated standard error

EXERCISES

1. Draw an X–Y axis through the middle of a 10×10 grid. The point where the X and Y lines intersect is known as the "origin" and is defined as the point at which both X and Y are equal to zero. Draw each of the following lines across the values of X from -5 to 5 and write the corresponding regression equation:

   (a) y-intercept = 2, slope = 2;

   (b) y-intercept = –2, slope = 2;

(c) y-intercept = 0, slope = –1;

(d) y-intercept = 2, slope = –2.

2. Solve each of the following mathematical expressions to yield a single component of the bivariate sample regression model:

(a) $\hat{\alpha} + \hat{\beta}X_i + \hat{u}_i$

(b) $Y_i - E(Y|X_i)$

(c) $\hat{\beta}X_i + \hat{u}_i - Y_i$

3. Using the data set "state.sav," we estimated a two-variable regression model using data from each U.S. state and the District of Columbia with per capita income ("pcinc" in our data set) as our dependent variable and the percentage of state residents with a college degree ("pctba" in our data set) as the independent variable. The estimated equation was:

$$\text{pcinc}_i = 11\,519.78 + 1028.96\text{pctba}_i.$$

Interpret the parameter estimate for the effect of a state's level of education on average income levels.

4. In the data set described in Exercise 3, the value of *pctba* for Illinois equals 29.9. What is the model's predicted per capita income for Illinois?

5. The estimated standard error for the slope parameter in the model described in Exercise 3 was 95.7. Construct a 95 percent confidence interval for this parameter estimate. Show your work. What does this tell you about the estimated relationship?

6. Test the hypothesis that the parameter for *pctba* is not equal to zero. Show your work. What does this tell you about the estimated relationship?

7. Test the hypothesis that the parameter for *pctba* is greater than zero. Show your work. What does this tell you about the estimated relationship?

8. The R-squared statistic for the model described in Exercise 3 is 0.70 and the root MSE = 3773.8. What do these numbers tell us about our model?

9. Estimate and interpret the results from a two-variable regression model different from the model in Exercise 3 using the data set "state.sav."

10. Think through the assumptions that you made when you carried out Exercise 9. Which do you feel least and most comfortable making? Explain your answers.

11. In Exercise 10 for Chapter 9, you calculated a correlation coefficient for the relationship between two continuous variables. Now, estimate a two-variable regression model for these same two variables. Produce a table of the results and write about what this table tells you about the relationship between education and income in 2018.

11 Multiple Regression

OVERVIEW

Despite what we have learned in the preceding chapters on hypothesis testing and statistical significance, we have not yet crossed all four of our hurdles for establishing causal relationships. Recall that all of the techniques we have learned in Chapters 9 and 10 are simply bivariate, X- and Y-type analyses. But, to fully assess whether X *causes* Y, we need to control for other possible causes of Y, which we have not yet done. In this chapter, we show how multiple regression – which is an extension of the two-variable model we covered in Chapter 10 – does exactly that. We explicitly connect the formulae that we include to the key issues of research design that tie the entire book together. We also discuss some of the problems in multiple regression models when key causes of the dependent variable are omitted, which ties this chapter to the fundamental principles presented in Chapters 3 and 4. We also provide introductory *discussions of* and *advice for* commonly encountered research scenarios involving dummy independent variables and interactive specifications.

11.1 MODELING MULTIVARIATE REALITY

From the very outset of this book, we have emphasized that almost all interesting phenomena in social reality have more than one cause. And yet most of our theories are simply bivariate in nature.

We have shown you (in Chapter 4) that there are distinct methods for dealing with the nature of reality in our designs for social research. If we are fortunate enough to be able to conduct an experiment, then the process of randomly assigning our participants to treatment groups will automatically "control for" those other possible causes that are not a part of our theory.

But in observational research – which represents the vast majority of sociological research – there is no automatic control for the other possible causes of our dependent variable; we have to control for them statistically. The main way that social scientists accomplish this is through multiple regression. The math in this model is an extension of the math involved in the two-variable regression model you just learned in Chapter 10. But first, we briefly divert to show how multivariate tabular analysis attempts to accomplish the same thing.

11.2 ADDING A *Z* VARIABLE TO A BIVARIATE TABULAR ANALYSIS

To ease the transition from the bivariate hypothesis testing procedures we covered in Chapters 9 and 10 to the multiple regression models examined in this chapter, we think it will be useful to illustrate what controlling for a *Z* variable actually looks like. In this section we introduce you to the logic and mechanics of control in the context of multivariate tabular analysis as a prelude to addressing control in multiple regression models.

Recall that in Chapter 9 (Section 9.4.1) we discussed bivariate tabular analysis and addressed why, in the absence of at least one *Z* variable, such tables do not allow us to infer causality. In this section we extend that discussion to a three-way tabular analysis by revisiting the example of gender differences in empathy that we introduced in Chapter 9. The relationship between empathy, our *Y* variable, and gender, our *X* variable, is then analyzed further by adding a *Z* variable, religiosity, to the mix in order to determine what effect, if any, religiosity has on the original gender–empathy relationship. As you will see, the logic (though not the mechanics) of controlling on a *Z* variable in a multivariate tabular analysis is identical to the logic of controlling on a *Z* variable in a multiple regression model; it also has the added benefit of requiring no new formulae to master!

Is there a credible causal mechanism linking gender and empathy? As we noted in Section 9.4.1, some research has shown that women are more likely than men to display empathy toward others because, the theory is, women are more often socialized to have prosocial, caring value orientations (Johnson and Marini, 1998). So the answer is yes, we have passed the first hurdle on the path to establishing causality. The second hurdle, ruling out the possibility that *Y* (religiosity) causes *X* (gender) instead of the reverse, is of course not an issue in this case.

Data for this illustration are drawn from the same 2012 and 2014 General Social Surveys we used in Chapter 9. Our measure of empathy is the same as that used earlier as well: "Please tell me whether you strongly agree, agree, neither agree nor disagree, disagree, or disagree strongly with the following statement. 'These days people need to look after themselves and not overly worry about others.' " As before, we combined responses of

Table 11.1 Gender and empathy, 2012 and 2014 GSS

Empathy	Female	Male	Row N
Empathetic	62.8%	53.5%	813
Not empathetic	37.2%	46.5%	1152
Column N	1086	879	1965

strongly agree and agree into a "non-empathetic" category and responses of disagree and disagree strongly into an "empathetic" category. Since the response "neither agree nor disagree" does not allow for placement into either the non-empathetic or empathetic category, we examine only respondents who did not choose this response option. We also eliminate respondents with missing data on either empathy or religiosity (there are no missing data on gender), leaving 1965 cases for analysis.[1]

Table 11.1 displays the zero-order relationship between gender and empathy. As in Chapter 9, the table shows that 62.8 percent of women, compared to 53.5 percent of men, are empathetic; and the χ^2 test statistic is significant ($p < 0.01$). Thus, the null hypothesis that gender and empathy are unrelated (i.e., statistically independent) can be safely rejected in favor of the research hypothesis that these variables covary significantly. We have passed the third hurdle on the path to establishing causality; X and Y covary.

On the basis of this finding, can we conclude that gender and empathy are causally related? As we discussed in Chapter 9, the answer to this question is "no, at least not yet." The fourth hurdle on the path to establishing causality – controlling on all confounding variables that might make the association between X and Y spurious – has not yet been addressed.

We can easily think of several Z variables that might be causally related to empathy and which, if controlled for in our tabular analysis, might alter or even negate the original relationship between gender and empathy. A respondent's education or income come to mind, as does the variable we use here, religiosity. We selected religiosity as our Z variable because of evidence showing that women exhibit higher levels of religiosity than men (Schnabel, 2015), which leads us to wonder whether the original relationship between gender and empathy might be a function of religiosity rather than of gender *per se*. In other words, does gender influence religiosity, and does religiosity, in turn, influence empathy, with no

[1] The total number of cases is slightly lower than in Chapter 9 due to missing data on the religiosity variable.

Table 11.2 Gender and empathy, controlling on religiosity, 2012 and 2014 GSS

Pray often

Empathy	Female	Male	Row N
Empathetic	62.7%	54.4%	894
Not empathetic	37.3%	45.6%	611
Column N	911	594	1505

Pray infrequently or never

Empathy	Female	Male	Row N
Empathetic	63.4%	51.6%	258
Not empathetic	36.6%	48.4%	202
Column N	175	285	460

direct causal link between gender and empathy? If this is the case, we would expect the original bivariate relationship between gender and empathy to substantially diminish, or perhaps even disappear, when religiosity is controlled for.

Table 11.2 displays the multivariate relationship between gender and empathy controlling on religiosity. In a tabular analysis, "controlling on" means recalculating the original bivariate relationship between X and Y within categories of the Z variable. For the purposes of this illustration, we have divided our measure of religiosity into two categories – those who pray several times a day, once a day, several times a week, or once a week; and those who pray less than once a week or not at all. What happens to the gender–empathy relationship when religiosity is included as our Z variable? The top panel of Table 11.2 shows that, among those who pray often, the gender gap in empathy that we saw in Table 11.1 is virtually unchanged, with 62.7 percent of women and 54.4 percent of men empathetic ($p < 0.01$). Similarly, among those who do not pray often, the gender gap in empathy is again virtually unchanged from Table 11.1, with 63.4 percent of women and 51.6 percent of men in the empathetic category. Thus, our conclusion is that the original bivariate association between gender and empathy persists intact when religiosity is controlled.[2]

What is the connection between introducing a Z variable in tabular analysis and introducing a Z variable in multiple regression analysis? As we noted above, the logic is the same in both cases – we control on Z variables

[2] Several other outcomes of controlling on Z variables are also possible. A classic social science book on this topic is Morris Rosenberg's (1968) *The Logic of Survey Analysis*.

in order to gain confidence in the accuracy of our causal inferences. If the original covariation between X and Y remains, or is only slightly reduced, after controlling on Z, confidence in our causal attributions increases. In this illustration we have found a bivariate association between gender and empathy and then confirmed that the association is not merely an artifact of religiosity; in other words, the association is not spurious (at least as far as religiosity is concerned). As a result, we have more faith now than we did after the bivariate analysis in Chapter 9 that the association may be causal. Still, we have controlled on only one possibly confounding variable. An important difference between tabular and multiple regression models in this context is that tabular analyses can examine only one or a few Z variables at a time and still produce tables that are interpretable, while multiple regression models can accommodate a large number of Z variables in a single model, thus allowing even more confidence on our path to causal inference. We discuss Z variables in multiple regression models in Section 11.4 below.

11.3 THE POPULATION REGRESSION FUNCTION

We can generalize the population regression model that we learned in Chapter 10 (Section 10.2),

$$\text{bivariate population regression model} \quad Y_i = \alpha + \beta X_i + u_i,$$

to include more than one systematic cause of Y, which we have been calling Z throughout this book,

$$\text{multiple population regression model} \quad Y_i = \alpha + \beta_1 X_i + \beta_2 Z_i + u_i.$$

The interpretation of the slope coefficients in the three-variable model is similar to interpreting bivariate coefficients, with one very important difference. In both, the coefficient in front of the variable X (β in the two-variable model, β_1 in the multiple regression model) represents the "rise-over-run" effect of X on Y. In the multiple regression case, though, β_1 actually represents the effect of X on Y *while holding constant the effects of* Z. If this distinction sounds important, it is. We show how these differences arise in the next section.

11.4 FROM TWO-VARIABLE TO MULTIPLE REGRESSION

Recall from Chapter 10 (Section 10.2) that the formula for a two-variable regression line (in a sample) is

$$Y_i = \hat{\alpha} + \hat{\beta} X_i + \hat{u}_i.$$

And recall that, to understand the nature of the effect that X has on Y, the estimated coefficient $\hat{\beta}$ tells us, on average, how many units of change in Y we should expect given a one-unit increase in X. The formula for $\hat{\beta}$ in the two-variable model, as we learned in Chapter 10, is

$$\hat{\beta} = \frac{\sum_{i=1}^{n}(X_i - \bar{X})(Y_i - \bar{Y})}{\sum_{i=1}^{n}(X_i - \bar{X})^2}.$$

Given that our goal is to control for the effects of some third variable, Z, how exactly is that accomplished in regression equations? If a scatter plot in two dimensions (X and Y) suggests the formula for a *line*, then adding a third dimension suggests the formula for a *plane*. And the formula for that plane is

$$Y_i = \alpha + \beta_1 X_i + \beta_2 Z_i.$$

That might seem deceptively simple. A formula representing a plane simply adds the additional $\beta_2 Z_i$ term to the formula for a line.[3]

Pay attention to how the notation has changed. In the two-variable formula for a line, there were no numeric subscripts for the β coefficient – because, well, there was only one of them. But now we have two independent variables, X and Z, that help to explain the variation in Y, and therefore we have two different coefficients β, and so we subscript them β_1 and β_2 to be clear that the values of these two effects are different from one another.[4]

The key message from this chapter is that, in the preceding formula, the coefficient β_1 represents more than the effect of X on Y; in the multiple regression formula, it represents *the effect of X on Y while controlling for the effect of Z*. Simultaneously, the coefficient β_2 represents *the effect of Z on Y while controlling for the effect of X*. And in observational research, this is the key to crossing our fourth causal hurdle that we introduced all the way back in Chapter 3.

How is it the case that the coefficient for β_1 actually controls for Z? After all, β_1 is not connected to Z in the formula; it is, quite obviously, connected to X. The first thing to realize here is that the preceding multiple regression formula for β_1 is different from the two-variable formula for β

[3] All of the subsequent math about adding one more independent variable, Z, generalizes quite easily to adding still more independent variables. We use the three-variable case for ease of illustration.

[4] In many other textbooks on regression analysis, just as we distinguish between β_1 and β_2, the authors choose to label their independent variables X_1, X_2, and so forth. We have consistently used the notation of X, Y, and Z to emphasize the concept of controlling for other variables while examining the relationship between an independent and a dependent variable of theoretical interest. Therefore we will stick with this notation throughout this chapter.

from Chapter 10. (We'll get to the formula shortly.) The key consequence of this is that the value of β derived from the two-variable formula, representing the effect of X on Y, will almost always be different – perhaps only trivially different, or perhaps wildly different – from the value of β_1 derived from the multiple regression formula, representing the effect of X on Y while controlling for the effects of Z.

But how does β_1 control for the effects of Z? Let's assume that X and Z are correlated. They need not be related in a *causal* sense, and they need not be related *strongly*. They simply have to be related to one another – that is, for this example, their covariance is not exactly equal to zero. Now, assuming that they are related somehow, we can write their relationship just like that of a two-variable regression model:

$$X_i = \hat{\alpha}' + \hat{\beta}' Z_i + \hat{e}_i.$$

Note some notational differences here. Instead of the parameters $\hat{\alpha}$ and $\hat{\beta}$, we are calling the estimated parameters $\hat{\alpha}'$ and $\hat{\beta}'$ just so you are aware that their values will be different from the $\hat{\alpha}$ and $\hat{\beta}$ estimates in previous equations. And note also that the residuals, which we labeled $\hat{u}_i$ in previous equations, are now labeled $\hat{e}_i$ here.

If we use Z to predict X, then the predicted value of X (or $\hat{X}$) based on Z is simply

$$\hat{X}_i = \hat{\alpha}' + \hat{\beta}' Z_i,$$

which is just the preceding equation, but without the error term, because it is expected (on average) to be zero. Now, we can just substitute the left-hand side of the preceding equation into the previous equation and get

$$X_i = \hat{X}_i + \hat{e}_i$$

or, equivalently,

$$\hat{e}_i = X_i - \hat{X}_i.$$

These $\hat{e}_i$, then, are the exact equivalents of the residuals from the two-variable regression of Y on X that you learned from Chapter 10. So their interpretation is identical, too. That being the case, the $\hat{e}_i$ are the portion of the variation in X that Z cannot explain. (The portion of X that Z *can* explain is the predicted portion, the $\hat{X}_i$.)

So what have we done here? We have just documented the relationship between Z and X and partitioned the variation in X into two parts – the portion that Z *can* explain (the $\hat{X}_i$) and the portion that Z *cannot* explain (the $\hat{e}_i$). Hold this thought.

We can do the exact same thing for the relationship between Z and Y that we just did for the relationship between Z and X. The process will look quite similar, with a bit of different notation to distinguish the processes. So we can model Y as a function of Z in the following way:

$$Y_i = \hat{\alpha}^* + \hat{\beta}^* Z_i + \hat{v}_i.$$

Here, the estimated slope is $\hat{\beta}^*$ and the error term is represented by $\hat{v}_i$.

Just as we did with Z and X, if we use Z to predict Y, then the predicted value of Y (or $\hat{Y}$) (which we will label $\hat{Y}^*$) based on Z is simply

$$\hat{Y}_i^* = \hat{\alpha}^* + \hat{\beta}^* Z_i,$$

which, as before, is identical to the preceding equation, but without the error term, because the residuals are expected (on average) to be zero. And again, as before, we can substitute the left-hand side of the preceding equation into the previous equation, and get

$$Y_i = \hat{Y}_i^* + \hat{v}_i$$

or, equivalently,

$$\hat{v}_i = Y_i - \hat{Y}_i^*.$$

These $\hat{v}_i$, then, are interpreted in an identical way to that of the preceding $\hat{e}_i$. They represent the portion of the variation in Y that Z cannot explain. (The portion of Y that Z *can* explain is the predicted portion, the $\hat{Y}_i^*$.)

Now what has this accomplished? We have just documented the relationship between Z and Y and partitioned the variation in Y into two parts – the portion that Z *can* explain and the portion that Z *cannot* explain.

So we have now let Z try to explain X and found the residuals (the $\hat{e}_i$ values); similarly, we have also now let Z try to explain Y, and found those residuals as well (the $\hat{v}_i$ values). Now back to our three-variable regression model that we have seen before, with Y as the dependent variable, and X and Z as the independent variables:

$$Y_i = \hat{\alpha} + \hat{\beta}_1 X_i + \hat{\beta}_2 Z_i + \hat{u}_i.$$

The formula for $\hat{\beta}_1$, representing the effect of X on Y while controlling for Z, is

$$\hat{\beta}_1 = \frac{\sum_{i=1}^{n} \hat{e}_i \hat{v}_i}{\sum_{i=1}^{n} \hat{e}_i^2}.$$

Now, we know what $\hat{e}_i$ and $\hat{v}_i$ are from the previous equations. So, substituting, we get

$$\hat{\beta}_1 = \frac{\sum_{i=1}^{n} (X_i - \hat{X}_i)(Y_i - \hat{Y}_i^*)}{\sum_{i=1}^{n} (X_i - \hat{X}_i)^2}.$$

Pay careful attention to this formula. The "hatted" components in these expressions are from the two-variable regressions involving Z that we previously learned about. The key components of the formula for the effect of X on Y, while controlling for Z, are the $\hat{e}_i$ and $\hat{v}_i$, which, as we just learned, are the portions of X and Y (respectively) that Z cannot account for. And that is how, in the multiple regression model, the parameter β_1, which represents the effects of X on Y, *controls for* the effects of Z. How? Because the only components of X and Y that it uses are components that Z cannot account for – that is, the $\hat{e}_i$ and $\hat{v}_i$.

Comparing this formula for estimating β_1 with the two-variable formula for estimating β is very revealing. Instead of using the factors $(X_i - \bar{X})$ and $(Y_i - \bar{Y})$ in the numerator, which were the components of the *two-variable* regression of Y on X from Chapter 10, in the multiple regression formula that controls for Z the factors in the numerator are $(X_i - \hat{X}_i)$ and $(Y_i - \hat{Y}_i^*)$, where, again, the hatted portions represent X as predicted by Z, and Y as predicted by Z.

Note something else in the comparison of the two-variable formula for estimating β and the multiple regression formula for estimating β_1. The result of $\hat{\beta}$ in the two-variable regression of Y and X and $\hat{\beta}_1$ in the three-variable regression of Y on X while controlling for Z will be different almost all the time. In fact, it is quite rare – though mathematically possible in theory – that those two values will be identical.[5]

And the formula for estimating β_2, likewise, represents the effects of Z on Y while controlling for the effects of X. These processes, in fact, happen simultaneously.

It's been a good number of chapters – seven of them, to be precise – between the first moment when we discussed the importance of controlling for Z and the point, just above, when we showed you precisely how to do it. The fourth causal hurdle has never been too far from front-and-center since Chapter 3, and now you know the process of crossing it.

Don't get too optimistic too quickly, though. As we noted, the three-variable setup we just mentioned can easily be generalized to more than three variables. But the formula for estimating β_1 controls only for the effects of the Z variable that are included in the regression equation. It does not control for other variables that are not measured and not included in the model. And what happens when we fail to include a relevant cause of Y in our regression model? Bad things. Those bad things will come into focus a bit later in this chapter. Next, we turn to the issues of how to

[5] Later in this chapter, you will see that there are two situations in which the two-variable and multiple regression parameter estimates of β will be the same.

Table 11.3 Three regression models of public support for government assistance to the poor

	A	B	C
Unemployment	1.04	—	0.87
	(0.56)	—	(0.50)
Degree	—	−0.42*	−0.39*
	—	(0.16)	(0.15)
Intercept	10.99*	26.97*	20.72*
	(3.62)	(3.68)	(5.03)
R^2	0.15	0.27	0.37
n	21	21	21

Notes: The dependent variable is the percentage of GSS respondents who support government assistance to the poor. Standard errors in parentheses. $^*p < 0.05$ (two-tailed t-test).

interpret regression tables using our running example of public support for government assistance to the poor.

11.5 INTERPRETING MULTIPLE REGRESSION

For an illustration of how to interpret multiple regression coefficients, let's return to our example from Chapter 10, in which we showed you the results of a regression of support for government assistance to the poor on the unemployment rate (see Figure 10.4). The model we estimated, you will recall, was support $= \alpha + (\beta \times \text{unemployment})$, and the estimated coefficients there were $\hat{\alpha} = 10.99$ and $\hat{\beta} = 1.04$. Those results are in column A of Table 11.3.

In column A, you can see the parameter estimates for the annual unemployment rate in the U.S. (in the row labeled "Unemployment"), and the standard error of that estimated slope, 0.56. In the row labeled "Intercept," you can see the estimated y-intercept for that regression, 10.99, and its associated standard error, 3.62. The parameter estimate for the intercept, but not for unemployment, is statistically significant.[6]

Recall that the interpretation of the slope coefficient in a two-variable regression indicates that, for every one-unit increase in the independent variable, we expect to see β units of change in the dependent variable.

[6] The p-value for the unemployment variable is 0.082, so it is very close to the 0.05 threshold for statistical significance.

In the current context, $\hat{\beta} = 1.04$ means that for every extra one percentage point in the unemployment rate, we expect to see, on average, an extra 1.04 percentage points in citizen support for government assistance to the poor.

But recall our admonition, throughout this book, about being too quick to interpret any bivariate analysis as evidence of a causal relationship. We have not shown, in column A of Table 11.3, that higher unemployment rates *cause* support for government assistance to the poor to be higher. To be sure, the evidence in column A is somewhat consistent with a causal connection, but it does not *prove* it. Why not? Because we have not controlled for other possible causes of support for government assistance. Surely there are other causes, in addition to how well or poorly the economy is performing, that might shape support for government assistance to the poor.

Consider, for instance, the possibility that higher aggregate levels of educational attainment change the population's calculus of the costs and benefits of liberal social policies. The better educated a society, the fewer people will see themselves as likely beneficiaries of assistance programs, and the more people will view themselves as likely payers for such programs. If this were the case, we would expect higher aggregate educational attainment to be negatively related to government assistance for the poor.

In column B of Table 11.3, we estimate another two-variable regression model, this time using the percentage of GSS respondents in each year between 1975 and 2014 for which data are available who have a bachelor's degree or higher – the variable is labeled "Degree" – as our independent variable. (Support for government assistance to the poor remains our dependent variable.) In the row labeled "Degree," we see that the parameter estimate is −0.42, which means that, on average, for every additional percentage point of respondents with at least a bachelor's degree, we expect to see a 0.42 percentage point decrease in support for government assistance to the poor. The coefficient is statistically significant.

Our separate two-variable regressions each show the relationship between the independent variable in the particular model and attitudes toward government assistance. But none of the parameter estimates in columns A or B controls for the other independent variable. We rectify that situation in column C, in which we estimate the effects of both the Unemployment and Degree variables on views of government assistance simultaneously.

Compare column C with columns A and B. In the row labeled "Degree," we see that the estimated parameter of $\hat{\beta} = -0.39$ indicates that, for every additional percentage point of respondents who have at least a bachelor's degree, we expect to see a 0.39 percentage point decrease in support of government aid to the poor, *while controlling for the effects of unemployment.* Note the additional clause in the interpretation as well as the emphasis that we place on it. Multiple regression coefficients always represent the effects of a one-point increase in that particular independent variable on the dependent variable, *while controlling for the effects of all other independent variables in the model.* The higher the percentage of college-educated respondents, the lower the support for government assistance should be, controlling for the unemployment rate.

But, critical to this chapter's focus on multiple regression, notice in column C how including the "Degree" variable changes the estimated effect of the "Unemployment" variable from an estimated 1.04 in column A to 0.87 in column C. The effect in column C is different because it *controls for the effects of "Degree."* That is, when the effects of high educational attainment are controlled for, the effects of unemployment fall a bit. The effect is still not statistically significant, however.[7] Note also that the R^2 statistic rises from 0.15 in column A to 0.37 in column C, which means that adding the "Degree" variable increased the proportion of the variance of our dependent variable that we have explained by 22 percent.[8]

In this particular example, the whole emphasis on controlling for other causes might seem like much ado about nothing. After all, comparing the three columns in Table 11.3 did not change our interpretation of whether unemployment rates affect attitudes toward government assistance. But we didn't know this until we tested for the effects of degree. And later in this chapter, we will see an example in which controlling for new causes of the dependent variable substantially changes our interpretations about

[7] And we can likewise compare the bivariate effect of Degree on Support for government assistance to the poor in column B with the multivariate results in column C, noting that the effect of Degree, in the multivariate context, fell by only 0.03 and remains statistically significant.

[8] It is important to be cautious when reporting contributions to R^2 statistics by individual independent variables, and this table provides a good example of why this is the case. If we were to estimate model A first and C second, we might be tempted to conclude that Unemployment explains 15 percent of the variance in Support for government assistance to the poor and Degree explains 22 percent. But if we estimated model B and then C, we might be tempted to conclude that Unemployment explains 10 percent of Support for government assistance and Degree explains 27 percent. Actually, both of these sets of conclusions are faulty. The R^2 is always a measure of the overall fit of the model to the dependent variable. So, all that we can say about the R^2 for model C is that Unemployment, Degree, and the intercept term together explain 37 percent of the variation in Support for government assistance. So, although we can talk about how the addition or subtraction of a particular variable to or from a model increases or decreases the model's R^2, we should not be tempted to attribute particular values of R^2 to specific independent variables. If we examine Figure 11.1, which appears in Section 11.8, we can get some intuition on why this is the case. The R^2 statistic for the model represented in this figure is $(f+d+b)/(a+f+d+b)$. It is the presence of area d that confounds our ability to make definitive statements about the contribution of individual variables to R^2.

causal relationships. We should be clear about one other thing regarding Table 11.3: Despite controlling for another variable, we still have a ways to go before we can say that we've controlled for all other possible causes of the dependent variable. As a result, we should be cautious about interpreting those results as proof of causality. However, as we continue to add independent variables to our regression model, we inch closer and closer to saying that we've controlled for every other possible cause that comes to mind. Recall that, all the way back in Chapter 1, we noted that one of the "rules of the road" of the scientific enterprise is to always be willing to consider new evidence. New evidence – in the form of controlling for other independent variables – can change our inferences about whether any particular independent variable is causally related to the dependent variable.

11.6 WHICH EFFECT IS "BIGGEST"?

In the preceding analysis, we might be tempted to look at the coefficients in column C of Table 11.3 for Unemployment (0.87) and for Degree (−0.39) and conclude that the effect for Unemployment is larger than the effect for Degree. As tempting as such a conclusion might be, it must be avoided for one critical reason: The two independent variables are measured in different metrics, which makes that comparison misleading. Unemployment rates are measured in a different metric – ranging from less than 4 percent for times during which the economy was performing well, all the way through weaker periods during which unemployment exceeded 9 percent per year – than are the percentage of respondents who have at least a bachelor's degree – which ranges from just over 9 percent in the data set to more than 18 percent. That makes comparing the coefficients misleading.

Because the coefficients in Table 11.3 each exist in the native metric of each variable, they are referred to as **unstandardized coefficients.** Although they are normally not comparable, there is a rather simple method to remove the metric of each variable to make them comparable with one another. As you might imagine, such coefficients, because they are on a standardized metric, are referred to as **standardized coefficients.** We compute them, quite simply, by taking the unstandardized coefficients and taking out the metrics – in the forms of the standard deviations – of both the independent and dependent variables:

$$\hat{\beta}_{\text{Std}} = \hat{\beta}\frac{s_X}{s_Y},$$

where $\hat{\beta}_{\text{Std}}$ is the standardized regression coefficient, $\hat{\beta}$ is the unstandardized coefficient (as in Table 11.3), and s_X and s_Y are the standard deviations of X and Y, respectively. The interpretation of the standardized coefficients changes, not surprisingly. Whereas the unstandardized coefficients represent the expected change in Y given a one-unit increase in X, the standardized coefficients represent the expected *standard deviation* change in Y given a *one-standard-deviation* increase in X. Now, because all parameter estimates are in the same units – that is, the standard deviations – they become comparable.

Implementing this formula for the unstandardized coefficients in column C of Table 11.3 produces the following results. First, for Unemployment,

$$\hat{\beta}_{\text{Std}} = 0.87 \left(\frac{1.419}{3.778} \right) = 0.33.$$

Next, for Degree,

$$\hat{\beta}_{\text{Std}} = -0.39 \left(\frac{4.630}{3.778} \right) = -0.47.$$

These coefficients would be interpreted as follows: For a one-standard-deviation increase in Unemployment, on average, we expect a 0.33-standard-deviation increase in the percentage supporting government assistance to the poor, controlling for the effect of Degree. And for a one-standard-deviation increase in Degree, we expect to see, on average, a 0.47-standard-deviation decrease in support, controlling for the effect of Unemployment. Note how, when looking at the unstandardized coefficients, we might have mistakenly thought that the effect of Unemployment was larger than the effect of Degree. But the standardized coefficients (correctly) tell the opposite story: The estimated effect of Unemployment is about two-thirds of the size of the effect of Degree.[9]

11.7 STATISTICAL AND SUBSTANTIVE SIGNIFICANCE

Related to the admonition about which effect is "biggest," consider the following, seemingly simpler, question: Are the effects found in column C of Table 11.3 "big"? A tempting answer to that question is "Well of course the effect of Degree is big, with a coefficient that is statistically significant.

[9] Some objections have been raised about the use of standardized coefficients (King, 1986). From a technical perspective, because standard deviations can differ across samples, this makes the results of standardized coefficients particularly sample-specific. Additionally, and from a broader perspective, one-unit or one-standard-deviation shifts in different independent variables have different substantive meanings regardless of the metrics in which the variables are measured. We might therefore logically conclude that there isn't much use in trying to figure out which effect is biggest.

Therefore, it's big. The effect of Unemployment, on the other hand, is not significant and, thus, not big."

That logic, although perhaps appealing, is faulty. Recall the discussion from Chapter 8 (specifically, Section 8.4.2) on the effects of sample size on the magnitude of the standard error of the mean. And we noted the same effects of sample size on the magnitude of the standard error of our regression coefficients (specifically, Section 10.4.4). What this means is that, even if the strength of the relationship (as measured by our coefficient estimates) remains constant, by merely increasing our sample size we can affect the statistical significance of those coefficients. Why? Because statistical significance is determined by a *t*-test (see Section 10.4.6) in which the standard error is in the denominator of that quotient. What you can remember is that larger sample sizes will shrink standard errors and therefore make finding statistically significant relationships more likely.[10] It is also apparent from Appendix B that, when the number of degrees of freedom is greater, it is easier to achieve statistical significance.

We hope that you can see that arbitrarily increasing the size of a sample, and therefore finding statistically significant relationships, does not in any way make an effect "bigger" or even "big." Recall that such changes to the standard errors have no bearing on the rise-over-run nature of the slope coefficients themselves.

How, then, should you judge whether an effect of one variable on another is "big"? One way is to use the method just described – using standardized coefficients. By placing the variances of X and Y on the same metric, it is possible to come to a judgment about how big an effect is. This is particularly helpful when the independent variables X and Z, or the dependent variable Y, or both, are measured in metrics that are unfamiliar or artificial.

When the metrics of the variables in a regression analysis are intuitive and well known, however, rendering a judgment about whether an effect is large or small becomes something of a matter of interpretation. For example, say we were interested in the effects of changes in the unemployment rate (X) on the President's approval rating (Y). It is very simple to interpret that a slope coefficient of, say, -1.51, means that, for every additional point of unemployment, we expect approval to go down by 1.51 points, controlling for other factors in the model. Is that effect large, small, or moderate? There is something of a judgment call to be made here, but at least in this

[10] To be certain, it's not always possible to increase sample sizes, and, even when possible, it is nearly always costly to do so. The research situations in which increasing sample size is most likely, albeit still expensive, is in mass-based survey research, as we discussed in Chapter 5.

case, the metrics of both X and Y are quite familiar; most people with even an elementary familiarity with politics will need no explanation as to what unemployment rates mean or what approval polls mean. Independent of the statistical significance of that estimate – which, you should note, we have not mentioned here – discussions of this sort represent attempts to judge the **substantive significance** of a coefficient estimate. Substantive significance is more difficult to judge than statistical significance because there are no numeric formulae for making such judgments. Instead, substantive significance is a judgment call about whether or not statistically significant relationships are "large" or "small" in terms of their real-world impact.

From time to time we will see a "large" parameter estimate that is not statistically significant. Although it is tempting to describe such a result as substantively significant, it is not. We can understand this by thinking about what it means for a particular result to be statistically significant. As we discussed in Chapter 10, in most cases we are testing the null hypothesis that the population parameter is equal to zero. In such cases, even when we have a large parameter estimate, if it is statistically insignificant, this means that it is not statistically distinguishable from zero. Therefore, a parameter estimate can be substantively significant only when it is also statistically significant.

11.8 WHAT HAPPENS WHEN WE FAIL TO CONTROL FOR Z

Controlling for the effects of other possible causes of our dependent variable Y, we have maintained, is critical to making the correct causal inferences. Some of you might be wondering something like the following: "How does omitting Z from a regression model affect my inference of whether X causes Y? Z isn't X, and Z isn't Y, so why should omitting Z matter?"

Consider the following three-variable regression model which involves our now-familiar trio of X, Y, and Z:

$$Y_i = \alpha + \beta_1 X_i + \beta_2 Z_i + u_i.$$

And assume, for the moment, that this is the *correct* model of reality. That is, the only systematic causes of Y are X and Z; and, to some degree, Y is also influenced by some random error component, u.

Now let's assume that, instead of estimating this correct model, we fail to estimate the effects of Z. That is, we estimate

$$Y_i = \alpha + \beta_1^* X_i + u_i^*.$$

As we previously hinted, the value of β_1 in the correct, three-variable equation and the value of β_1^* will not be identical under most circumstances. (We'll see the exceptions in a moment.) And that, right there, should be enough to raise red flags. For, if we know that the three-variable model is the *correct* model – and what that means, of course, is that the estimated value of β_1 that we obtain from the data will be equal to the true population value – and if we know that β_1 will not be equal to β_1^*, then there is a problem with the estimated value of β_1^*. That problem is a statistical problem called **bias**, which means that the expected value of the parameter estimate that we obtain from a sample will not be equal to the true population parameter. The specific type of bias that results from the failure to include a variable that belongs in our regression model is called **omitted-variables bias.**

Let's get specific about the nature of omitted-variables bias. If, instead of estimating the true three-variable model, we estimate the incorrect two-variable model, the formula for the slope β_1^* will be

$$\hat{\beta}_1^* = \frac{\sum_{i=1}^{n}(X_i - \bar{X})(Y_i - \bar{Y})}{\sum_{i=1}^{n}(X_i - \bar{X})^2}.$$

Notice that this is simply the bivariate formula for the effect of X on Y. (Of course, the model we just estimated is a bivariate model, in spite of the fact that we know that Z, as well as X, affects Y.) But because we know that Z *should* be in the model, and we know from Chapter 10 that regression lines travel through the mean value of each variable, we can figure out that the following is true:

$$(Y_i - \bar{Y}) = \beta_1(X_i - \bar{X}) + \beta_2(Z_i - \bar{Z}) + (u_i - \bar{u}).$$

We can do this because we know that the plane will travel through each variable's mean.

Now notice that the left-hand side of the preceding equation, the $(Y_i - \bar{Y})$, is identical to one portion of the numerator of the slope for $\hat{\beta}_1^*$. Therefore we can substitute the right-hand side of the preceding equation – yes, that entire mess – into the numerator of the formula for $\hat{\beta}_1^*$.

The resulting math isn't anything that is beyond your skills in algebra, but it is cumbersome, so we won't derive it here. After a few lines of multiplying and reducing, though, the formula for $\hat{\beta}_1^*$ will reduce to

$$E(\hat{\beta}_1^*) = \beta_1 + \beta_2 \frac{\sum_{i=1}^{n}(X_i - \bar{X})(Z_i - \bar{Z})}{\sum_{i=1}^{n}(X_i - \bar{X})^2}.$$

This might seem like a mouthful – a fact that's rather hard to deny – but there is a very important message in it. What the equation says is that the estimated effect of X on Y, $\hat{\beta}_1^*$, in which we do not include the effects of

Z on Y (but should have), will be equal to the true β_1 – that is, the effect with Z taken into account – plus a bundle of other stuff. That other stuff, strictly speaking, is bias. And because this bias came about as a result of omitting a variable (Z) that should have been in the model, this type of bias is known as omitted-variables bias.

Obviously, we'd like the expected value of our $\hat{\beta}_1^*$ (estimated without Z) to equal the true β_1 (as if we had estimated the equation with Z). And if the product on the right-hand side of the "+" sign in the preceding equation equals zero, it will. When will that happen?[11] In two circumstances, neither of which is particularly likely. First, $\hat{\beta}_1^* = \beta_1$ if $\beta_2 = 0$. Second, $\hat{\beta}_1^* = \beta_1$ if the large quotient at the end of the equation, the

$$\frac{\sum_{i=1}^{n}(X_i - \bar{X})(Z_i - \bar{Z})}{\sum_{i=1}^{n}(X_i - \bar{X})^2},$$

is equal to zero. What is that quotient? It should look familiar; in fact, it is the bivariate slope parameter of a regression of Z on X.

In the first of these two special circumstances, the bias term will equal zero if and only if the effect of Z on Y – that is, the parameter β_2 – is zero. Okay, so it's safe to omit an independent variable from a regression equation if it has no effect on the dependent variable. (If that seems obvious to you, good.) The second circumstance is a bit more interesting: It's safe to omit an independent variable Z from an equation if it is entirely unrelated to the other independent variable X. Of course, if we omit Z in such circumstances, we'll still be deprived of understanding how Z affects Y; but at least, so long as Z and X are absolutely unrelated, omitting Z will not adversely affect our estimate of the effect of X on Y.[12]

We emphasize that this second condition is unlikely to occur in practice. Therefore, if Z affects Y, and Z and X are related, then if we omit Z from our model, our bias term will not equal zero. In the end, omitting Z will cause us to misestimate the effect of X on Y.

This result has many practical implications. Foremost among them is the fact that, even if you aren't interested theoretically in the connection between Z and Y, you need to control for it, statistically, in order to get an unbiased estimate of the impact of X, which is the focus of the theoretical investigation.

That might seem unfair, but it's true. If we estimate a regression model that omits an independent variable (Z) that belongs in the model, then the effects of that Z will somehow work their way into the parameter estimates for the independent variable that we do estimate (X) and pollute our estimate of the effect of X on Y.

[11] To be very clear, for a mathematical product to equal zero, either one or both of the components must be zero.

[12] Omitting Z from our regression model also drives down the R^2 statistic.

The preceding equation also suggests when the magnitude of the bias is likely to be large and when it is likely to be small. If either or both of the components of the bias term, i.e., β_2 and

$$\frac{\sum_{i=1}^{n}(X_i - \bar{X})(Z_i - \bar{Z})}{\sum_{i=1}^{n}(X_i - \bar{X})^2}, \tag{11.1}$$

are *close to* zero, then the bias is likely to be small (because the bias term is the product of both components); but if both are likely to be large, then the bias is likely to be quite large.

Moreover, the equation also suggests the likely *direction* of the bias. All we have said thus far is that the coefficient $\hat{\beta}_1^*$ will be biased – that is, it will not equal its true value. But will it be too large or too small? If we have good guesses about the values of β_2 and the correlation between X and Z – that is, whether or not they are positive or negative – then we can suspect the direction of the bias. For example, suppose that β_1, β_2, and the correlation between X and Z are all positive. That means that our estimated coefficient $\hat{\beta}_1^*$ will be larger than it is supposed to be, because a positive number plus the product of two positive numbers will be a still-larger positive number. And so on.[13]

To better understand the importance of controlling for other possible causes of the dependent variable and the importance of the relationship (or the lack of one) between X and Z, consider the following graphical illustrations. In Figure 11.1, we represent the total variation of Y, X, and Z each with a circle.[14] The covariation between any of these two variables – or among all three – is represented by the places where the circles overlap. Thus, in the figure, the total variation in Y is represented as the sum of the area $a + b + d + f$. The covariation between Y and X is represented by the area $b + d$.

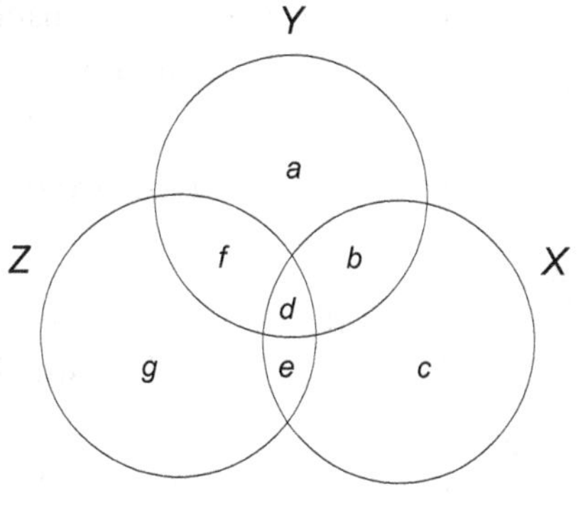

Figure 11.1 Venn diagram in which X, Y, and Z are correlated

Note in Figure 11.1, though, that the variable Z is related to both Y and X (because the circle for Z overlaps with both Y and X). In particular, the relationship between Y and Z is accounted for by the area

13 With more than two independent variables, it becomes more complex to figure out the direction of the bias.

14 Recall from Chapter 10 how we introduced Venn diagrams to represent variation (the circles) and covariation (the overlapping portion of the circles).

$f + d$, and the relationship between Z and X is accounted for by the area $d + e$. As we have already seen, d is also a portion of the relationship between Y and X. If, hypothetically, we erased the circle for Z from Figure 11.1, we would (incorrectly) attribute all of the area $b + d$ to X, when in fact the d portion of the variation in Y is shared by *both* X and Z. This is why, when Z is related to both X and Y, if we fail to control for Z, we will end up with a biased estimate of X's effect on Y.

Consider the alternative scenario, in which both X and Z affect Y, but X and Z are completely unrelated to one another. That scenario is portrayed graphically in Figure 11.2. There, the circles for both X and Z overlap with the circle for Y, but they do not overlap at all with one another. In that case – which, we have noted, is unlikely in applied research – we can safely omit consideration of Z when considering the effects of X on Y. In Figure 11.2, the relationship between X and Y, the area b, is unaffected by the presence (or absence) of Z in the model.[15]

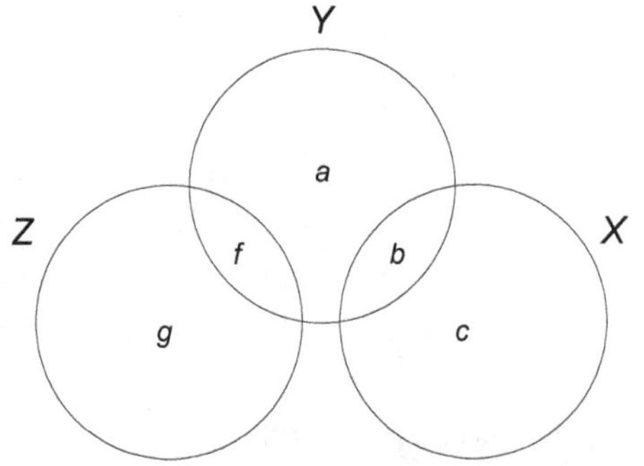

Figure 11.2 Venn diagram in which X and Z are correlated with Y, but not with each other

11.8.1 An Additional Minimal Mathematical Requirement in Multiple Regression

We outlined a set of assumptions and minimal mathematical requirements for the two-variable regression model in Chapter 10. In multiple regression, all of these assumptions are made and all of the same minimal mathematical requirements remain in place. In addition to those, however, we need to add one more minimal mathematical requirement to be able to estimate our multiple regression models: It must be the case that *there is no exact linear relationship* between any two or more of our independent variables (which we have called X and Z). This is also called the assumption of no **perfect multicollinearity** (by which we mean that X and Z cannot be *perfectly* collinear, with a correlation coefficient of $r = 1.0$).

What does it mean to say that X and Z cannot exist in an exact linear relationship? Refer back to Figure 11.1. If X and Z had an *exact*

[15] For identical reasons, we could safely estimate the effect of Z on Y, the area f, without considering the effect of X.

linear relationship, instead of having some degree of overlap – that is, some imperfect degree of correlation – the circles would be exactly on top of one another. In such cases, it is literally impossible to estimate the regression model, as separating out the effects of X on Y from the effects of Z on Y is impossible.

This is not to say that we must assume that X and Z are entirely uncorrelated with one another (as in Figure 11.2). In fact, in almost all applications, X and Z will have some degree of correlation between them. Things become complicated only as that correlation approaches 1.0; and when it hits 1.0, the regression model will fail to be estimable with both X and Z as independent variables.

11.9 BEING SMART WITH DUMMY INDEPENDENT VARIABLES IN OLS

In Chapter 7 we discussed how an important part of knowing your data involves knowing the metric in which each of your variables is measured. Throughout the examples that we have examined thus far, almost all of the variables, both the independent and dependent variables, have been continuous. This is not by accident. We chose examples with continuous variables because they are, in many cases, easier to interpret than models in which the variables are noncontinuous. In this section, though, we consider a series of scenarios involving independent variables that are *not* continuous. We begin with a relatively simple case in which we have a categorical independent variable that takes on one of two possible values for all cases. Categorical variables like this are commonly referred to as **dummy variables.** Although any two values will do, the most common form of dummy variable is one that takes on values of one or zero. These variables are also sometimes referred to as "indicator variables" when a value of one indicates the presence of a particular characteristic and a value of zero indicates the absence of that characteristic. After considering dummy variables that reflect two possible values, we then consider more complicated examples in which we have an independent variable that is categorical with more than two values. We conclude this section with an examination of how to handle models in which we have multiple dummy variables representing multiple and overlapping classifications of cases.

11.9.1 Using Dummy Variables to Test Hypotheses about a Categorical Independent Variable with Only Two Values

We know from a long tradition of social science research that education and gender, among other factors, play key roles in determining income.

Coefficients[a]

Model	Unstandardized Coefficients B	Std. Error	Standardized Coefficients Beta	t	Sig.
1 (Constant)	6.897	.712		9.690	.000
Female	-2.512	.281	-.206	-8.925	.000
Educ	.677	.049	.320	18.849	.000

[a] Dependent Variable: Rincom16

Excluded Variables

Model	Beta In	t	Sig	Partial Correlation	Collinearity Statistics Tolerance
1 Male	.[b]	.	.	.	.000

[a] Dependent Variable: Rincom16
[b] Predictors: (Constant), Educ, Female

Figure 11.3 SPSS output when we include both gender dummy variables in our model

Throughout the next few examples we will use individual (as opposed to household) income as our dependent variable and education and gender as our independent variables. The 2016 GSS is our data set. For the sake of these examples, we are going to assume that our dependent variable, income, is continuous, as is our independent variable, education; gender is measured as a dichotomy (male or female).[16] Initially, each respondent's gender was coded as equaling either 1 for "male" or 2 for "female." Although we could leave this gender variable as it is and run our analyses, we chose to use this variable to create two new dummy variables, "male" equaling 1 for "yes" and 0 for "no," and "female" equaling 1 for "yes" and 0 for "no."

Our first inclination is to estimate an OLS model in which the specification is the following:

$$\text{Income}_i = \alpha + \beta_1 \text{Education}_i + \beta_2 \text{Male}_i + \beta_3 \text{Female}_i + u_i.$$

But if we try to estimate this model, our statistical computer program will revolt and give us an error message.[17] Figure 11.3 shows a screenshot of what this output looks like in SPSS. We can see that SPSS has reported the results from the following model instead of what we asked for:

$$\text{Income}_i = \alpha + \beta_1 \text{Education}_i + \beta_2 \text{Female}_i + u_i.$$

Instead of the estimates for β_2 on the second row of parameter estimates, we see in the "excluded variables" panel of the output that the variable "Male" was dropped from the model. This is the case because

[16] In this survey, a respondent's annual income is measured on a scale ranging from 1 (less than $1000) to 26 ($170,000 or more).

[17] Most programs will throw one of the two variables out of the model and report the results from the resulting model along with an error message.

we have failed to meet the additional minimal mathematical criteria that we introduced when we moved from two-variable OLS to multiple OLS earlier in this chapter – "no perfect multicollinearity." The reason that we have failed to meet this is that, for two of the independent variables in our model, Male_i and Female_i, it is the case that

$$\text{Male}_i + \text{Female}_i = 1 \quad \forall\, i.$$

In other words, our variables "Male" and "Female" are perfectly correlated: If we know a respondent's value on the "Male" variable, then we know their value on the "Female" variable with perfect certainty.

When this happens with dummy variables, we call this situation the **dummy-variable trap**. To avoid the dummy-variable trap, we have to omit one of our dummy variables. But we want to be able to compare the effects of being male with the effects of being female to test our hypothesis. How can we do this if we have to omit one of our two variables that measure gender? Before we answer this question, let's look at the results in Table 11.4 from the two different models in which we omit one of these two variables. We can learn a lot by looking at what is and what is not the same across these two models. In both models, the parameter estimate and standard error for education are identical. The R^2 statistics are also identical. The parameter estimate and the standard error for the intercept are different across the two models. The parameter estimate for male is 2.51, whereas that for female is −2.51, although the standard error for each of these parameter estimates is 0.28. If you're starting to think that all of these similarities cannot have happened by coincidence, you are correct.

Table 11.4 Two models of the effects of gender and education on income

Independent variable	Model 1	Model 2
Male	—	2.51***
		(0.28)
Female	−2.51***	—
	(0.28)	
Education	0.68***	0.68***
	(0.05)	(0.05)
Intercept	6.90***	4.39***
	(0.71)	(0.73)
n	1631	1631
R^2	0.14	0.14

Notes: The dependent variable in both models is the respondent's income. Standard errors in parentheses. Two-sided t-tests: *** $p < 0.01$.

In fact, these two models are, mathematically speaking, the same model. All of the $\hat{Y}$ values and residuals for the individual cases are *exactly* the same. With education held constant, the estimated difference between being male and being female is 2.51. The sign on this parameter estimate switches from negative to positive when we go from model 1 to model 2 because we are phrasing the question differently across the two models:

- For model 1: "What is the estimated difference for a female compared with a male?"
- For model 2: "What is the estimated difference for a male compared with a female?"

So why are the intercepts different? Think back to our discussion in Chapter 10 about the interpretation of the intercept – it is the estimated value of the dependent variable when the independent variables are all equal to zero. In model 1 this means the estimated value of the dependent variable for a man with no education. In model 2 this means the estimated value of the dependent variable for a woman with no education. And the difference between these two values – you guessed it – is $6.90-4.39 = 2.51$!

What does the regression line from model 1 or model 2 look like? The answer is that it depends on the gender of the individual for which we are plotting the line, but that it does not depend on which of these two models we use. For men, where $\text{Female}_i = 0$ and $\text{Male}_i = 1$, the predicted values are calculated as follows:

Model 1 for men:

$$\begin{aligned}\hat{Y}_i &= 6.90 - (2.51 \times \text{Female}_i) + (0.68 \times \text{Education}_i)\\ &= 6.90 - (2.51 \times 0) + (0.68 \times \text{Education}_i)\\ &= 6.90 + (0.68 \times \text{Education}_i).\end{aligned}$$

Model 2 for men:

$$\begin{aligned}\hat{Y}_i &= 4.39 + (2.51 \times \text{Male}_i) + (0.68 \times \text{Education}_i)\\ &= 4.39 + (2.51 \times 1) + (0.68 \times \text{Education}_i)\\ &= 6.90 + (0.68 \times \text{Education}_i).\end{aligned}$$

So we can see that, for men, regardless of whether we use the results from model 1 or model 2, the formula for predicted values is the same. For women, where $\text{Female}_i = 1$ and $\text{Male}_i = 0$, the predicted values are calculated as follows:

Model 1 for women:

$$\begin{aligned}\hat{Y}_i &= 6.90 - (2.51 \times \text{Female}_i) + (0.68 \times \text{Education}_i)\\ &= 6.90 - (2.51 \times 1) + (0.68 \times \text{Education}_i)\\ &= 4.39 + (0.68 \times \text{Education}_i).\end{aligned}$$

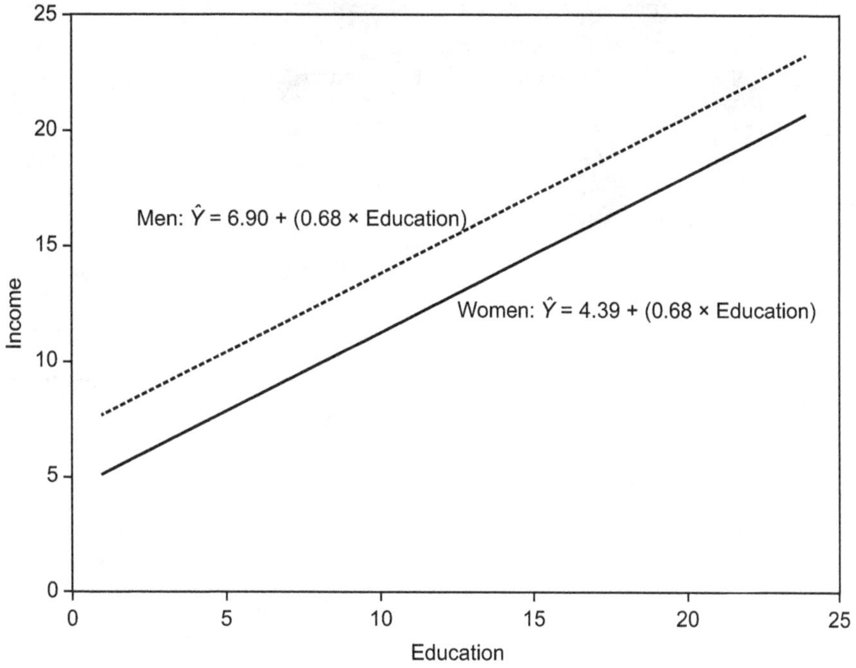

Figure 11.4 Regression lines from the model with a dummy variable for gender

Model 2 for women:

$$\begin{aligned}\hat{Y}_i &= 4.39 + (2.51 \times \text{Male}_i) + (0.68 \times \text{Education}_i)\\ &= 4.39 + (2.51 \times 0) + (0.68 \times \text{Education}_i)\\ &= 4.39 + (0.68 \times \text{Education}_i).\end{aligned}$$

Again, the formula from model 1 is the same as the formula from model 2 for women. To illustrate these two sets of predictions, we have plotted them in Figure 11.4. Given that the two predictive formulae have the same slope, it is not surprising to see that the two lines in this figure are parallel to each other with the intercept difference determining the space between the two lines.

11.9.2 Using Dummy Variables to Test Hypotheses about a Categorical Independent Variable with More Than Two Values

As you might imagine, when we have a categorical variable with more than two categories and we want to include it in an OLS model, things get more complicated. We'll keep with our running example of modeling respondents' income as a function of their educational attainments. In this section we work with a respondent's race/ethnicity as a categorical

Table 11.5 Racial/ethnic identification in the 2016 GSS

Value	Category	Frequency	Percent
0	White	2088	75.4
1	Black	487	17.6
2	Asian	90	3.3
3	Hispanic	103	3.7
	Totals	1631	100.0

independent variable. The frequency of different responses to this item in the 2016 GSS is displayed in Table 11.5.

Could we use the race/ethnicity variable as it is in our regression models? That would be a bad idea. Remember, this is a categorical variable, in which the values of the variable are not ordered from lowest to highest. Indeed, there is no such thing as "lowest" or "highest" on this variable. So running a regression model with the data as is would be meaningless. But beware: *Your statistics package does not know that this is a categorical variable.* It will be more than happy to run the regression and report parameter estimates to you, even though these estimates will be nonsensical.

In the previous subsection, in which we had a categorical variable (gender) with only two possible values, we saw that, when we switched which value was represented by "1" and which by "0," the estimated parameter switched signs. This was the case because we were asking a different question. With a categorical independent variable that has more than two values, we have more than two possible questions that we can ask. Because using the variable as is is not an option, the best strategy for modeling the effects of such an independent variable is to include a dummy variable for all values of that independent variable *except one.*[18] The value of the independent variable for which we do not include a dummy variable is known as the **reference category**. This is the case because the parameter estimates for all of the dummy variables representing the other values of the independent variable are estimated with reference to that value of the independent variable. So let's say that we choose to estimate the following model:

$$\text{Income}_i = \alpha + \beta_1 \text{Education}_i + \beta_2 \text{White}_i + \beta_3 \text{Asian}_i + \beta_4 \text{Hispanic}_i + u_i.$$

For this model we would be using "Black" as our reference category for race/ethnicity. This would mean that $\hat{\beta}_2$ would be the estimated effect

[18] If our theory was that only one category, such as Hispanics, was different from all of the others, then we would collapse the remaining categories of the variable in question

of being White *relative to* being Black, and we could use this value along with its standard error to test the hypothesis that this effect was statistically significant, controlling for the effects of education. The remaining parameter estimates ($\hat{\beta}_3$ and $\hat{\beta}_4$) would both also be interpreted as the estimated effect of being in the each of the remaining categories relative to "Blacks." The value that we choose to use as our reference category does not matter, as long as we interpret our results appropriately. But we can use the choice of the reference category to focus on the relationships in which we are particularly interested. For each possible pair of categories of the independent variable, we can conduct a separate hypothesis test. The easiest way to get all of the p-values in which we are interested is to estimate the model multiple times with different reference categories. Table 11.6 displays a model of income scores with the four different choices of reference categories. It is worth emphasizing that this is *not* a table with four different models, but it *is* a table with the same model displayed four different ways. From this table we can see that, when we control for the

Table 11.6 The same model of race/ethnicity and education effects on income with different reference categories

Independent variable	Model 1	Model 2	Model 3	Model 4
Education	0.602**	0.597**	0.619**	0.612**
	(0.051)	(0.051)	(0.050)	(0.051)
White	2.053**	1.948**	0.750	—
	(0.361)	(0.594)	(0.592)	
Asian	2.970**	2.872**	—	1.005
	(0.844)	(0.972)	—	(0.797)
Hispanic	0.719	—	−0.538	−1.203
	(0.830)	—	(0.962)	(0.792)
Black	—	−0.005	−1.188	−1.840**
		(0.661)	(0.666)	(0.383)
Intercept	5.050**	5.228**	6.108**	6.848**
	(0.757)	(0.839)	(0.926)	(0.744)
n	1631	1631	1631	1631
R^2	0.11	0.11	0.11	0.11

Notes: The dependent variable in all models is the respondent's income. Standard errors in parentheses. Two-sided t-tests: ** $p < 0.05$.

together and we would have a two-category independent variable. We should do this only if we have a theoretical justification for doing so.

effects of education, some of the categories of race/ethnicity are statistically different from each other on income whereas others are not. This raises an interesting question: Can we say that the effect of race/ethnicity, controlling for education, is statistically significant? The answer is that it depends on which categories of race/ethnicity we want to compare.

11.9.3 Using Dummy Variables to Test Hypotheses about Multiple Independent Variables

It is often the case that we will want to use multiple dummy independent variables in the same model. Consider the model presented in Table 11.7, which was estimated from the 2016 GSS data. The dependent variable is respondents' income. The model has two continuous independent variables (education and age) and two dummy independent variables (residence and gender). As Table 11.8 indicates, all four possible combinations of these two dummy variables occurred in the sample of cases on which the model presented in Table 11.7 was estimated.

So, how do we interpret these results? It's actually not as hard as it might first appear. Remember from earlier in this chapter that, when we move from a bivariate regression model to a multiple regression model, we have to interpret each parameter estimate as the estimated effect of a

Table 11.7 Model with two continuous independent variables and two dummy independent variables

Independent variable	Parameter estimate
Education	0.655**
	(0.048)
Age	0.069**
	(0.010)
Urban	0.811*
	(0.406)
Male	2.510**
	(0.278)
Intercept	0.933
	(0.878)
n	1626
R^2	0.16

Notes: The dependent variable is the respondent's income. Standard errors in parentheses. Two-sided t-tests: ** $p < 0.01$; * $p < 0.05$.

Table 11.8 Two overlapping dummy variables in models from the 2016 GSS

		Gender	
		Female (0)	Male (1)
Residence	Nonurban (0)	120	101
	Urban (1)	711	694

Note: Numbers in cells represent the number of cases.

one-point increase in that particular independent variable on the dependent variable, *while controlling for the effects of all other independent variables in the model*. This has not changed. Instead, what is a little different from the examples that we have considered before is that we have two dummy independent variables that can vary independently of each other. So, when we interpret the estimated effect of each continuous independent variable, we interpret the parameter estimate as the estimated effect of a one-point increase in that particular independent variable on the dependent variable, while controlling for the effects of all other independent variables in the model, including the two dummy variables. And, when we interpret the estimated effect of each dummy independent variable, we interpret the parameter estimate as the estimated effect of that variable having a value of one versus zero on the dependent variable, while controlling for the effects of all other independent variables in the model, including the other dummy variable. For instance, the estimated effect of a one-unit increase in education, holding everything else constant, is a 0.655 dollar increase in income. And, the estimated effect of residing in an urban (versus a nonurban) area, holding everything else constant, is a 0.811 dollar increase in income.

11.10 TESTING INTERACTIVE HYPOTHESES WITH DUMMY VARIABLES

All of the OLS models that we have examined so far have been what we could call "additive models." To calculate the $\hat{Y}$ value for a particular case from an additive model, we simply multiply each independent variable value for that case by the appropriate parameter estimate and *add* these values together. In this section we explore some **interactive models**. Interactive models contain at least one independent variable that we create by multiplying together two or more independent variables. When we specify interactive models, we are testing theories about how the effects of one independent variable on our dependent variable may be contingent on the value of another independent variable. We will continue with our running example of modeling respondents' income. We begin with an additive model with the following specification:

$$\text{Income}_i = \alpha + \beta_1 \text{Education}_i + \beta_2 \text{Male}_i + u_i.$$

In this model we are testing the theory that a respondent's income is a function of his or her education and gender. This specification seems pretty reasonable, but we also want to test an additional theory that education has a stronger effect on income among men than it does among women. Notice the difference in phrasing there. In essence, we want to test the hypothesis that the slope of the line representing the relationship between education and income is *steeper* for men than it is for women. To test this hypothesis, we need to create a new variable that is the product of the two independent variables in our model and include this new variable in our model:

$$\begin{aligned}\text{Income}_i = \alpha + \beta_1 \text{Education}_i + \beta_2 \text{Male}_i \\ + \beta_3 (\text{Education}_i \times \text{Male}_i) + u_i.\end{aligned}$$

By specifying our model as such, we have created two different models for women and men. So we can rewrite our model as follows:

$$\begin{aligned}&\text{For Women (Male} = 0\text{):}\\ &\quad \text{Income}_i = \alpha + \beta_1 \text{Education}_i + u_i.\\ &\text{For Men (Male} = 1\text{):}\\ &\quad \text{Income}_i = \alpha + \beta_1 \text{Education}_i\\ &\qquad\qquad + (\beta_2 + \beta_3)(\text{Education}_i) + u_i.\end{aligned}$$

And we can rewrite the formula for men as follows:

$$\begin{aligned}&\text{For Men (Male} = 1\text{):}\\ &\quad \text{Income}_i = (\alpha + \beta_2) + (\beta_1 + \beta_3)(\text{Education}_i) + u_i.\end{aligned}$$

What this all boils down to is that we are allowing our regression line to be different for men and women. For women, the intercept is α and the slope is β_1. For men, the intercept is $\alpha + \beta_2$ and the slope is $\beta_1 + \beta_3$. However, if $\beta_2 = 0$ and $\beta_3 = 0$, then the regression lines for men and women will be the same. Table 11.9 shows the results for our additive and interactive models of the effects of gender and education on income. We can see from the interactive model that we can reject the null hypothesis that $\beta_2 = 0$ and the null hypothesis that $\beta_3 = 0$, so our regression lines for men and women are different. We can also see that the intercept for the line for men $(\alpha + \beta_2)$ is higher than the intercept for women (α). However, contrary to our expectations based on the literature, the estimated effect of education for men is less than the effect of education for women.

Table 11.9 The effects of gender and education on income

Independent variable	Additive model	Interactive model
Education	0.68**	0.83**
	(0.05)	(0.07)
Male	2.51**	6.96**
	(0.28)	(1.41)
Education × Male	—	−0.31**
		(0.10)
Intercept	4.39**	2.13*
	(0.73)	(1.01)
n	1631	1631
R^2	0.14	0.14

Notes: The dependent variable in both models is the respondent's income. Standard errors in parentheses. Two-sided *t*-tests: ** $p < 0.01$; * $p < 0.05$.

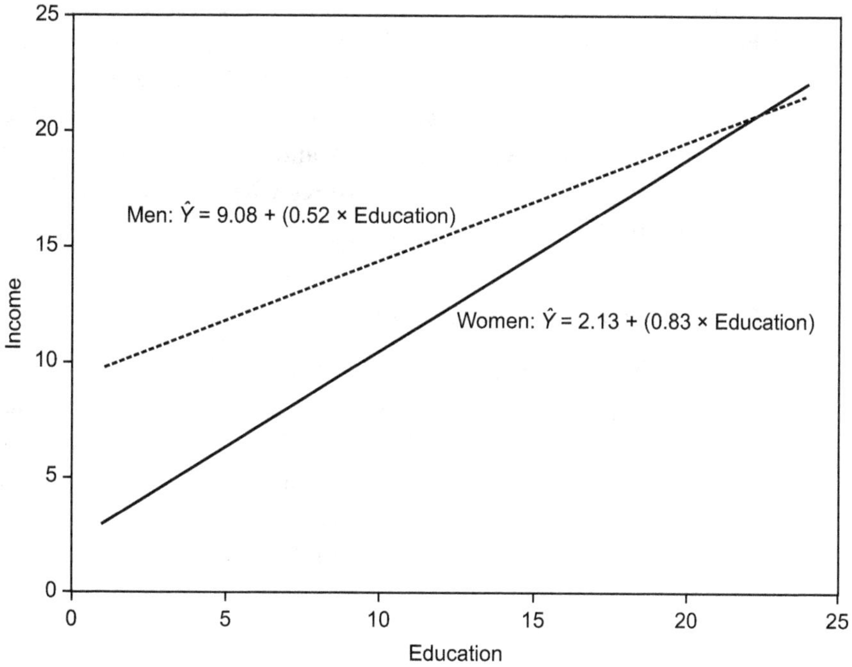

Figure 11.5 Regression lines from the interactive model

The best way to see the combined effect of all of the results from the interactive model in Table 11.9 is to look at them graphically in a figure such as Figure 11.5. From Figure 11.5 we can see the regression lines for men and for women across the range of the independent variable. It is clear from Figure 11.5 that, although men tend to have higher incomes than women, this gender gap narrows when we compare those individuals who have higher levels of education.

11.11 DUMMY DEPENDENT VARIABLES

Thus far, our discussion of dummy variables has been limited to situations in which the variable in question is one of the independent variables in our model. The obstacles in those models are relatively straightforward. Things get a bit more complicated, however, when our dependent variable is a dummy variable.

Certainly, many of the dependent variables of theoretical interest to sociologists are not continuous. Very often, this means that we need to move to a statistical model other than OLS if we want to get reasonable estimates for our hypothesis testing. One exception to this is the **linear probability model** (LPM). The LPM is an OLS model in which the dependent variable is a dummy variable. It is called a "probability" model because we can interpret the $\hat{Y}$ values as "predicted probabilities." But, as we will see, it is not without problems. Because of these problems, many sociologists do not use the LPM. We provide a brief discussion of the popular alternatives to the LPM and then conclude this section with a discussion of goodness-of-fit measures when the dependent variable is a dummy variable.

11.11.1 The Linear Probability Model

As an example of a dummy dependent variable, we use the choice that most U.S. voters in the 2004 presidential election made between voting for the incumbent George W. Bush and his Democratic challenger John Kerry.[19] Our dependent variable, which we will call "Bush," is equal to one for respondents who reported voting for Bush and equal to zero for respondents who reported voting for Kerry. For our model we theorize

[19] There was only a handful of respondents to the ANES who refused to reveal their vote to the interviewers or voted for a different candidate. But there were a large number of respondents who reported that they did not vote. By excluding all of these categories, we are defining the population about which we want to make inferences as those who voted for Kerry or Bush. Including respondents who voted for other candidates, refused to report their vote, or those who did not vote would amount to changing from a dichotomous categorical dependent variable to a multichotomous categorical dependent variable. The types of models used for this type of dependent variable are substantially more complicated, and are beyond the scope of this book.

Table 11.10 The effects of partisanship and performance evaluations on votes for Bush in 2004

Independent variable	Parameter estimate
Party identification	0.09**
	(0.01)
Evaluation: War on terror	0.08**
	(0.01)
Evaluation: Health of the economy	0.08**
	(0.01)
Intercept	0.60**
	(0.01)
R^2	0.73
n	780

Notes: The dependent variable is equal to one if the respondent voted for Bush and equal to zero if they voted for Kerry. Standard errors in parentheses. Two-sided t-tests: ** $p < 0.01$; * $p < 0.05$.

that the decision to vote for Bush or Kerry is a function of an individual's partisan identification (ranging from –3 for strong Democrats, to 0 for Independents, to +3 for strong Republican identifiers) and their evaluation of the job that Bush did in handling the war on terror and the health of the economy (both of these evaluations range from +2 for "approve strongly" to –2 for "disapprove strongly"). The formula for this model is:

$$\text{Bush}_i = \alpha + \beta_1 \text{Party ID}_i + \beta_2 \text{War evaluation}_i + \beta_3 \text{Economic evaluation}_i + u_i.$$

Table 11.10 presents the OLS results from this model. We can see from the table that all of the parameter estimates are statistically significantis often the case that we in the expected (positive) direction. Not surprisingly, we see that people who identified with the Republican Party and who had more approving evaluations of the President's handling of the war and the economy were more likely to vote for him.

To examine how the interpretation of this model is different from that of a regular OLS model, let's calculate some individual $\hat{Y}$ values. We know from Table 11.10 that the formula for $\hat{Y}$ is:

$$\hat{Y}_i = 0.6 + 0.09 \times \text{Party ID}_i + 0.08 \times \text{War evaluation}_i + 0.08 \times \text{Economic evaluation}_i.$$

For a respondent who reported being a pure Independent (Party ID = 0) with a somewhat approving evaluation of Bush's handling of the war on terror (War evaluation = 1) and a somewhat disapproving evaluation of Bush's handling of the economy (Economic evaluation = −1), we would calculate $\hat{Y}_i$ as follows:

$$\hat{Y}_i = 0.6 + (0.09 \times 0) + (0.08 \times 1) + (0.08 \times -1) = 0.6.$$

One way to interpret this predicted value is to think of it as a **predicted probability** that the dummy dependent variable is equal to one, or, in other words, the predicted probability of this respondent voting for Bush. Using the example for which we just calculated $\hat{Y}_i$, we would predict that such an individual would have a 0.6 probability (or 60 percent chance) of voting for Bush in 2004. As you can imagine, if we change the values of our three independent variables around, the predicted probability of the individual voting for Bush changes correspondingly. This means that the LPM is a special case of OLS for which we can think of the predicted values of the dependent variable as predicted probabilities. From here on, we represent predicted probabilities for a particular case as "$\hat{P}_i$" or "$\hat{P}(Y_i = 1)$" and we can summarize this special property of the LPM as $\hat{P}_i = \hat{P}(Y_i = 1) = \hat{Y}_i$.

One of the problems with the LPM comes when we arrive at extreme values of the predicted probabilities. Consider, for instance, a respondent who reported being a strong Republican (Party ID = 3) with a strongly approving evaluation of Bush's handling of the war on terror (War evaluation = 2) and a strongly approving evaluation of Bush's handling of the economy (Economic evaluation = 2). For this individual, we would calculate $\hat{P}_i$ as follows:

$$\hat{P}_i = \hat{Y}_i = 0.6 + (0.09 \times 3) + (0.08 \times 2) + (0.08 \times 2) = 1.19.$$

This means that we would predict that such an individual would have a 119 percent chance of voting for Bush in 2004. To be sure, if we went to the other extremes for the values of our independent variables, it would be similarly possible to obtain a predicted probability of less than zero. Such predicted probabilities are, of course, nonsensical because probabilities cannot be smaller than zero or greater than one. So one of the problems with the LPM is that it can produce such values. In the greater scheme of things, though, this problem is not so severe, as we can make sensible interpretations of predicted values higher than one or lower than zero – these are cases for which we are very confident that probability is close to one (for $\hat{P}_i > 1$) or close to zero (for $\hat{P}_i < 0$).

To the extent that the LPM has potentially more serious problems, they come in two forms: heteroscedasticity and functional form. We discussed heteroscedasticity in Chapter 10 when we noted that, any time that we estimate an OLS model, we assume that there is homoscedasticity (or equal error variance). We can see that this assumption is particularly problematic with the LPM because the values of the dependent variable are all equal to zero or one, but the $\hat{Y}$ or predicted values range anywhere between zero and one (or even beyond these values). This means that the errors (or residual values) will tend to be largest for cases for which the predicted value is close to 0.5. Any nonuniform pattern of model error variance such as this is called heteroscedasticity, which means that the estimated standard errors may be too high or too low. We care about this because standard errors that are too high or too low will have bad effects on our hypothesis testing, and thus ultimately on our conclusions about the presence or absence of causal relationships.

The problem of functional form is related to the assumption of parametric linearity that we also discussed in Chapter 10. In the context of the LPM, this assumption amounts to saying that the impact of a one-unit increase in an independent variable X is equal to the corresponding parameter estimate $\hat{\beta}$ regardless of the value of X or any other independent variable. This assumption may be particularly problematic for LPMs because the effect of a change in an independent variable may be greater for cases that would otherwise be at 0.5 than for those cases for which the predicted probability would otherwise be close to zero or one. Obviously the extent of both of these problems will vary across different models.

For these reasons, the typical solution to having a dummy dependent variable is to avoid using the LPM. Most applications that you will come across in sociological research will use a **binomial logit** (BNL) or **binomial probit** (BNP) model instead of the LPM for models in which the dependent variable is a dummy variable. BNL and BNP models are similar to regression models in many ways, but they involve an additional step in interpreting them. In the next subsection we provide a brief overview of these types of models.

11.11.2 Binomial Logit and Binomial Probit

In cases in which their dependent variable is dichotomous, most sociologists use a BNL or a BNP model instead of an LPM. In this subsection we provide a brief introduction to these two models, using the same example that we used for our LPM in the previous subsection.

To understand these models, let's first rewrite our LPM from our preceding example in terms of a probability statement:

$$P_i = P(Y_i = 1) = \alpha + \beta_1 \times \text{Party ID}_i + \beta_2 \times \text{War evaluation}_i \\ + \beta_3 \times \text{Economic evaluation}_i + u_i.$$

This is just a way of expressing the probability part of the LPM in a formula in which "$P(Y_i = 1)$" translates to "the probability that Y_i is equal to one," which in the case of our running example is the probability that the individual cast a vote for Bush. We then further collapse this to

$$P_i = P(Y_i = 1) = \alpha + \beta_1 X_{1i} + \beta_2 X_{2i} + \beta_3 X_{3i} + u_i,$$

and yet further to

$$P_i = P(Y_i = 1) = X_i\beta + u_i,$$

where we define $X_i\beta$ as the systematic component of Y such that $X_i\beta = \alpha + \beta_1 X_{1i} + \beta_2 X_{2i} + \beta_3 X_{3i}$.[20] The term u_i continues to represent the stochastic or random component of Y. So if we think about our predicted probability for a given case, we can write this as:

$$\hat{Y}_i = \hat{P}_i = \hat{P}(Y_i = 1) = X_i\hat{\beta} = \hat{\alpha} + \hat{\beta}_1 X_{1i} + \hat{\beta}_2 X_{2i} + \hat{\beta}_3 X_{3i}.$$

A BNL model with the same variables would be written as:

$$P_i = P(Y_i = 1) = \Lambda(\alpha + \beta_1 X_{1i} + \beta_2 X_{2i} + \beta_3 X_{3i} + u_i) = \Lambda(X_i\beta + u_i).$$

The predicted probabilities from this model would be written as:

$$\hat{P}_i = \hat{P}(Y_i = 1) = \Lambda(\hat{\alpha} + \hat{\beta}_1 X_{1i} + \hat{\beta}_2 X_{2i} + \hat{\beta}_3 X_{3i} = \Lambda(X_i\hat{\beta}).$$

A BNP with the same variables would be written as:

$$P_i = P(Y_i = 1) = \Phi(\alpha + \beta_1 X_{1i} + \beta_2 X_{2i} + \beta_3 X_{3i} + u_i) = \Phi(X_i\beta + u_i).$$

The predicted probabilities from this model would be written as:

$$\hat{P}_i = \hat{P}(Y_i = 1) = \Phi(\hat{\alpha} + \hat{\beta}_1 X_{1i} + \hat{\beta}_2 X_{2i} + \hat{\beta}_3 X_{3i} = \Phi(X_i\hat{\beta}).$$

The difference between the BNL model and the LPM is the Λ, and the difference between the BNP model and the LPM is the Φ. The Λ and Φ are known as **link functions**. A link function *links* the linear component of a logit or probit model, $X_i\hat{\beta}$, to the quantity in which we are interested, the predicted probability that the dummy dependent variable equals one, $\hat{P}(Y_i = 1)$ or $\hat{P}_i$. A major result of using these link functions is that the relationship between our independent and dependent variables is no longer assumed to be linear. In the case of a logit model, the link function, abbreviated as Λ, uses the cumulative logistic distribution function (and thus the name "logit") to link the linear component to the probability that $Y_i = 1$. In the case of the probit function, the link function, abbreviated as Φ, uses the cumulative normal distribution function to link the linear component to the predicted probability that $Y_i = 1$. Appendices C (for the BNL) and D (for the BNP) provide tables for converting $X_i\hat{\beta}$ values into predicted probabilities.

[20] This shorthand comes from matrix algebra. Although matrix algebra is a very useful tool in statistics, it is not needed to master the material in this text.

Table 11.11 The effects of partisanship and performance evaluations on votes for Bush in 2004: three different types of models

	LPM	BNL	BNP
Party identification	0.09**	0.82**	0.45**
	(0.01)	(0.09)	(0.04)
Evaluation: War on terror	0.08**	0.60**	0.32**
	(0.01)	(0.09)	(0.05)
Evaluation: Health of the economy	0.08**	0.59**	0.32**
	(0.01)	(0.10)	(0.06)
Intercept	0.60**	1.11**	0.58**
	(0.01)	(0.20)	(0.10)

Notes: The dependent variable is equal to one if the respondent voted for Bush and equal to zero if they voted for Kerry. Standard errors in parentheses. Two-sided *t*-tests: ** $p < 0.01$; * $p < 0.05$.

The best way to understand how the LPM, BNL, and BNP work similarly to and differently from each other is to look at them all with the same model and data. An example of this is presented in Table 11.11. From this table it is apparent that, across the three models, the parameter estimate for each independent variable has the same sign and significance level. But it is also apparent that the magnitudes of these parameter estimates are different across the three models. This is mainly due to the difference of link functions.

To better illustrate the differences between the three models presented in Table 11.11, we plotted the predicted probabilities from them in Figure 11.6. These predicted probabilities are for an individual who strongly approved of the Bush administration's handling of the war on terror but who strongly disapproved of the Bush administration's handling of the economy.[21] The horizontal axis in Figure 11.6 is this individual's party identification, ranging from strong Democratic Party identifiers on the left end to strong Republican Party identifiers on the right end. The vertical axis is the predicted probability of voting for Bush. We can see from this figure that the three models make very similar predictions. The main differences come as we move away from a predicted probability of 0.5.

[21] These were the modal answers to the two evaluative questions that were included in the model presented in Table 11.11. It is a fairly common practice to illustrate the estimated impact of a variable of interest from this type of model by holding all other variables constant at their mean or modal values and then varying that one variable to see how the predicted probabilities change.

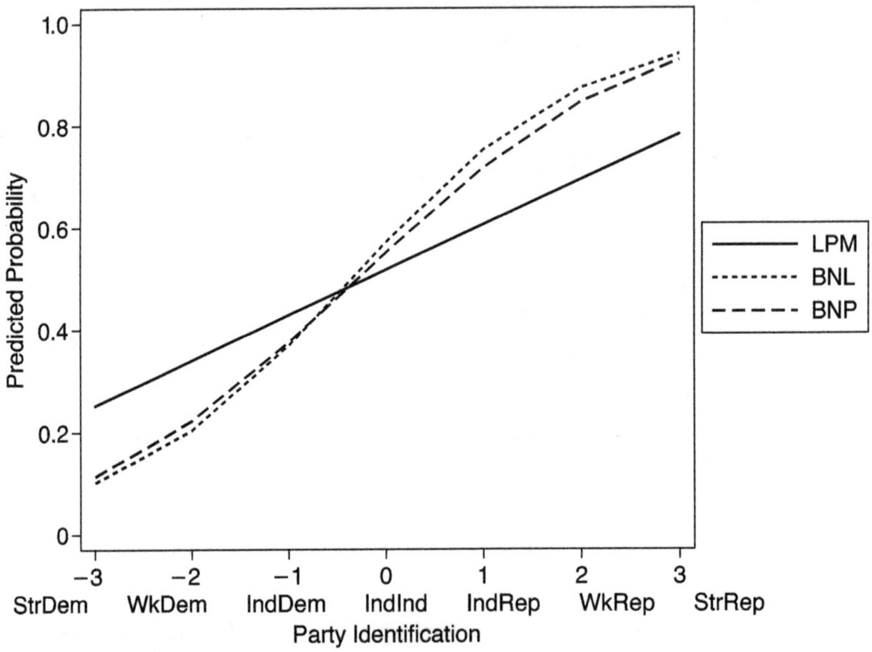

Figure 11.6 Three different models of Bush vote

The LPM line has, by definition, a constant slope across the entire range of X. The BNL and BNP lines of predicted probabilities change their slope such that they slope more and more gently as we move farther from predicted probabilities of 0.5. The differences between the BNL and BNP lines are trivial. This means that the effect of a movement in Party Identification on the predicted probability is constant for the LPM. But for the BNL and BNP, the effect of a movement in Party Identification *depends* on the value of the other variables in the model. It is important to realize that the differences between the LPM and the other two types of model are by construction instead of some novel finding. In other words, our choice of model determines the shape of our predicted probability line.

11.11.3 Goodness-of-Fit with Dummy Dependent Variables

Although we can calculate an R^2 statistic when we estimate a linear probability model, R^2 doesn't quite capture what we are doing when we want to assess the fit of such a model. What we are trying to assess is the ability of our model to separate our cases into those in which $Y = 1$ and those in which $Y = 0$. So it is helpful to think about this in terms of a 2×2 table of model-based expectations and actual values. To figure out the model's expected values, we need to choose a cutoff point at which we interpret the model as predicting that $Y = 1$. An obvious value to use

Table 11.12 Classification table from LPM of the effects of partisanship and performance evaluations on votes for Bush in 2004

	Model-based expectations	
Actual vote	**Bush**	**Kerry**
Bush	361	36
Kerry	28	355

Notes: Cell entries are the number of cases. Predictions are based on a cutoff of $\hat{Y} > 0.5$.

for this cutoff point is $\hat{Y} > 0.5$. Table 11.12 shows the results of this in what we call a **classification table.** Classification tables compare model-based expectations with actual values of the dependent variable.

In Table 11.12, we can see the differences between the LPM's predictions and the actual votes reported by survey respondents to the 2004 ANES. One fairly straightforward measure of the fit of this model is to look at the percentage of cases that were correctly classified through use of the model. So if we add up the cases correctly classified and divide by the total number of cases we get:

$$\text{correctly classified LPM}_{0.5} = \frac{361 + 355}{780} = \frac{716}{780} = 0.918.$$

So our LPM managed to correctly classify 0.918 or 91.8 percent of the respondents and to erroneously classify the remaining 0.082 or 8.2 percent.

Although this might seem like a pretty high classification rate, we don't really know what we should be comparing it with. One option is to compare our model's classification rate with the classification rate for a naive model (NM) that predicts that all cases will be in the modal category. In this case, the NM would predict that all respondents voted for Bush. So, if we calculate the correctly classified cases for the NM:

$$\text{correctly classified NM} = \frac{361 + 36}{780} = \frac{397}{780} = 0.509.$$

This means that the NM correctly classified 0.509, or 50.9 percent, of the respondents and erroneously classified the remaining 0.491, or 49.1 percent.

Turning now to the business of comparing the performance of our model with that of the NM, we can calculate the **proportionate reduction of error** when we move from the NM to our LPM with party identification and two performance evaluations as independent variables. The percentage erroneously classified in the naive model was 49.1 and the percentage erroneously classified in our LPM was 8.2. So we have reduced the error proportion by 49.1 – 8.2 = 40.9. If we now divide this by the total error percentage of the naive model, we get 40.9/49.1 = 0.833. This means that we have a proportionate reduction of error equal to 0.833. Another way of saying this is that when we moved from the NM to our LPM we reduced the classification errors by 83.3 percent.

11.12 IMPLICATIONS

What are the implications of this chapter? One of the key take-home points of this chapter – that failing to control for all relevant independent variables will often lead to mistaken causal inferences for the variables that do make it into our models – applies in several contexts. If you are reading a research article in one of your other classes, and it shows a regression analysis between two variables, but fails to control for the effects of some other possible cause of the dependent variable, then you have some reason to be skeptical about the reported findings. In particular, if you can think of another independent variable that is likely to be related to *both* the independent variable and the dependent variable, then the relationship that the article does show that fails to control for that variable is likely to be plagued with bias. And if that's the case, then there is substantial reason to doubt the findings. The findings *might* be right, but you can't know that from the evidence presented in the article; in particular, you'd need to control for the omitted variable to know for sure.

But this critical issue isn't just encountered in research articles. When you read a news article from your favorite media website that reports a relationship between some presumed cause and some presumed effect – news articles don't usually talk about "independent variables" or "dependent variables" – but fails to account for some other cause that you can imagine might be related to both the independent and dependent variables, then you have reason to doubt the conclusions.

It might be tempting to react to omitted-variables bias by saying, "Omitted-variables bias is such a potentially serious problem that I don't want to use regression analysis." That would be a mistake. In fact, the logic of omitted-variables bias applies to any type of research, no matter what type of statistical technique is used – in fact, no matter whether the research is qualitative or quantitative.

Sometimes, as we have seen, controlling for other causes of the dependent variable changes the discovered effects only at the margins. That happens on occasion in applied research. At other times, however, failure to control for a relevant cause of the dependent variable can have serious consequences for our causal inferences about the real world.

CONCEPTS INTRODUCED IN THIS CHAPTER

- bias – a statistical problem that occurs when the expected value of the parameter estimate that we obtain from a sample will not be equal to the true population parameter
- binomial logit (BNL) – a model of a dummy dependent variable that uses the logistic distribution to convert predicted values into predicted probabilities
- binomial probit (BNP) – a model of a dummy dependent variable that uses the cumulative normal distribution to convert predicted values into predicted probabilities
- classification table – tables that compare model-based expectations with actual values of the dependent variable
- dummy variable – a variable that takes on one of two values (usually one or zero)
- dummy variable trap – perfect multicollinearity that results from the inclusion of dummy variables representing each possible value of a categorical variable
- interactive models – multiple regression models that contain at least one independent variable that we create by multiplying together two or more independent variables
- linear probability model (LPM) – an OLS model in which the dependent variable is a dummy variable
- link functions – functions that convert the linear component of a nonlinear model to a quantity of interest
- omitted-variables bias – the specific type of bias that results from the failure to include a variable that belongs in our regression model
- perfect multicollinearity – when there is an exact linear relationship between any two or more of a regression model's independent variables
- predicted probability – in models with a dummy dependent variable, the expected value of the dependent variable conditioned on the values of the independent variable(s)
- proportionate reduction of error – a calculation used to assess the usefulness of a model by comparing its predictive accuracy with that of a naive model (NM) that always predicts the modal category of the dependent variable
- reference category – in a multiple regression model, the value of a categorical independent variable for which we do not include a dummy variable

- standardized coefficients – regression coefficients such that the rise-over-run interpretation is expressed in standard-deviation units of each variable
- substantive significance – a judgment call about whether or not statistically significant relationships are "large" or "small" in terms of their real-world impact
- unstandardized coefficients – regression coefficients such that the rise-over-run interpretation is expressed in the original metric of each variable

EXERCISES

1. Identify an article from a social science journal approved by your instructor that reports a causal relationship between two variables. Can you think of another variable that may be related to both the independent variable and the dependent variable? Print and turn in a copy of the article with your answers.
2. In Exercise 1, estimate the direction of the bias resulting from omitting the third variable.
3. Fill in the values in the third column of Table 11.13.
4. In your own research you have found evidence from a bivariate regression model that supports your theory that your independent variable X_i is positively related to your dependent variable Y_i (the slope parameter for X_i was statistically significant and positive when you estimated a bivariate regression model). You go to a research presentation in which other researchers present a theory that their independent variable Z_i is negatively related to their dependent variable Y_i. They report the results from a bivariate regression model in which the slope parameter for Z_i was statistically significant and negative. Your Y_i and

Table 11.13 Bias in $\hat{\beta}_1$ when the true population model is $Y_i = \alpha + \beta_1 X_i + \beta_2 Z_i + u_i$ but we leave out Z

β_2	$\frac{\sum_{i=1}^{n}(X_i-\bar{X})(Z_i-\bar{Z})}{\sum_{i=1}^{n}(X_i-\bar{X})^2}$	Resulting bias in $\hat{\beta}_1$
0	+	?
0	–	?
+	0	?
–	0	?
+	+	?
–	–	?
+	–	?
–	+	?

Table 11.14 Three regression models of teacher salaries in the U.S. states and the District of Columbia

	A	B	C
Percentage of state residents with a college degree	704.02*	—	24.56
	(140.22)	—	(231.72)
Per capita income	—	0.68*	0.66*
	—	(0.11)	(0.19)
Intercept	28 768.01*	21 168.11*	21 161.07*
	(3913.27)	(4102.40)	(4144.96)
R^2	0.34	0.47	0.47
n	51	51	51

Notes: The dependent variable is the average salary of public elementary and secondary school teachers. Standard errors in parentheses. * $p < 0.05$ (two-tailed t-test).

their Y_i are the same variable. What would be your reaction to these findings under each of the following circumstances?

(a) You are confident that the correlation between Z_i and X_i is equal to zero.

(b) You think that the correlation between Z_i and X_i is positive.

(c) You think that the correlation between Z_i and X_i is negative.

5. Using the results depicted in Table 11.14, interpret the results of the bivariate models displayed in columns A and B.
6. Using the results depicted in Table 11.14, interpret the results of the multiple regression model displayed in column C. Compare the results in column C with those in both columns A and B.
7. Draw a Venn diagram that depicts what is going on between the three variables based on the results in Table 11.14.
8. Using the model presented in Table 11.7, what is your prediction of income for female respondents who are 28 years of age, have 16 years of education, and reside in urban areas?
9. Using the model presented in Table 11.7, interpret the parameter estimate for the variable "Age."
10. Using the model presented in Table 11.7, interpret the parameter estimate for the variable "Male."
11. Using the data set "GSS2018," investigate two possible causes of a respondent's attitudes toward abortion (which you will, for the purposes of this exercise, need to treat as a continuous variable), using the respondent's gender and the

respondent's level of education as your two key independent variables. First, construct an additive multiple regression model investigating the effects of gender and education on abortion attitudes. Next, construct an interactive multiple regression model that adds an interaction term for gender and education. Present the results of both models in a single table. Interpret, first, the additive regression model, and then interpret the interactive model. Does education have the same, a smaller, or a larger effect on abortion attitudes for women as it does for men?

12. Imagine a respondent who reported being a strong Republican (Party ID = 3) with a strongly disapproving evaluation of Bush's handling of the war on terror (War evaluation = −2) and a strongly disapproving evaluation of Bush's handling of the health of the economy (Economic evaluation = −2). Using the results from the linear probability model in Table 11.11, calculate the predicted probability of this individual voting for Bush. Show all of your work.

13. Using the binomial logit model in Table 11.11, calculate the predicted probability of the individual described in Exercise 12 voting for Bush. Show all of your work.

14. Using the binomial probit model in Table 11.11, calculate the predicted probability of the individual described in Exercise 12 voting for Bush. Show all of your work.

15. Table 11.15 is the classification table from a binomial probit model in which the dependent variable was a dummy variable equal to one if the respondent reported voting for Obama and equal to zero if the respondent reported voting for McCain. The independent variables in this model were measures of party identification and respondents' expectations about economic and foreign policy performances with each of the two major party candidates as the President. Calculate the percentage of respondents classified correctly by this model. Show all of your work.

Table 11.15 Classification table from a BNP of the effects of partisanship and prospective expectations on votes for Obama in 2008

	Model-based expectations	
Actual vote	**Obama**	**McCain**
Obama	1575	233
McCain	180	1201

Notes: Cell entries are the number of cases. Predictions are based on a cutoff of $\hat{Y} > 0.5$.

16. Using Table 11.15, calculate the percentage of respondents that would be correctly classified by a naive model that predicts that all respondents choose the modal category of the dependent variable. Show all of your work.
17. Using the calculations that you made in Exercises 15 and 16, calculate the proportionate reduction of error when we move from the naive model to the binomial probit model. Show all of your work.

12 Putting It All Together to Produce Effective Research

OVERVIEW

In Chapter 2 we discussed the art of theory building. In this chapter we discuss the art of putting it all together to produce effective research. As is the case with theory building, there is no magic formula for putting together an effective research manuscript, but there certainly are good manuscript-assembling strategies. We will begin this chapter with an elaboration on some of the themes discussed in Chapter 2. We then turn to a more in-depth discussion of how to examine published research which takes advantage of the fact that you have now absorbed the lessons and strategies presented in this book. As such, we can now discuss the dissection of previous research at a higher level, and prepare you to start producing research of your own.

Amat victoria curam
(Victory loves preparation)
—Latin proverb

If I have seen further, it is by standing on the shoulders of giants
—Isaac Newton

12.1 TWO ROUTES TOWARD A NEW SCIENTIFIC PROJECT

We began this book with three goals. First, to make you a better consumer of information. Second, to enable you to understand theoretical debates more easily in your other sociology classes. And third, to motivate and equip you to begin to do your own research. This last chapter is dedicated to this third objective.

As we said at the beginning of this book, the twin goals of all science, including social science, are to generate new causal theories about the world, and then to test those theories. You have learned throughout this book that one of the keys to testing a theory is to control for other possible explanations of the dependent variable.

And if we've been successful in these pages, some of you are feeling anxious to start research projects of your own – perhaps as an independent study, or a summer research project, or a senior honors thesis. But how can you get started on a big new project like the ones just mentioned? In this section, we will suggest two major strategies (and one offshoot) for starting new research agendas. These strategies, to be sure, represent a simplification of the ways in which sociologists generate their own research programs. But sometimes simplifying things is helpful, especially when faced with a possibly daunting task.

Consistent with the way we have been describing dependent variables as Y and a key independent variable as X, the two routes to formulating a new project are:

1. A new Y (and some X).
2. An existing Y and a new X.

We take them in turn, and then look at some variants.

12.1.1 Project Type 1: A New Y (and Some X)

The first type of project involves the creation of, invention of, or discovery of some new type of dependent variable, and then theorizing about some independent variable that might cause the dependent variable to vary. What makes projects like this distinctive – and difficult! – is the word "new." A research project of this type is exceedingly creative, and also rather rare. Social scientists don't just arrive in their offices in the morning, take that first swig of coffee, and confront the day with the thought, "Okay, here we go. Today I'm going to create another new dependent variable to analyze." If only it were that simple!

The burden of creating a new concept to represent a brand-new dependent variable is considerable. Moreover, because research never occurs in a metaphorical vacuum, it has to be a concept that other scholars will find interesting. Otherwise, your work is unfortunately quite likely to be ignored.

If you can conceptualize something genuinely new, and then proceed to measure it, then the next (and critical!) step is to theorize some X that might cause this new Y to vary. Again, this is sometimes a formidable task, but, on the other hand, it's likely that, if you are able to imagine a new dependent variable, you might already have a clue about what force or forces might cause it to vary.

Projects of this type can break new paths toward scientific knowledge – paths that other scholars can follow, and which can lead to new theories and findings about how the world works. An example of a project like this is David Sears and Donald Kinder's (1971) study "Racial tensions and voting in Los Angeles," in *Los Angeles: Viability and Prospects for Metropolitan Leadership*, edited by Werner Hirsch. In this study Sears and Kinder coined the term "symbolic racism" to refer to a new kind of racial prejudice among whites. They argued that the cornerstone of whites' racial animus has shifted from traditional or "old-fashioned" racism's overt bigotry and belief in the biological inferiority of blacks to a subtle, more covert set of beliefs that emphasizes blacks' supposed "cultural deficiencies." According to Sears and Kinder (1971) the sources of whites' symbolic racism are rooted in early racial socialization experiences; in the view that racial discrimination against blacks, though widespread in the past, no longer exists; and in the belief that African Americans violate such traditional socio-cultural values as individualism, self-reliance, and hard work. The study by Sears and Kinder exemplifies this type of project – a new Y (symbolic racism) and some X (see below) – since no previous scholars had thought of symbolic racism as a possible dependent variable in need of explanation.[1] In terms of X variables, recent research has shown that increasing education and adherence to egalitarian norms tend to decrease, and political conservatism and stereotypical thinking tend to increase, symbolic racism, though more research on predictors is needed (Simmons and Bobo, 2018). The symbolic racism concept has generated substantial scholarly interest, and lively debate, among (and between) sociologists, political scientists, and social psychologists.[2]

So how do you find a new Y? First, you have to know that it is, indeed, *new*, by which we mean that no previous scholar has already conducted research on this particular dependent variable. This requires conducting a thorough research of the existing literature, likely using Google Scholar and some variations on keywords.[3] Beyond that, there is no magical formula, no recipe to follow that will lead to a new dependent variable that begs explanation. What we can say, to hearken back to our analogy in

[1] Subsequent studies have found that symbolic racism – now commonly referred to as "modern racism" or "racial resentment" (Kinder and Sanders, 1996) – is also an important explanatory variable shaping whites' attitudes toward policies designed to ameliorate racial disadvantage (see, for example, Tuch and Hughes, 2011, and sources cited therein).

[2] See, for example, Carmines, Sniderman, and Easter (2011), Feldman and Huddy (2005), Henry and Sears (2009), Hughes (1997), Roos, Hughes, and Reichelmann (2019), Schuman (2000), Sears and Henry (2005), Simmons and Bobo (2018), and Sniderman, Crosby, and Howell (2000).

[3] Google Scholar is found at scholar.google.com, and is distinct from the main Google search engine, found at www.google.com. Be careful not to confuse the two.

Chapter 2, is that the best way to get struck by metaphorical lightning is to read academic works. Read with a hunger that points toward questions like, "What *don't* we know yet?" This is a theme we'll return to later in this chapter.

12.1.2 Project Type 2: An Existing Y and a New X

Perhaps you will find that creating a new dependent variable from scratch is too challenging for your project. If so, you're in very good company. Many researchers come to the conclusion that all of the good dependent variables are already taken. And if you find yourself in this position, perhaps it's time to consider our second type of research project: Taking an existing Y and theorizing how a new X might cause it.

You'll note that projects like these also have the word "new" in them – though this time, what's new isn't the dependent variable, but the independent variable. The burden of producing something new – by which we mean a relationship between X and Y that some other scholar has not already examined in the same way that you're proposing – is still considerable. But in projects like this, the sense that a new scholar is "standing on the shoulders of giants" is far more evident. Previous scholars may have already examined a particular dependent variable, proposing several causes that might explain its variation. Those causes, to be sure, might be competing with one another, or they might complement one another. The heart of projects of this type is identifying some *other* possible cause of Y that has not been adequately examined.

The burden of novelty requires thorough canvassing of the existing literature on the particular phenomenon that interests you. For example, if you are interested in explaining variation in why some citizens seem more trusting of government, whereas others seem less trusting of government, this means that you will have to consume that literature, systematically noting what independent variables – or categories of independent variables (like "the economy") – have already been examined by previous researchers.

A project becomes an original project once you propose a new X that has not been tested to see if it relates to Y. Controlling for a new variable, as we have seen time and again in this book – but especially in Chapter 11 – sometimes alters the patterns of findings that have been previously accepted. That is, controlling for your new independent variable might change how some of the previously investigated independent variables relate to the dependent variable once the effects of your variable are controlled for. This is how science often moves forward.

Therefore, when embarking on a project of this type, it is absolutely critical to be sure that you do, indeed, control for these previous explanations. This can happen by way of research design – especially if you're able to conduct an experiment – or by statistical controls, in the event that you're using an observational research design. If you'll be using an observational design, then of course you'll need to be sure to gather data for the established independent variables so that you'll be able to control for their effects statistically.

12.1.3 Variants on the Two Project Types

We have emphasized that there are two major types of new projects. In reality, that is something of a simplification. In this section, we consider a third type of new project that can help create scientific knowledge.

A third path to an original project can be to examine a previously examined *X*–*Y* relationship in a new context. Again, notice the word "new" here; in order for your work to make an original contribution, something has to be new. In this variant, sometimes the new-ness comes from testing an established *X*–*Y* relationship in a new time period, either an earlier one or a later one. Perhaps more commonly, the new-ness can come from testing an established *X*–*Y* relationship in a new geographic context. Or alternatively, we might think of a theoretically interesting comparison of an established *X*–*Y* relationship across different groups of cases within a sample in which the *X*–*Y* relationship has already been established. (See Firebaugh (2008) for an excellent discussion of other variants.)

The hope with a project like this is that, when the existing relationship is tested in a new context, interesting patterns will emerge that can create further opportunities for research. A useful way to think about this movement to a new context is to think about it as moving from an examination of an established *X*–*Y* relationship in one particular sample of cases to a comparison of this same *X*–*Y* relationship across different subsamples of cases. As we have emphasized throughout the book, we continue to use these sample findings to make inferences about unobservable populations. In the context of this type of design, we can think about theoretically interesting ways to divide our cases into different subpopulations.

To take an example where the new-ness comes from a new time, consider that, at least since the work of Converse (1964), it has been noticed that, among members of the American public, there was not a particularly strong relationship between an individual's party identification (*X*) and their policy attitudes (*Y*). That is, there was a correlation between being a Republican and espousing more conservative policy attitudes, but the correlations were always very modest. More recent research, though, particularly by Levendusky (2009), that investigates this same X–Y connection in a newer time period, has shown that the correlations have become quite a bit stronger in recent years. That is, in what Levendusky calls "the partisan sort," something has happened to make the correlation between an individual's partisanship and their policy preferences much more strong. This led Levendusky, of course, to ask what made this happen, and opened up considerable space for additional research in the study of American public opinion.

Other projects investigate an existing X–Y connection in different geographic contexts. One example we have used in this book is the example of the relationship between the U.S. economy and incumbent party electoral fortunes. Indeed, much of the pioneering work on what is called economic voting took place in the U.S. context. Those findings, as you have seen, show that a strong economy clearly benefits the candidate of the incumbent party, and a weak economy hurts the incumbent party's electoral fortunes. Scholars naturally wondered if these patterns would also be found in other democracies. Fascinatingly, in some countries, an X–Y connection existed similar to that in the U.S., but in others, no such connection could be found. Naturally, that led scholars to wonder why evidence of economic voting was strong in some countries, and absent in others. Powell and Whitten (1993) show that the strength of the economic vote is driven by, among other things, what they call the "clarity of responsibility" of the governing party's handling of the economy. In countries with coalition governments, where multiple parties share power, for example, it's much less clear who deserves credit or blame for the health of the economy than it is in a country where control over the economic policy is concentrated in the hands of a single party.

12.2 USING THE LITERATURE WITHOUT GETTING BURIED IN IT

If you are going to embark on an original research project, you first have to be aware of what scholarly work has already been done in that area of inquiry. How do you go about doing that? This section is devoted to how to identify the giants whose shoulders you would like to stand upon.

12.2.1 Identifying the Important Work on a Subject – Using Citation Counts

One of the most daunting tasks faced by a researcher starting out in an area is to identify what has been done before. Most keyword searches will yield a phone-book-sized return of articles and other publications. Even the most avid reader will be overwhelmed. Thankfully citations provide a powerful shortcut for sorting out which of the many published works on a topic are the most important.

By now you have probably had some experience with having to produce a written work with citations of sources. Citations are one of the most valued currencies in which scientific researchers conduct their business. To be cited is to be relevant; to be uncited is to be ignored. For this reason, citations have formed the basis for a wide range of indices by which individual scientists, scientific journals, academic departments, and even entire universities are ranked relative to each other. We can safely say that academia today is obsessed with citations.

As such, we recommend taking advantage of the fact that citations are a powerful tool for distinguishing among the many articles any time that you do a search using Google Scholar or similar tools. So, an obvious next question is how many citations does a publication need for it to be regarded as having a substantial impact? As a rough rule of thumb, we suggest that you use twenty citations. Of course, as you might imagine, the number of citations that a publication has is, in part, a function of time. Thus, an article that was published in 2018 that already has ten citations in 2020 is probably going to have a substantial influence.

12.2.2 Oh No! Someone Else Has Already Done What I Was Planning to Do. What Do I Do Now?

One of the most frustrating things that can happen during a search of the literature is that you find that someone else has already done what you had in mind and published an article or book testing your theory or something close to it. As frustrating as this may be at first, it is actually a good sign because it means that what you had in mind was in fact a good idea. If this happens to you, you should read the work and think about how it can be improved upon.

12.2.3 Dissecting the Research by Other Scholars

Once you have identified the important work in your topic area, it is important to take it apart in order to be able to put it to work for your purposes. We recommend making notes on the answers to the following questions:

- What was the research question/puzzle?
- What was their theory?

- What was their research design?
- How did they do with the four hurdles?
- What did they conclude?
- Can their theory be applied elsewhere in an interesting fashion?

For example, in an article about consumer confidence and presidential approval by MacKuen, Erikson, and Stimson (1992), a paragraph-long synopsis of that article might take the following form:

> In their article, MacKuen, Erikson, and Stimson (1992) address the question of how changes in the economy translate into shifts in presidential approval ratings. Whereas the conventional wisdom held that objective economic reality – usually in the form of inflation and unemployment – drives approval ratings, their theory argues that the more subjective consumer confidence is what causes approval to rise and fall over time. To test their theory, they conducted a time-series observational study over the period 1954–1988, controlling for a number of non-economic factors that also shape approval. They found that, once controlling for consumer sentiment, inflation and unemployment no longer were statistically significant predictors of approval ratings, whereas consumer confidence was.

By systematically going through previous research, as we've done here, and summarizing it compactly, it becomes possible to see what the literature, as a collection, teaches us about what we do know, and what we don't know, about a particular phenomenon.

12.2.4 Read Effectively to Write Effectively

One of the best ways to learn strategies for effectively communicating your research ideas is to examine the ways in which other researchers communicate their ideas. Pay attention to how others write: you can learn a lot from both good and bad writing. When you are reading, be particularly conscious of the way in which causal arguments are presented. Make notes about those arguments that you find immediately persuasive and those arguments that are less so. What did the authors do to enhance or hurt their arguments?

To be clear, we are not recommending that you copy the writing of someone else; that would be plagiarism. Instead, what we are recommending is that you think consciously about the strategic decisions that the authors whose work you are reading have made. What is it about a particular turn of phrase or style of argument that convinces you that they are right or leaves you unconvinced?

As an example of effective writing, consider Lawrence Bobo and Victor Hutchings' (1996) article "Perceptions of racial group competition: extending Blumer's theory of group position to a multiracial social context" in the *American Sociological Review*. The abstract of Bobo and Hutchings' article begins (p.351):

> Perceptions of threat occupy a central place in race relations in Blumer's theory of prejudice but few direct efforts to study such perceptions exist. Extending Blumer's reasoning, we hypothesize that such perceptions are driven by a group's feelings of racial alienation within the larger social order. The more that members of a particular racial group feel collectively oppressed and unfairly treated by society, the more likely they are to perceive members of other groups as potential threats. We also examine whether such perceptions spring from simple self-interest, orthodox prejudice such as negative feelings and stereotyping, or broad beliefs about social stratification and inequality.

Notice how unambiguously Bobo and Hutchings frame their study at the outset. Although perceptions of competitive threat are key to Herbert Blumer's (1958) (now classic) group position theory of prejudice, they argue, scholars had not previously studied such perceptions. Bobo and Hutchings then hypothesize that these perceptions are "driven by" – in other words, caused by – a group's sense of racial alienation. They also note other potential causes of perceptions of threat – self-interest, stereotyping, and beliefs about the determinants of inequality – all of which are fully discussed later in their article. In these few, authoritatively written sentences, Bobo and Hutchings accomplish several key goals: they (1) clearly identify the topic of their research; (2) pose a causal mechanism to be explored in their data analysis; (3) identify alternative causal factors that may account for their *Y* variable that they will also examine; and (4) indicate how their study will contribute something new to the existing literature on racial prejudice. Bobo and Hutchings conclude their introduction with this sentence (p.352): "Hence, an examination of feelings of competitive threat among Whites, African Americans, Latinos, and Asian Americans provides a unique chance to test these ideas empirically and to generalize Blumer's model to an increasingly important case: relations within and between racial minority groups."

The authoritative yet accessible tone with which Bobo and Hutchings (1996) wrote the abstract to their paper makes readers want to read more. In just a few short sentences, they have introduced the subject and established themselves as authorities. They have presented the essential elements of their theoretical ideas about the causal processes at work and have told readers what to expect in their article.

12.3 WRITING EFFECTIVELY ABOUT YOUR RESEARCH

Writing is thinking

—Deirdre McCloskey

In this section we discuss a set of strategies for writing effectively about your research. We cannot overstate the importance of writing in social science research. Writing is an extremely important part of the research process. Even the most exciting statistical results can be buried by bad writing. Good scientific writing is achieved through clarity – clear thinking and clear writing.

12.3.1 Write Early, Write Often (Because Writing is Thinking)

"Writing is thinking." This simple phrase is the title of a chapter in Deirdre McCloskey's (1999) classic book *Economical Writing* (p.6). We could not agree more. Whenever you have an idea about research, we strongly encourage you to start writing. We can tell you from experience that it is simply amazing how often taking some time to write about an idea helps you to clarify your thinking. Sometimes you will find that writing helps you to cut through the fog of a collection of loosely thrown-together ideas. Other times, writing will expose logical problems in a theory that seemed to be very solid when it was just a thought in your head. In either situation, it is best to know sooner rather than later where you stand with a particular idea.

So why do people wait to write? An easy answer is that writing is hard and other activities may seem more fun and immediately rewarding. With modern social science research, one frequent occurrence is that researchers get excited about their data and do a lot of analysis before writing. Sometimes this works just fine, but other times when they start writing they realize that they have been missing something major and have to go back to the drawing board in terms of their analyses. Our suggestion is to think of writing and conducting analyses as an integrated process rather than as step one and step two in a research project. One way to effectively integrate writing and analyses is to document your code.

12.3.2 Document Your Code – Writing and Thinking While You Compute

Although analyses in SPSS, Stata, or R (or other software platforms) can be conducted using pull-down menus, we highly recommend that researchers create program scripts (what are called "syntax files" in the parlance of SPSS) to conduct their analyses. Syntax files, which are identified in SPSS with an ".sps" extension, contain the actual programming codes that are embedded in the drop-down menus and which produce our statistical results. For example, you might name the syntax file that contains the code for the first assignment in your statistics class "assgn_1." SPSS will automatically append the extension .sps to the file and "assgn_1.sps" will be created and saved on your computer. While this way of working may seem slow and perhaps even a bit tedious compared to simply "pointing-and-clicking," we have found that it serves a very important purpose. When you document and save your code, you produce work that can be replicated. In an excellent article written as a guide to programming for political science researchers, but which applies equally well to sociologists, Jonathan Nagler (1995) outlines the goals as "First, the researcher should be able to replicate his or her own work six hours later, six months later, and even six years later. Second, others should be able to look at the code and understand what was being done (and preferably why it was being done)." By creating and saving syntax files, these goals can be achieved.

12.3.3 Divide and Conquer – a Section-by-Section Strategy for Building Your Project

Thinking about writing an entire manuscript can be pretty intimidating. For this reason, we recommend an initial approach in which you divide your project into the following six sections: "Introduction," "Literature Review," "Theory," "Research Design and Data," "Findings/Results," and "Implications and Conclusions." More advanced writers may want to work with a different set of section headings, but this basic list of six has, in our experience, been a good structure to start working with.

We recommend putting these section headings into your document, choosing one section, and starting to write. Yes, that's right, there is no need to start at the beginning. You will find that even if you start writing your introduction, you will likely change it down the line. So pick the section that you feel most comfortable writing and have at it. We will now discuss briefly the essential components that should be contained within each section.

Introduction

The introduction section should answer the question "What is the contribution of this work?" As such, the introduction should provide an overview of the theory that is going to be tested. You don't have to provide all of the details of the causal mechanism behind your theory; that's what the theory section of the project is for. But you should at least give a broad overview of the theoretical contribution that you intend to make. If the importance of the subject matter being covered is not obviously clear, it needs to be made so early in the introduction.

Beginning researchers will often be tempted to load their introduction up with citations of published research. We strongly advise against this. Instead, we suggest selecting at most three major works to cite in this section. The point of this section is to introduce readers to what you are going to do and to make them want to read on. Many authors end the introduction of their projects with a roadmap-style brief discussion of the sections that are coming.

In our experience, shorter introductions are more effective. You want to use this section to set up the rest of the project and move on.

Literature Review

The literature review section is where you describe the relevant literature for your purposes. You don't need to reference every work that has ever been carried out on your topic. Instead, you should write authoritatively about the parts of the literature that are most relevant to what you are going to do in your manuscript. It is important to be strategic in your crafting of this section. You want readers to be able to anticipate what your contribution to the literature will be.

This section of your project should answer, for the reader, the twin questions that are likely to be on their mind. First, what does the literature teach us about the causes of the dependent variable of interest? Second, what do we still not know about those causes? These two questions provide the basis for the section, the essential subtext beneath your actual sentences and paragraphs.

While it is certainly reasonable to be critical of published research, we recommend that any criticism should be carefully and tactfully phrased. As we discussed in Chapter 1, part of taking a scientific approach to the study of sociology is being skeptical and challenging when we consider the research of other scientists. This can lead to a tendency to want to tear into research conducted by other scholars. But it's important to keep in mind that, by harshly criticizing the work of other researchers, you may be criticizing work that your readers like. And this, in turn, may make them read your work with a more negative eye. It's important to keep in mind that flaws in the research of other scholars provide us with opportunities to make improvements. And, at the end of the day, if a work is completely useless, why are you citing it?

Theory

The theory section is where you need to definitively answer the first causal hurdle question, "Is there a credible causal mechanism that connects X to Y?" This can be done in a variety of ways, but it needs to be done well. As we discussed in Section 12.2.4, we highly recommend taking some time to analyze what does and doesn't work in the writing of other researchers. This is particularly helpful in terms of the presentation of theories.

You may also want to use this section of the project to answer the question "Can we rule out the possibility that Y could cause X?" However, if you think that you have answered this question in the way that you set up your research design, you should address this question in the "Research Design and Data" section of your project.

Writing theory sections is hard. There's just no way around that fact. One of the benefits, though, of structuring research projects in the way we have suggested is that, by seeing a separate "Theory" section, and realizing that it has to contain *new* causal ideas, it helps us to realize just how important theoretical ideas are. By requiring the summary and critique of the previous literature to be in a separate section, the "Theory" section must then contain new causal claims, complete with new mechanisms linking your independent variable to your dependent variable. By separating these two sections, the originality of your project is showcased. In other words, a "Theory" section is not where you would insert *other* scholars' causal ideas; those belong in the "Literature Review" section. Sometimes, this leaves nearly empty "Theory" sections, or perhaps just very short ones. What this should signal to you is that the theoretical contribution of your project needs some clarifying.

Research Design and Data

In the research design and data section, you need to write clearly about how you operationalized your variables and how the cases studied were chosen. Did you conduct an experimental or an observational study? Why? If it was an observational study, was it a cross-sectional or a time-series study? Why? Where did your data come from? How were your variables measured? What is the sample of cases, and what is the population to which you will make your inferences from this sample? All of these questions need to be answered in this section.

Findings/Results

In Section 12.4 we provide discussions of preparing and presenting tables and figures. This type of work will make up the bulk of what you will do in this section of your project. In addition to walking readers through your results, it is important that in this section you weigh in on the degree to which your hypotheses have been supported from the analyses that you are presenting.

Implications and Conclusions

In this final section, you should come back to your original theory and discuss the degree to which it has been supported from the analyses that you have presented. This section should be one in which you write more broadly about the implications of what you have found. This is also a section where you should discuss how what you have found in this work leads to other ideas about work in the future, and how your project fits in with the literature that you reviewed in Section 12.3.3.

12.3.4 Proofread, Proofread, and then Proofread Again

Once you've written a draft, there's a tendency to feel very satisfied. You should. However, for the serious scholar, there is still a lot of work to be done. Proofreading is critically important to writing effectively about any subject, but especially so when you are writing about a technical undertaking such as theory testing. The more technical the subject on which you are writing, the more important proofreading becomes. You want your readers to be able to glide seamlessly through your writing so that they can clearly understand what you are trying to communicate. This can only be achieved through the hard work of proofreading.

Beginning students will often equate proofreading with running a spell-checking program. Spell-checking is important, but even the best programs can't tell when you use a word that is actually a word, but clearly not the word you intended. (Consider the phrase "pubic opinion," which all three authors of this book have seen in final course projects submitted by their students. If this doesn't convince you that a spell-checker is not enough, then perhaps nothing will.) There is simply no substitute for reading your work carefully.

There are multiple ways in which you can and should proofread each project that you write. If you have time – and you will if you are writing early and often – you should proofread multiple times with a different focus. We also recommend thinking about proofreading at different levels – micro-level to macro-level proofreading. By micro-proofreading, we mean proofreading your project sentence by sentence making sure that each sentence is grammatically correct and that each sentence flows well on its own. At a middle level of proofreading focus, read your project with a focus on the flow and rhythm of each paragraph. At this level you should also proofread once with a focus on cutting unnecessary words and phrases. At a more macro-level, go through your project and write above each paragraph a single sentence that explains the point of that paragraph. We recommend doing this in italics so that it stands out from the rest of the text. If you cannot write a single sentence that explains the point of the paragraph, you probably need to restructure your paragraphs until this can be done. At this point, we recommend looking at the last sentence of each paragraph and the first sentence of the following paragraph. Your goal should be that these two sentences are written in such a fashion that they enhance the overall flow of your project.

Although it can be a rather painful exercise, we highly recommend asking someone else to read your writing out loud to you. Perhaps you can dull the pain of this exercise by agreeing to do the same for a colleague in your class. When someone else reads your prose out loud to you, it will usually be quite obvious where your prose does and does not flow well.

12.4 MAKING EFFECTIVE USE OF TABLES AND FIGURES

We strongly recommend that you spend a lot of time constructing the tables and figures that you include in your projects. When they first pick up your written work (or open it electronically), many readers will take a quick look at the title and introduction and then go directly to your tables and figures. This is certainly a reasonable thing to do when someone is trying to evaluate whether or not they should invest further time reviewing your work. Thus, although they may appear at the back of your project, tables and figures often determine the first impression that potential readers have of your project. As such, we recommend that you construct your tables and figures so they stand on their own and draw readers in. With these two goals in mind, we have a set of recommendations for what you should and should not do as you put your tables and figures together. We also recommend that you tell readers in the text of your project what they should see in your tables and figures. This is another part of the craft where we echo the lessons of Section 12.2.4 – take time to analyze what works and what doesn't work in terms of other scholars' use of tables and figures.

12.4.1 Constructing Regression Tables

As we have made clear in earlier chapters, multiple regression analyses are the main tool that researchers in sociology use to test their causal claims.

Consumers of sociological research are well trained to read regression tables and make assessments based on what they see in them. In addition to making assessments about the specific results presented in a table, readers will also use what they see and don't see in regression tables to make assessments about the technical competence of the person who has constructed the table. Since this will have a major impact on the overall assessment of your project, you will want to be careful and thorough in your construction of regression tables.

The construction of regression tables involves moving back and forth between results in a statistics program and the table-making facilities in whatever word-processing program you are using. The easiest and *worst* way to do this is to simply copy and paste your statistical output into your word-processing program. This is a bad way to proceed for at least six reasons. First of all, it just doesn't look good. Second, statistical programs tend to give you a lot of information when you estimate a regression model. This information is often way more than what you will need to report in your regression table. Third, the default reporting of results from the statistical program may be different from what is appropriate for your purposes. For instance, as we discussed in Chapter 10, almost all statistical programs report the results from two-tailed hypothesis tests when most of our hypotheses in sociology are directional (and thus should be assessed with one-tailed tests). Fourth, statistical programs report the names of your variables as they appear in your data sets. While the abbreviations that you have chosen for your variables probably make sense to you, they will almost surely be confusing to your readers. Fifth, computer programs usually report statistics in fractions that go way beyond what you need to report. As a general rule, we recommend rounding to two decimal places. And sixth, computer programs report model results with variables in a particular order, but that order may not be the best for emphasizing the important aspects of your results.

Having established what you *should not* do in constructing your tables, let's now talk about what you *should* do. Remember that your goals are to make your table of results stand on its own and draw potential readers in. As such, you want your tables to transmit to other researchers what you have done. Your regression table should include:

- a title that communicates the purpose of the model and/or the most important implications,
- names for the independent variables that are as clear as possible,
- your independent variables in an order that fits your purposes (usually with your main theoretical variable(s) at the top and control variables listed below),

- the estimated effect of each independent variable (usually the estimated parameter),
- some indication of the uncertainty/statistical significance of each estimated effect (standard errors or t-statistics in parentheses underneath a parameter estimate),
- some indication of which results have been found to be statistically significant according to a particular standard (e.g., putting asterisks next to results for which $p < 0.05$),
- some indication of what is the dependent variable,
- some overall diagnostics to communicate the model's fit and the number of cases on which the model was estimated,
- a set of notes to help readers decode anything they need to decode (e.g., that "***" means "$p < 0.01$," and
- any other information that needs to be communicated in order to convey the importance of the findings.

As an example of a table of regression results, consider Table 12.1.[4] If we go through the list of what a table should contain, we can evaluate how well this table does with each item. The title is fairly informative about what is going on in the model depicted in the table, and conveys the most important implications. It also identifies the dependent variable, attitudes toward physicians. The names of the independent variables are mostly clear, though "Global health status" and "Insurance" might have been described in more detail. The table clearly contains parameter estimates, though no indication (in the form of standard errors) of the uncertainty about them, which is not ideal. In addition, we can tell from the note beneath the table that the asterisks in the table convey different levels of statistical significance. The notes beneath the table also make clear what the excluded categories of the dummy variables are. So, overall, while this table is fairly clear, it could certainly be improved upon.

As we have seen in Chapter 11, it is often the case that we will want to report the results from several regression models in the same table. When we do this, it is important to make sure that we are setting up our comparisons across models in a fashion that conveys exactly what we want. There are two types of comparisons that we typically make when we are presenting multiple regression models in the same table: comparisons of different model specifications with the same sample of data, or comparisons of the same model specification across different samples of data. It is very important not to mix these two types of model specifications.

[4] Table 12.1 is from Pescosolido, Tuch, and Martin (2001).

Table 12.1 Estimates for the regression of negative and positive attitudes toward physicians on socio-demographic characteristics, self-reported health status, and medical insurance status, 1976 Access to Medical Care in the U.S. and 1998 General Social Survey

	Negative attitudes		Positive attitudes	
	1976	1998	1976	1998
Socio-demographics				
Gender (1 = women)	0.030	0.126	0.131***	−0.163***
Race (1 = whites)	−0.294***	0.014	−0.065	−0.264***
Age (years)	−0.006***	0.004	0.009***	0.008***
Income	−0.001*	0.019	0.001	−0.032***
Education	−0.042**	0.045***	−0.081***	−0.028*
Never married[a]	0.097	−0.141	−0.110	−0.027
Div./sep.[a]	0.083	0.032	−0.009	−0.284**
Widowed[a]	0.005	−0.215	0.093	0.020
Urban[b]	0.059	0.059	0.059	−0.065
Rural[b]	−0.079	0.304***	0.083	−0.285***
Health variables				
Global health status	−0.181***	0.169***	0.002	0.118
Insurance (1 = yes)	0.040	0.265**	−0.030	0.280*
Intercept	2.631	2.800	1.653	1.732
R-squared	0.040***	0.050***	0.059***	0.080***

Notes: $^{***}p < 0.001$; $^{**}p < 0.010$; $^{*}p < 0.050$ (two-tailed tests).
[a] Reference category = married.
[b] Reference category = suburban.

Consider, for instance, Table 11.3. In this table we present different model specifications across the same sample. What we can see very well as we move across the columns in this table is the changes in the estimated effects of our variables as we change our model. In other words, the effect of unemployment (or degree) on public support for assistance to the poor differs depending on whether or not degree (or unemployment) is in the model. But, it is important to note that if the sample in Table 11.3 was not *exactly* the same across the columns, we would not know why the estimated effects were changing. In such a case, changes could be due to a change in the sample or a change in the model.

As an example of the second type of comparison, where we look at the same model specification but across different samples, consider Table 12.2. This table is an example of the type of research design discussed in Section 12.1.3 where we are interested in differences across subpopulations of cases in terms of the relationship between X and Y. Table 12.2 shows such a

Table 12.2 Alternative presentation of the effects of gender and education on income

	Sample		
Independent variable	**All**	**Male**	**Female**
Education	0.68**	0.52**	0.83**
	(0.05)	(0.07)	(0.07)
Intercept	6.90	9.08	2.13**
	(0.71)	(1.00)	(0.99)
n	1631	798	833
R^2	0.14	0.07	0.15

Notes: The dependent variable in both models is the respondent's income. Standard errors in parentheses. Two-sided t-tests: **indicates $p < 0.01$.

comparison using the example that we presented in Chapter 11 of looking at the relationship between education and income across men and women. In Chapter 11, we discussed how we can make this comparison by creating an interaction term. But here we show this difference in the relationship between X and Y by presenting the bivariate regression model with income as the dependent variable and education as the independent variable on the entire sample and then subsamples of cases defined by the gender of the respondent. We can see from this table that, although the sample changes across the columns, the model specification is the same. And we can tell from this comparison that there are differences across the columns in terms of the estimated relationships. As we illustrated with this same example in Chapter 11, we can also get leverage on this type of difference in the relationship between X and Y across subpopulations through the use of an interactive model specification.

12.4.2 Writing about Regression Tables

Although our goal in constructing tables is to make them stand well on their own, when writing about regression tables, it is important to do a little bit of handholding. In other words, *tell* your readers what they should take away from each table. Consider the way in which we just ended Section 12.4.1. Although this table is competently constructed, we don't know for sure which parts of the table are going to catch the eye of our readers. All that we have told readers is that there are differences across groups. Instead of leaving this up to chance, we should tell them what they should see from this table – for instance, that the largest effect of education on income appears among women. Moreover, we know from the discussion of this finding in Chapter 11 that the difference between men and women is statistically significant.

The bottom line with writing about regression tables is that you want to tell your readers what they should see. This will help you to maximize the impact of what you have found and to keep your audience focused on what you are trying to communicate.

12.4.3 Other Types of Tables and Figures

We have emphasized the creation of and writing about regression tables, and for good reason: Regression analysis is the workhorse of social science research. But there might be other types of tables or figures that you might find useful, largely depending on what type of research design you use, and what new project type you're adopting. These decisions should be guided, we emphasize, by an anticipation of what you expect your readers will be most interested in seeing.

For example, if your new project type is the first variant – that is, you've created a new Y and are exploring whether it is caused by some X – then in general it is incumbent upon you to somehow describe your new dependent variable. This can be done in a table or a figure, or both, depending on the circumstances. In his work on the causes of the U.S. public's preferences for liberal or conservative racial policies, for example, Kellstedt (2000) created an index that represented the public's aggregate preferences for liberal or conservative racial policies over a fifty-year period. Because his dependent variable was new, Kellstedt included a figure showing the variable that would become his dependent variable of interest. In fact, because his key independent variables – media coverage about race in the U.S. – were also new, he included figures showing the over-time movement of those series as well. The point is to give the reader a mental picture (which may, of course, also be a literal picture) of what the dependent variable "looks like."

Though figures like this might also be useful in cross-sectional research, they are particularly valuable in time-series observational studies. In a cross-sectional study, it's perhaps more typical to show a frequency table with the likely values for a new dependent variable. The intent in these circumstances is to give the reader a sense of both the central tendency and the variability in the new dependent variable.

Showing a figure or creating a frequency table for the dependent variable is less useful when your project is of our second type – ones with an existing Y and a new X. Instead, in those circumstances, it is generally wise to showcase what is *new* – and in this case, it's a new X. If this is a time-series design, then a figure is perhaps most appropriate. If the design is cross-sectional, it would likely be a frequency table.

In general, the strategy we recommend is to showcase what is new – and therefore, both intriguing and unfamiliar – to your readers.

EXERCISES

1. In five words or less, write the phrase that best describes your current research interest. Conduct a citation search for this phrase using Google Scholar or some other citation search engine. Write about what you find.
2. Select three articles from a social science journal approved by your instructor. Discuss how the abstracts of each of these articles either pique, or fail to pique, your interest in the topic.
3. Read one of the articles from the journal that you selected in Exercise 2. Provide answers to each of the following questions:

   (a) What was the research question?

   (b) What theory did the author(s) test?

   (c) What was their research design?

   (d) How did they do with the four hurdles?

   (e) What did they conclude?

   (f) Can their theory be applied elsewhere in an interesting fashion?

4. Table 2.1 contains the fifty most frequently downloaded articles from the American Sociological Association's journals in 2018. Search one of these articles on Google Scholar. What is the most recently published paper that cites the article you have chosen? Obtain a copy of this article and figure out what is the research question. Write about what you have learned from doing this.

APPENDIX A

Critical Values of Chi-Squared

	Level of significance				
df	**0.10**	**0.05**	**0.025**	**0.01**	**0.001**
1	2.706	3.841	5.024	6.635	10.828
2	4.605	5.991	7.378	9.210	13.816
3	6.251	7.815	9.348	11.345	16.266
4	7.779	9.488	11.143	13.277	18.467
5	9.236	11.070	12.833	15.086	20.515
6	10.645	12.592	14.449	16.812	22.458
7	12.017	14.067	16.013	18.475	24.322
8	13.362	15.507	17.535	20.090	26.125
9	14.684	16.919	19.023	21.666	27.877
10	15.987	18.307	20.483	23.209	29.588
11	17.275	19.675	21.920	24.725	31.264
12	18.549	21.026	23.337	26.217	32.910
13	19.812	22.362	24.736	27.688	34.528
14	21.064	23.685	26.119	29.141	36.123
15	22.307	24.996	27.488	30.578	37.697
20	28.412	31.410	34.170	37.566	45.315
25	34.382	37.652	40.646	44.314	52.620
30	40.256	43.773	46.979	50.892	59.703
35	46.059	49.802	53.203	57.342	66.619
40	51.805	55.758	59.342	63.691	73.402
50	63.167	67.505	71.420	76.154	86.661
60	74.397	79.082	83.298	88.379	99.607
70	85.527	90.531	95.023	100.425	112.317
75	91.061	96.217	100.839	106.393	118.599
80	96.578	101.879	106.629	112.329	124.839
90	107.565	113.145	118.136	124.116	137.208
100	118.498	124.342	129.561	135.807	149.449

APPENDIX B

Critical Values of *t*

df	Level of significance					
	0.10	0.05	0.025	0.01	.005	0.001
1	3.078	6.314	12.706	31.821	63.657	318.313
2	1.886	2.920	4.303	6.965	9.925	22.327
3	1.638	2.353	3.182	4.541	5.841	10.215
4	1.533	2.132	2.776	3.747	4.604	7.173
5	1.476	2.015	2.571	3.365	4.032	5.893
6	1.440	1.943	2.447	3.143	3.707	5.208
7	1.415	1.895	2.365	2.998	3.499	4.782
8	1.397	1.860	2.306	2.896	3.355	4.499
9	1.383	1.833	2.262	2.821	3.250	4.296
10	1.372	1.812	2.228	2.764	3.169	4.143
11	1.363	1.796	2.201	2.718	3.106	4.024
12	1.356	1.782	2.179	2.681	3.055	3.929
13	1.350	1.771	2.160	2.650	3.012	3.852
14	1.345	1.761	2.145	2.624	2.977	3.787
15	1.341	1.753	2.131	2.602	2.947	3.733
20	1.325	1.725	2.086	2.528	2.845	3.552
25	1.316	1.708	2.060	2.485	2.787	3.450
30	1.310	1.697	2.042	2.457	2.750	3.385
40	1.303	1.684	2.021	2.423	2.704	3.307
50	1.299	1.676	2.009	2.403	2.678	3.261
60	1.296	1.671	2.000	2.390	2.660	3.232
70	1.294	1.667	1.994	2.381	2.648	3.211
75	1.293	1.665	1.992	2.377	2.643	3.202
80	1.292	1.664	1.990	2.374	2.639	3.195
90	1.291	1.662	1.987	2.368	2.632	3.183
100	1.290	1.660	1.984	2.364	2.626	3.174
∞	1.282	1.645	1.960	2.326	2.576	3.090

The Λ Link Function for Binomial Logit Models

	Translating negative $X_i\hat{\beta}$ values into predicted probabilities ($\hat{P}_i$)									
$X_i\hat{\beta}$	−0.00	−0.01	−0.02	−0.03	−0.04	−0.05	−0.06	−0.07	−0.08	−0.09
−4.5	0.0110	0.0109	0.0108	0.0107	0.0106	0.0105	0.0104	0.0103	0.0102	0.0101
−4.0	0.0180	0.0178	0.0176	0.0175	0.0173	0.0171	0.0170	0.0168	0.0166	0.0165
−3.5	0.0293	0.0290	0.0287	0.0285	0.0282	0.0279	0.0277	0.0274	0.0271	0.0269
−3.0	0.0474	0.0470	0.0465	0.0461	0.0457	0.0452	0.0448	0.0444	0.0439	0.0435
−2.5	0.0759	0.0752	0.0745	0.0738	0.0731	0.0724	0.0718	0.0711	0.0704	0.0698
−2.0	0.1192	0.1182	0.1171	0.1161	0.1151	0.1141	0.1130	0.1120	0.1111	0.1101
−1.9	0.1301	0.1290	0.1279	0.1268	0.1256	0.1246	0.1235	0.1224	0.1213	0.1203
−1.8	0.1419	0.1406	0.1394	0.1382	0.1371	0.1359	0.1347	0.1335	0.1324	0.1312
−1.7	0.1545	0.1532	0.1519	0.1506	0.1493	0.1480	0.1468	0.1455	0.1443	0.1431
−1.6	0.1680	0.1666	0.1652	0.1638	0.1625	0.1611	0.1598	0.1584	0.1571	0.1558
−1.5	0.1824	0.1809	0.1795	0.1780	0.1765	0.1751	0.1736	0.1722	0.1708	0.1694
−1.4	0.1978	0.1962	0.1947	0.1931	0.1915	0.1900	0.1885	0.1869	0.1854	0.1839
−1.3	0.2142	0.2125	0.2108	0.2092	0.2075	0.2059	0.2042	0.2026	0.2010	0.1994
−1.2	0.2315	0.2297	0.2279	0.2262	0.2244	0.2227	0.2210	0.2193	0.2176	0.2159
−1.1	0.2497	0.2479	0.2460	0.2442	0.2423	0.2405	0.2387	0.2369	0.2351	0.2333
−1.0	0.2689	0.2670	0.2650	0.2631	0.2611	0.2592	0.2573	0.2554	0.2535	0.2516
−0.9	0.2891	0.2870	0.2850	0.2829	0.2809	0.2789	0.2769	0.2749	0.2729	0.2709
−0.8	0.3100	0.3079	0.3058	0.3036	0.3015	0.2994	0.2973	0.2953	0.2932	0.2911
−0.7	0.3318	0.3296	0.3274	0.3252	0.3230	0.3208	0.3186	0.3165	0.3143	0.3112
−0.6	0.3543	0.3521	0.3498	0.3475	0.3452	0.3430	0.3407	0.3385	0.3363	0.3340
−0.5	0.3775	0.3752	0.3729	0.3705	0.3682	0.3659	0.3635	0.3612	0.3589	0.3566
−0.4	0.4013	0.3989	0.3965	0.3941	0.3917	0.3894	0.3870	0.3846	0.3823	0.3799
−0.3	0.4256	0.4231	0.4207	0.4182	0.4158	0.4134	0.4110	0.4085	0.4061	0.4037
−0.2	0.4502	0.4477	0.4452	0.4428	0.4403	0.4378	0.4354	0.4329	0.4305	0.4280
−0.1	0.4750	0.4725	0.4700	0.4675	0.4651	0.4626	0.4601	0.4576	0.4551	0.4526
−0.0	0.5000	0.4975	0.4950	0.4925	0.4900	0.4875	0.4850	0.4825	0.4800	0.4775

(continued)

Appendix C (*continued*)

	Translating positive $X_i\hat{\beta}$ values into predicted probabilities ($\hat{P}_i$)									
$X_i\hat{\beta}$	+0.00	+0.01	+0.02	+0.03	+0.04	+0.05	+0.06	+0.07	+0.08	+0.09
0.0	0.5000	0.5025	0.5050	0.5075	0.5100	0.5125	0.5150	0.5175	0.5200	0.5225
0.1	0.5250	0.5275	0.5300	0.5325	0.5349	0.5374	0.5399	0.5424	0.5449	0.5474
0.2	0.5498	0.5523	0.5548	0.5572	0.5597	0.5622	0.5646	0.5671	0.5695	0.5720
0.3	0.5744	0.5769	0.5793	0.5818	0.5842	0.5866	0.5890	0.5915	0.5939	0.5963
0.4	0.5987	0.6011	0.6035	0.6059	0.6083	0.6106	0.6130	0.6154	0.6177	0.6201
0.5	0.6225	0.6248	0.6271	0.6295	0.6318	0.6341	0.6365	0.6388	0.6411	0.6434
0.6	0.6457	0.6479	0.6502	0.6525	0.6548	0.6570	0.6593	0.6615	0.6637	0.6660
0.7	0.6682	0.6704	0.6726	0.6748	0.6770	0.6792	0.6814	0.6835	0.6857	0.6878
0.8	0.6900	0.6921	0.6942	0.6964	0.6985	0.7006	0.7027	0.7047	0.7068	0.7089
0.9	0.7109	0.7130	0.7150	0.7171	0.7191	0.7211	0.7231	0.7251	0.7271	0.7291
1.0	0.7311	0.7330	0.7350	0.7369	0.7389	0.7408	0.7427	0.7446	0.7465	0.7484
1.1	0.7503	0.7521	0.7540	0.7558	0.7577	0.7595	0.7613	0.7631	0.7649	0.7667
1.2	0.7685	0.7703	0.7721	0.7738	0.7756	0.7773	0.7790	0.7807	0.7824	0.7841
1.3	0.7858	0.7875	0.7892	0.7908	0.7925	0.7941	0.7958	0.7974	0.7990	0.8006
1.4	0.8022	0.8038	0.8053	0.8069	0.8085	0.8100	0.8115	0.8131	0.8146	0.8161
1.5	0.8176	0.8191	0.8205	0.8220	0.8235	0.8249	0.8264	0.8278	0.8292	0.8306
1.6	0.8320	0.8334	0.8348	0.8362	0.8375	0.8389	0.8402	0.8416	0.8429	0.8442
1.7	0.8455	0.8468	0.8481	0.8494	0.8507	0.8520	0.8532	0.8545	0.8557	0.8569
1.8	0.8581	0.8594	0.8606	0.8618	0.8629	0.8641	0.8653	0.8665	0.8676	0.8688
1.9	0.8699	0.8710	0.8721	0.8732	0.8744	0.8754	0.8765	0.8776	0.8787	0.8797
2.0	0.8808	0.8818	0.8829	0.8839	0.8849	0.8859	0.8870	0.8880	0.8889	0.8899
2.5	0.9241	0.9248	0.9255	0.9262	0.9269	0.9276	0.9282	0.9289	0.9296	0.9302
3.0	0.9526	0.9530	0.9535	0.9539	0.9543	0.9548	0.9552	0.9556	0.9561	0.9565
3.5	0.9707	0.9710	0.9713	0.9715	0.9718	0.9721	0.9723	0.9726	0.9729	0.9731
4.0	0.9820	0.9822	0.9824	0.9825	0.9827	0.9829	0.9830	0.9832	0.9834	0.9835
4.5	0.9890	0.9891	0.9892	0.9893	0.9894	0.9895	0.9896	0.9897	0.9898	0.9899

APPENDIX D

The Φ Link Function for Binomial Probit Models

	Translating negative $X_i\hat{\beta}$ values into predicted probabilities ($\hat{P}_i$)									
$X_i\hat{\beta}$	**−0.00**	**−0.01**	**−0.02**	**−0.03**	**−0.04**	**−0.05**	**−0.06**	**−0.07**	**−0.08**	**−0.09**
−3.4	0.0003	0.0003	0.0003	0.0003	0.0003	0.0003	0.0003	0.0003	0.0003	0.0002
−3.0	0.0013	0.0013	0.0013	0.0012	0.0012	0.0011	0.0011	0.0011	0.0010	0.0010
−2.5	0.0062	0.0060	0.0059	0.0057	0.0055	0.0054	0.0052	0.0051	0.0049	0.0048
−2.0	0.0228	0.0222	0.0217	0.0212	0.0207	0.0202	0.0197	0.0192	0.0188	0.0183
−1.9	0.0287	0.0281	0.0274	0.0268	0.0262	0.0256	0.0250	0.0244	0.0239	0.0233
−1.8	0.0359	0.0351	0.0344	0.0336	0.0329	0.0322	0.0314	0.0307	0.0301	0.0294
−1.7	0.0446	0.0436	0.0427	0.0418	0.0409	0.0401	0.0392	0.0384	0.0375	0.0367
−1.6	0.0548	0.0537	0.0526	0.0516	0.0505	0.0495	0.0485	0.0475	0.0465	0.0455
−1.5	0.0668	0.0655	0.0643	0.0630	0.0618	0.0606	0.0594	0.0582	0.0571	0.0559
−1.4	0.0808	0.0793	0.0778	0.0764	0.0749	0.0735	0.0721	0.0708	0.0694	0.0681
−1.3	0.0968	0.0951	0.0934	0.0918	0.0901	0.0885	0.0869	0.0853	0.0838	0.0823
−1.2	0.1151	0.1131	0.1112	0.1093	0.1075	0.1056	0.1038	0.1020	0.1003	0.0985
−1.1	0.1357	0.1335	0.1314	0.1292	0.1271	0.1251	0.1230	0.1210	0.1190	0.1170
−1.0	0.1587	0.1562	0.1539	0.1515	0.1492	0.1469	0.1446	0.1423	0.1401	0.1379
−0.9	0.1841	0.1814	0.1788	0.1762	0.1736	0.1711	0.1685	0.1660	0.1635	0.1611
−0.8	0.2119	0.2090	0.2061	0.2033	0.2005	0.1977	0.1949	0.1922	0.1894	0.1867
−0.7	0.2420	0.2389	0.2358	0.2327	0.2296	0.2266	0.2236	0.2206	0.2177	0.2148
−0.6	0.2743	0.2709	0.2676	0.2643	0.2611	0.2578	0.2546	0.2514	0.2483	0.2451
−0.5	0.3085	0.3050	0.3015	0.2981	0.2946	0.2912	0.2877	0.2843	0.2810	0.2776
−0.4	0.3446	0.3409	0.3372	0.3336	0.3300	0.3264	0.3228	0.3192	0.3156	0.3121
−0.3	0.3821	0.3783	0.3745	0.3707	0.3669	0.3632	0.3594	0.3557	0.3520	0.3483
−0.2	0.4207	0.4168	0.4129	0.4090	0.4052	0.4013	0.3974	0.3936	0.3897	0.3859
−0.1	0.4602	0.4562	0.4522	0.4483	0.4443	0.4404	0.4364	0.4325	0.4286	0.4247
−0.0	0.5000	0.4960	0.4920	0.4880	0.4840	0.4801	0.4761	0.4721	0.4681	0.4641

(continued)

Appendix D (*continued*)

$X_i\hat{\beta}$	Translating positive $X_i\hat{\beta}$ values into predicted probabilities ($\hat{P}_i$)									
	+0.00	+0.01	+0.02	+0.03	+0.04	+0.05	+0.06	+0.07	+0.08	+0.09
+0.0	0.5000	0.5040	0.5080	0.5120	0.5160	0.5199	0.5239	0.5279	0.5319	0.5359
+0.1	0.5398	0.5438	0.5478	0.5517	0.5557	0.5596	0.5636	0.5675	0.5714	0.5753
+0.2	0.5793	0.5832	0.5871	0.5910	0.5948	0.5987	0.6026	0.6064	0.6103	0.6141
+0.3	0.6179	0.6217	0.6255	0.6293	0.6331	0.6368	0.6406	0.6443	0.6480	0.6517
+0.4	0.6554	0.6591	0.6628	0.6664	0.6700	0.6736	0.6772	0.6808	0.6844	0.6879
+0.5	0.6915	0.6950	0.6985	0.7019	0.7054	0.7088	0.7123	0.7157	0.7190	0.7224
+0.6	0.7257	0.7291	0.7324	0.7357	0.7389	0.7422	0.7454	0.7486	0.7517	0.7549
+0.7	0.7580	0.7611	0.7642	0.7673	0.7704	0.7734	0.7764	0.7794	0.7823	0.7852
+0.8	0.7881	0.7910	0.7939	0.7967	0.7995	0.8023	0.8051	0.8078	0.8106	0.8133
+0.9	0.8159	0.8186	0.8212	0.8238	0.8264	0.8289	0.8315	0.8340	0.8365	0.8389
+1.0	0.8413	0.8438	0.8461	0.8485	0.8508	0.8531	0.8554	0.8577	0.8599	0.8621
+1.1	0.8643	0.8665	0.8686	0.8708	0.8729	0.8749	0.8770	0.8790	0.8810	0.8830
+1.2	0.8849	0.8869	0.8888	0.8907	0.8925	0.8944	0.8962	0.8980	0.8997	0.9015
+1.3	0.9032	0.9049	0.9066	0.9082	0.9099	0.9115	0.9131	0.9147	0.9162	0.9177
+1.4	0.9192	0.9207	0.9222	0.9236	0.9251	0.9265	0.9279	0.9292	0.9306	0.9319
+1.5	0.9332	0.9345	0.9357	0.9370	0.9382	0.9394	0.9406	0.9418	0.9429	0.9441
+1.6	0.9452	0.9463	0.9474	0.9484	0.9495	0.9505	0.9515	0.9525	0.9535	0.9545
+1.7	0.9554	0.9564	0.9573	0.9582	0.9591	0.9599	0.9608	0.9616	0.9625	0.9633
+1.8	0.9641	0.9649	0.9656	0.9664	0.9671	0.9678	0.9686	0.9693	0.9699	0.9706
+1.9	0.9713	0.9719	0.9726	0.9732	0.9738	0.9744	0.9750	0.9756	0.9761	0.9767
+2.0	0.9772	0.9778	0.9783	0.9788	0.9793	0.9798	0.9803	0.9808	0.9812	0.9817
+2.5	0.9938	0.9940	0.9941	0.9943	0.9945	0.9946	0.9948	0.9949	0.9951	0.9952
+3.0	0.9987	0.9987	0.9987	0.9988	0.9988	0.9989	0.9989	0.9989	0.9990	0.9990
+3.4	0.9997	0.9997	0.9997	0.9997	0.9997	0.9997	0.9997	0.9997	0.9997	0.9998

References

Allport, Gordon Willard, Kenneth Clark, and Thomas Pettigrew. 1954. *The Nature of Prejudice*. Reading, MA: Addison-Wesley.

ANES (American National Election Studies). 2021. *ANES 2020 Time Series Study Full Release* [dataset and documentation]. July 19, 2021 version. www.electionstudies.org.

Arceneaux, Kevin, and Martin Johnson. 2011. "Does Media Fragmentation Produce Mass Polarization? Selective Exposure and a New Era of Minimal Effects." Unpublished manuscript.

ASA (American Sociological Association). 2018. *ASA Code of Ethics*. Washington, DC: American Sociological Association. www.asanet.org/code-ethics.

Berrens, Robert P., Alok K. Bohara, Hank Jenkins-Smith, Carol Silva, and David L. Weimer. 2003. "The Advent of Internet Surveys for Political Research: A Comparison of Telephone and Internet Samples." *Political Analysis* 11(1):1–22.

Beutel, Ann M., and Margaret Mooney Marini. 1995. "Gender and Values." *American Sociological Review* 60:436–448.

Blumberg, Stephen J., and V. Luke Julian. 2017. "Wireless Substitution: Early Release of Estimates from the National Health Interview Survey, January–June 2017." National Center for Health Statistics. www.cdc.gov/nchs/data/nhis/earlyrelease/wireless201712.pdf.

Blumberg, Stephen J., and Julian V. Luke. 2021. "Wireless Substitution: Early Release of Estimates from the National Health Interview Survey, January–June 2021." National Center for Health Statistics, Hyattsville, MD. https://doi.org/10.15620/cdc:111171.

Blumer, Herbert. 1958. "Race Relations as a Sense of Group Position." *Pacific Sociological Review* 1(1):3–7.

Bobo, Lawrence, and Victor Hutchings. 1996. "Perceptions of Racial Group Competition: Extending Blumer's Theory of Group Position to a Multiracial Social Context." *American Sociological Review* 61(6):951–972.

Brady, Henry E. 2002. "Models of Causal Inference: Going Beyond the Neyman–Rubin–Holland Theory." Paper presented at the Annual Meeting of the Political Methodology Society, Seattle, WA.

Brady, Henry E. 2004. "Introduction." *Perspectives on Politics* 2:295–300.

Campbell, Donald T., and Julian C. Stanley. 1963. *Experimental and Quasi-Experimental Designs for Research*. Chicago: Rand McNally.

Carmines, Edward G., Paul M. Sniderman, and Beth C. Easter. 2011. "On the Meaning, Measurement, and Implications of Racial Resentment." *Annals of the American Academy of Political and Social Science* 634(1):98–116.

Chang, Linchiat, and Jon A. Krosnick. 2009. "National Surveys via RDD Telephone Interviewing Versus the Internet: Comparing Sample Representativeness and Response Quality." *Public Opinion Quarterly* 73(4):641–678.

Converse, Philip E. 1964. "The Nature of Belief Systems in Mass Publics." In *Ideology and Discontent*, ed. David E. Apter. New York: The Free Press, pp. 206–261.

Copernicus, Nicolaus. 2004. *On the Revolutions of Heavenly Spheres*. Philadelphia: Running Press Book Publishers. [Translation of 1543 book in Latin]

Couper, Mick P. 2017. "New Developments in Survey Data Collection." *Annual Review of Sociology* 43(1):121–145.

Couper, Mick P., and Michael Bosnjak. 2010. "Internet Surveys." *Handbook of Survey Research* 2:527–550.

Currie, Janet, and Duncan Thomas. 1995. "Does Head Start Make a Difference?" *American Economic Review* 85:341–364.

Danziger, Sheldon, and Peter Gottschalk. 1983. "The Measurement of Poverty: Implications for Antipoverty Policy." *American Behavioral Scientist* 26:739–756.

Desforges, Donna M., Charles G. Lord, Shawna L. Ramsey, Julie A. Mason, Marilyn D. Van Leeuwen, Sylvia C. West, and Mark R. Lepper. 1991. "Effects of Structured Cooperative Contact on Changing Negative Attitudes Toward Stigmatized Social Groups." *Journal of Personality and Social Psychology* 60(4):531.

Dillman, Don A. 2011. *Mail and Internet Surveys: The Tailored Design Method–2007 Update with New Internet, Visual, and Mixed-Mode Guide*. New York: John Wiley & Sons.

Dillman, Don A., Jolene D. Smyth, and Leah Melani Christian. 2014. *Internet, Phone, Mail, and Mixed-Mode Surveys: The Tailored Design Method*. New York: John Wiley & Sons.

Duflo, Esther, Michael Kremer, and Jonathan Robinson. 2011. "Nudging Farmers to Use Fertilizer: Theory and Experimental Evidence from Kenya." *American Economic Review* 101:2350–2390.

Edmonds, David, and John Eidinow. 2003. *Wittgenstein's Poker: The Story of a Ten-Minute Argument Between Two Great Philosophers*. New York: Harper Perennial.

Feldman, Stanley, and Leonie Huddy. 2005. "Racial Resentment and White Opposition to Race-Conscious Programs: Principles or Prejudice?" *American Journal of Political Science* 49(1):168–183.

Firebaugh, Glenn. 2008. *Seven Rules for Social Research*. Princeton, NJ: Princeton University Press.

Guggenheim, Lauren, Colleen McClain, Yioryos Nardis, and Ted Brader. N.d. "Comparing Face-to-Face and Web Modes in the ANES 2016 Time Series Study." *ANES Technical Report*. Forthcoming.

Haney, Craig, Curtis Banks, and Philip Zimbardo. 1973. "Interpersonal Dynamics in a Simulated Prison." *Sociology of Corrections*. New York: John Wiley & Sons, pp. 65–92.

Hanson, Sandra L. 2006. "Insights from Vignettes: African American Women's Perceptions of Discrimination in the Science Classroom." *Journal of Women and Minorities in Science and Engineering* 12(1).

Henry, Patrick J., and David O. Sears. 2009. "The Crystallization of Contemporary Racial Prejudice across the Lifespan." *Political Psychology* 30(4):569–590.

Huddy, Leonie, and Stanley Feldman. 2009. "On Assessing the Political Effects of Racial Prejudice." *Annual Review of Political Science* 12:423–447.

Hughes, Michael. 1997. "Symbolic Racism, Old-Fashioned Racism, and Whites' Opposition to Affirmative Action." *Racial Attitudes in the 1990s: Continuity and Change*. Westport, CT: Praeger, pp. 45–75.

Humphreys, Laud. 1975. *Tearoom Trade, Impersonal Sex in Public Places*. Enlarged Edition. Chicago: Aldine Transaction Publishers.

Inglehart, Ronald, Christian Haerpfer, Alejandro Moreno, Christian Welzel, Kseniya Kizilova, Jaime Diez-Medrano, et al. 2014. *World Values Survey: Round Six-Country-Pooled Datafile Version*. Madrid: JD Systems Institute, p. 12.

ISSP Research Group. (2016). *International Social Survey Programme*. GESIS Data Archive, Cologne. ZA5900 Data file Version 4.0.0. https://doi.org/10.4232/1.12661.

Johnson, Monica Kirkpatrick, and Margaret Mooney Marini. 1998. "Bridging the Racial Divide in the United States: The Effect of Gender." *Social Psychology Quarterly* 61(3):247–258.

Kellstedt, Paul M. 2000. "Media Framing and the Dynamics of Racial Policy Preferences." *American Journal of Political Science* 44:245–260.

Kinder, Donald R., and Lynn M. Sanders. 1996. *Divided by Color: Racial Politics and Democratic Ideals*. Chicago: University of Chicago Press.

King, Gary. 1986. "How Not to Lie with Statistics: Avoiding Common Mistakes in Quantitative Political Science." *American Journal of Political Science* 30: 666–687.

Kuhn, Thomas S. 1962. *The Structure of Scientific Revolutions*. Chicago: University of Chicago Press.

Lavrakas, Paul J., Grant Benson, Stephen Blumberg, Ismael Flores Cervantes, Leah Christian, David Dutwin, et al. 2017. "Report from the AAPOR Task Force on 'The Future of US General Population Telephone Survey Research'." Technical Report. www.aapor.org/Education-Resources/Reports.

Lazarsfeld, Paul F., Bernard R. Berelson, and Hazel Gaudet. 1948. *The People's Choice: How the Voter Makes Up His Mind in a Presidential Campaign*, 1st edn. New York: Columbia University Press.

Levendusky, Matthew. 2009. *The Partisan Sort*. Chicago: University of Chicago Press.

Lewis-Beck, Michael S. 1997. "Who's the Chef? Economic Voting Under a Dual Executive." *European Journal of Political Research* 31:315–325.

Logan, John R., and Brian J. Stults. 2011. "The Persistence of Segregation in the Metropolis: New Findings from the 2010 Census." *Census Brief Prepared for Project US2010*, p. 24.

MacKuen, Michael B., Robert S. Erikson, and James A. Stimson. 1992. "Peasants or Bankers? The American Electorate and the US Economy." *American Political Science Review* 86(3):597–611.

Marsden, Peter V., and James D. Wright. 2010. *Handbook of Survey Research*. Bingley, UK: Emerald Group Publishing.

Massey, Douglas, and Nancy A. Denton. 1993. *American Apartheid: Segregation and the Making of the Underclass*. Cambridge, MA: Harvard University Press.

Mathews, Jay. 2000. "Scores Improve for D.C. Pupils with Vouchers." *The Washington Post*, August 28, page A1.

McCloskey, Deirdre N. 1999. *Economical Writing*, 2nd end. Long Grove, IL: Waveland Press.

Milgram, Stanley. 1963. "Behavioral study of obedience." *Journal of Abnormal and Social Psychology* 67(4):371.

Morton, Rebecca B., and Kenneth C. Williams. 2010. *Experimental Political Science and the Study of Causality: From Nature to the Lab*. New York: Cambridge University Press.

Mueller, John. 1973. *War, Presidents and Public Opinion*. New York: John Wiley & Sons.

Nagler, Jonathan. 1995. "Coding Style and Good Computing Practices." *PS: Political Science & Politics* 28(3):488–492.

Niemi, Richard G., and M. Kent Jennings. 1974. *The Political Character of Adolescence: The Influence of Families and Schools*. Princeton, NJ: Princeton University Press.

Olson, Kristen, Jolene D. Smyth, Rachel Horwitz, Scott Keeter, Virginia Lesser, Stephanie Marken, et al. 2021. "Transitions from Telephone Surveys to Self-Administered and Mixed-Mode Surveys: AAPOR Task Force Report." *Journal of Survey Statistics and Methodology* 9(3):381–411.

Pearl, Judea. 2000. *Causality: Models, Reasoning, and Inference*. New York: Cambridge University Press.

Pescosolido, Bernice A., Steven A. Tuch, and Jack K. Martin. 2001. "The Profession of Medicine and the Public: Examining Americans' Changing Confidence in Physician Authority from the Beginning of the 'Health Care Crisis' to the Era of Health Care Reform." *Journal of Health and Social Behavior* 42:1–16.

Pettigrew, Thomas F. 1998. "Intergroup Contact Theory." *Annual Review of Psychology* 49(1):65–85.

Piazza, Thomas, Paul M. Sniderman, and Philip E. Tetlock. 1990. "Analysis of the Dynamics of Political Reasoning: A General-Purpose Computer-Assisted Methodology." *Political Analysis* 1:99–120.

Posner, Daniel N. 2004. "The Political Salience of Cultural Difference: Why Chewas and Tumbukas Are Allies in Zambia and Adversaries in Malawi." *American Political Science Review* 98:529–545.

Powell, G. Bingham Jr., and Guy D. Whitten. 1993. "A Cross-National Analysis of Economic Voting: Taking Account of the Political Context." *American Journal of Political Science* 37:391–414.

Richards, Diana, T. Clifton Morgan, Rick Wilson, Valerie L. Schwebach, and Garry D. Young. 1993. "Good Times, Bad Times and the Diversionary Use of Force: A Tale of Some Not So Free Agents." *Journal of Conflict Resolution* 37:504–535.

Rollins, Judith. 1985. *Between Women: Domestics and Their Employers*. Philadelphia: Temple University Press.

Roos, J. Micah, Michael Hughes, and Ashley V. Reichelmann. 2019. "A Puzzle of Racial Attitudes: A Measurement Analysis of Racial Attitudes and Policy Indicators." *Socius* 5:2378023119842738.

Rosenberg, Morris. 1968. *The Logic of Survey Analysis*. New York: Basic Books.

Salmon, Wesley C. 1993. "Probabilistic Causality." In *Causation*, ed. Ernest Sosa, and Michael Tooley. Oxford: Oxford University Press, chapter 8, pp. 137–153.

Schnabel, Landon. 2015. "How Religious Are American Women and Men? Gender Differences and Similarities." *Journal for the Scientific Study of Religion* 54(3):616–622.

Schuman, Howard. 2000. "The Perils of Correlation, the Lure of Labels, and the Beauty of Negative Results." In *Racialized Politics: The Debate About Racism in America*, eds David O. Sears, James Sidanius, and Lawrence Bobo. Chicago: University of Chicago Press, chapter 10, pp. 302–323.

Sears, David O., and Patrick J. Henry. 2005. "Over Thirty Years Later: A Contemporary Look at Symbolic Racism." *Advances in Experimental Social Psychology* 37(1):95–125.

Sears, David, and Donald Kinder. 1971. "Racial Tensions and Voting in Los Angeles." In *Los Angeles: Viability and Prospects for Metropolitan Leadership*, ed. Werner Hirsch. New York: Praeger.

Sherif, Muzafer, and Institute of Group Relations, University of Oklahoma. 1961. *Intergroup Conflict and Cooperation: The Robbers Cave Experiment*. Norman, OK: University Book Exchange.

Sherman, Lawrence W., and Richard A. Berk. 1984. "The Specific Deterrent Effects of Arrest for Domestic Assault." *American Sociological Review* 49:261–272.

Simmons, Alicia D., and Lawrence D. Bobo. 2015. "Can Non-Full-Probability Internet Surveys Yield Useful Data? A Comparison with Full-Probability Face-to-Face Surveys in the Domain of Race and Social Inequality Attitudes." *Sociological Methodology* 45(1):357–387.

Simmons, Alicia D., and Lawrence D. Bobo. 2018. "Understanding 'no special favors': A Quantitative and Qualitative Mapping of the Meaning of Responses to the Racial Resentment Scale." *Du Bois Review: Social Science Research on Race* 15(2):323–352.

Smith, Tom W., Michael Davern, Jeremy Freese, and Stephen L. Morgan. 2019. *General Social Surveys, 1972–2018*. NORC, University of Chicago.

Sniderman, Paul M., Gretchen C. Crosby, and William G. Howell. 2000. "The Politics of Race." In *Racialized Politics: The Debate About Racism in America*, eds David O. Sears, Jim Sidanius, and Lawrence Bobo. Chicago: University of Chicago Press, pp. 236–279.

Sniderman, Paul M., and J.N. Druckman. 2011. "The Logic and Design of the Survey Experiment." In *Cambridge Handbook of Experimental Political Science*, eds James N. Druckman, Donald P. Green, James H. Kuklinski, and Arthur Lupia. New York: Cambridge University Press, Chapter 8, pp. 102–114.

Sniderman, Paul M., and Thomas Piazza. 1993. *The Scar of Race*. Cambridge, MA: Harvard University Press.

Tijms, Henk. 2004. *Understanding Probability: Chance Rules in Everyday Life*. Cambridge: Cambridge University Press.

Tourangeau, Roger. 2004. "Survey Research and Societal Change." *Annual Review of Psychology* 55:775–801.

Tuch, Steven A., and Michael Hughes. 2011. "Whites' Racial Policy Attitudes in the 21st Century: The Continuing Significance of Racial Resentment." *Annals of the American Academy of Political and Social Science* 634:134–152.

Verba, Sidney, Kay Lehman Schlozman, Henry Brady, and Norman H. Nie. 1993. "Race, Ethnicity and Political Resources: Participation in the United States." *British Journal of Political Science* 23:453–497.

Wallace, Walter L. 1971. *The Logic of Science in Sociology*. Abingdon, UK: Routledge.

Weitzer, Ronald, and Steven A. Tuch. 2006. *Race and Policing in America: Conflict and Reform*. New York: Cambridge University Press.

Yeager, David S., Jon A. Krosnick, LinChiat Chang, Harold S. Javitz, Matthew S. Levendusky, Alberto Simpser, and Rui Wang. 2011. "Comparing the Accuracy of RDD Telephone Surveys and Internet Surveys Conducted with Probability and Non-Probability Samples." *Public Opinion Quarterly* 75(4):709–747.

Index

CPSIA information can be obtained
at www.ICGtesting.com
Printed in the USA
LVHW010314010922
727354LV00011B/624

9 781107 569164